Portuguese Table Wines

Portuguese Table Wines

The New Generation of Wines and Wine Makers

Giles MacDonogh

London

First published in 2001 by
Grub Street
The Basement
10 Chivalry Road
London SW11 1HT
Email: food@grubstreet.co.uk
www.grubstreet.co.uk

British Library Cataloguing in Publication Data
MacDonogh, Giles, 1955-
Portuguese table wines
1. Wine and winemaking – Portugal – History
I. Title
641.2'2'09469

ISBN 1902304861

Printed and bound in Spain by Bookprint, S.L., Barcelona

acknowledgements

It was Luis Avides Moreira of ICEP - Portugal's overseas trade organisation - who first suggested the idea to me of writing a useful, short work that presented an accurate picture of Portuguese wine today, after the many changes that have taken place in the past two decades. The project was taken up by João Renano Henriques, then President of Vini Portugal, with whom I made a series of visits to Portugal; and his successor Vasco d'Avillez, who looked after me in Portugal during the final stages of the book, where, on occasion, he and his wife Mary Anne were kind enough to entertain me and my family in their home. Others in Portugal who offered help or encouragement were Sophia Bergquist, Vasco Magalhães, Jerry Luper, Anselmo Mendes, Dirk Niepoort, Maria João Colares Pereira, Iain Richardson, George Sandeman and Paul Symington and Jackie Thurn Valsassina.

In London thanks are due to Geoffrey Kelly, an early supporter of the idea, with whom I travelled in Portugal and experienced some of its best hotels and restaurants; also Richard Mayson (an invaluable guide to all things Portuguese) Carolyn Cavele, Debbie Collinson, James Craig-Wood, Joanna Delaforce, Sue Glasgow and Claire O'Connor, Raymond Reynolds, Dino Ventura and Emma Wellings. Erika Schüle-Grosso of *Relais et Châteaux* – who kindly arranged accommodation for me in Portugal. My thanks also to Jill James at the *Financial Times*, Susan Keevil, sometime editor of *Decanter,* and Amy Wislocki, its present editor, and James Steen, the quondam editor of *Punch*, as well as Richard Brass, its current editor, who allowed me to try out a few ideas in print.

Particular thanks are due to Edite Vieira for reading the manuscript and correcting my many mistakes in Portuguese orthography.

I have visited every one of the wine-producing regions of Portugal. My absences from home were noted. To Candida and Isolde I apologize for any strain this has caused.

in memoriam

Ron Pisarkiewicz, (1943 - 2001) late of the Vienna Philharmonic Orchestra –
a consummate musician who found the odd moment for wine.

Não mais Musa, não mais, que a Lira tenho

Destemperada e a voz enrouquecida,

E não do canto, mas de ver que venho

Cantar a gente surda e endurecida.

contents

foreword

VINI PORTUGAL is very proud to present this book on Portuguese table wines to the English-speaking public. The reader may be curious about the appropriately named organization that first suggested a need for this book and had many discussions with the author over its contents. We are a private interprofessional association, composed of both public and private entities that are involved in the production and marketing of wine and have an acknowledged status in the wine trade.

The objective of this work is to provide the average consumer with basic information about Portuguese table wines and to spread knowledge of the 'silent revolution' that has taken place in Portugal in the last ten or fifteen years, which has transformed the quality of the wines placed on the market.

Portuguese table wines deserve promotion, and that is what we are trying to achieve in order to increase their sales. One of the riches of Portuguese wines is the vast quantity of the indigenous grape varietals, which are capable of producing wines with differing styles of aroma, flavour and body, as well as a characteristic after-taste – all of which admirably complement the Mediterranean cuisine of the country. The appealing combination of price and quality in most Portuguese wines is notable, as are the numerous flavours that the vast amount of different, indigenous castas, (varieties of grapes) grown there, infuse into them.

We are certain that this book will be a success, since it is educative and informative and at the same time entertaining and easy to read.

It was indeed a pleasure to have had the opportunity to show the Portuguese countryside to Giles MacDonogh, and to enjoy his dry, Oxonian sense of humour, which is, we are sure, reflected in his writing.

We hope you will enjoy the book – and even more, the wines it talks about.

Vasco d'Avillez
President of VINI PORTUGAL

introduction

This book is intended as an introduction and practical guide to the new table wines of Portugal. Neither the Douro nor Madeira has been included for their fortified wines, as the presence of either would expand these pages beyond manageable length. Port and Madeira are both special wines and require specialised treatment. It has been my intention to give the book a little more shelf life than is generally the case; for that reason alone I have tried to avoid mentioning vintages and have given a composite picture of the different wines.

I have also chosen to include a section on food, as I believe that a country's cooking is vital in understanding the way a wine tastes as it does. I have included a few notes on restaurants and hotels, only when I have personally eaten or stayed in them. I have given some tips on what to see when travelling in Portugal: wine will punctuate their stay, but few people, after all, travel for wine alone. For more complete coverage I refer the reader to the *Guide*

Bleu, the *Michelin* or the *Rough Guide*, from all three of which I have benefited from on occasion.

In the spring of 1981, I visited Portugal for the second time in my life. I drove down from Paris with a friend. We stopped at one or two places along the way, spending one night in Spain in the great university city of Salamanca. It was about nine by the time we were ready to go out. We wandered into the plaza Major in search of dinner. The restaurants were either empty or still closed. We were told to come back at 10.30 or 11.00. The next morning we set out for Portugal. The car developed a limp on the far side of Viseu and we didn't arrive in Oporto until after eight; and by the time we had dressed it was gone nine. We tried a restaurant in the main business area that offered lampreys. We pushed open the door in hungry anticipation. It was too late, however, they said the chef had already gone home.

Had I been given the chance then I would have found the food very different too. In Spain it was all baby lambs, cooked on embers, or in a bread oven; but not in Portugal. More likely I'd have found salt cod, sardines, fresh grilled fish - with an inevitable side portion of rice, Brobdingnagian chips and tomato salad. If I had wanted meat I might have been offered roast kid in most inland regions, or suckling pig in Bairrada, or the country's most idiosyncratic dish, the combination of pork and clams which was invented in Lisbon, but which is always claimed for the Alentejo.

The Portuguese are not Spaniards. In fact, they resemble their neighbours very little, not even physically; which is odder still, considering the raw material is much the same. Here are the same Celts mixed with Latin elements coupled with a smattering of Visigothic or Swabian Germanity that you would find in Galicia or the Asturias, but somehow they failed to develop along the same lines as their neighbours. It would be hard to find two peoples which live so close to one another and which behave so differently.

Portugal is truly unique. As I rapidly came to realise, its identity has been shaped by a number of factors: historical, political, geographical and linguistic. On my one previous visit I had a drink with a man whose family had been prominent in the port wine trade a century before, and who now ran a travel agency. He pointed out that Portugal's borders had remained virtually unchanged since the country came into being in the twelfth century; that they were some of the oldest in Europe. Behind its geological walls it had been able to plot its own course. Despite repeated attempts, mountain, stream and racing torrent – not to mention the odd fort – had kept the Spanish at bay. With the exception of the sixty-year *dominio filipino* when the Portuguese crown went into abeyance, successful Spanish incursions have been remarkably few.

The Portuguese language, most similar to the Galician encountered in the north-western corner of Spain, had also developed on its own lines, and what lines! That phenomenal linguist, the Bible-propagandist and gypsy-fancier George Borrow, compared the idiom of a Lisbon boatman to 'the scream of a hyena blended with the bark of a terrier'. With its many nasal sounds, diphthongs and elisions, on first acquaintance it doesn't seem Latin at all, but it is. As Camões puts it proudly:

> *... na língua, na qual quando imagina,*
> *Com pouca corrupção crê que é a Latina.*

> ... the language, which an inventive mind
> Could mistake for Latin, passably declined.
> *Trans. Landeg White*

A man from Madrid can make himself understood very easily, but he cannot speak Portuguese.

Separate linguistic or historical development aside, Portugal's character is also determined by orientation. It faces out to sea. The ocean calls. Even

the vines heed the Atlantic. Its geography is
altogether different to its neighbour. In general the
meseta, that great arid Castillian plain, stops where
Portugal begins. In the north Portugal is one great
granite rock, in the middle it is calcarious, occasionally
dotted with *terra rossa* soils. Then there is flatter,
sleeker, sandier earth south of the Tagus, ending up
with a little bit of Africa in the Algarve.

Portugal has changed a lot since those first visits of
mine; more than any country in Western Europe. I
noticed then the habit of drinking a noggin of sweet
wine with some sugary egg-yolk confection in a bar. I
also observed the fondness for rough brandy
(*aguardente* or *bagaceira*) but this was not just on
the part of the Portuguese, it was also true of long-
standing residents. In the English Club in Oporto I
watched open-mouthed as I saw the quantities put
away by one old member as he lectured a devout
Portuguese on the non-existence of God and the
gross futility of belief.

The brandy was rough stuff; probably not so
different to that drunk in the first half of the
nineteenth century when Borrow found many old
soldiers, who had served either in Napoleon's or
Wellington's armies, crapulous as a result of their
consumption of native brandy. Now you may savour a
refined version made from Alvarinho grapes in the
Minho, or a superb brandy such as Adega Velha, which

can stand comparison with the best in the world.

Twenty years ago Portuguese wine also looked
considerably more rustic than it does today. On my
initial visit I travelled down to Coimbra and on to Tomar,
where a lyrical hotelier who sang to a guitar entertained
me. Down by the river I watched the *passeio* of the
town's young men and women on the bridge at sunset. I
encountered ordinary wines in bars and restaurants. I
remember a *tasca* next to the magnificent abbey in
Batalha, with its swing doors opening onto little tables,
each set with a huge bottle of red wine. You paid a
pittance for whatever you drank. It was wholesome,
and thoroughly unpretentious. In the Minho vinho
verde, white and red, was drawn from venerable casks
lodged in the corner of the bar. It came out cloudy, and
in the summertime it was already distinctly sour. The
locals, I was sure, were looking forward to the fruit
from the new harvest. If you wanted something a bit
cleaner you drank one of the main bottled brands:

Gatão, or the sweetish Casal Mendes.

Before I returned to France I took advice from the port shipper Johnnie Graham as to what I should take back to Paris to show wine-loving friends. He worked for Cockburns then and the port-houses generally made a little up-market *consumo* for the use of their directors that was never sold to the general public. I remember he thought J.M. da Fonseca's Periquita a reliable wine, but pointed me in the direction of a merchant where I was faced by an array of ancient *garrafeiras* all with seemingly inscrutable labels: a series of initials and a date, and that was all. I bought a few, as well as some bottles of Colares, the one non-fortified Portuguese wine I knew to possess an historical reputation – but had never tried – as well as a medley of *vinhos verdes* and bore them home to France.

A few years later the news began to filter through that some excellent new-wave Portuguese wines were being made in the Alentejo and the Setúbal Peninsula. I only became familiar with them once I had returned to Britain in the mid-eighties and began to buy such excellent, good value wines as Tinto da Ânfora, and the Quinta da Bacalhôa. They were the first signals of a more general reform, in this instance worked by the presence of a brilliant Australian oenologist who has since put down roots: Peter Bright. Take-off had begun.

It had been sudden. When Dan Stanislawksi wrote his pioneering study of Portuguese viticulture, *Landscape of Bacchus,* in 1979, only three regions had been properly demarcated: the Minho, Douro and Dão, while protective legislation had also been introduced for four other wines, Colares, Bucelas, Carcavelos and Moscatel de Setúbal, the future of all of which looked uncertain at the time, and in the case of two of them, looks even less so now.

Since that time Portugal has entered the European Union and its wine regions have been brought into line with the rest of the Continent. There are now controlled appellations or *Denominação de Origem Controlada* for all the main regions – with numerous subdivisions – for the fortified wines of Port and Madeira, but also a host of IPRs (*Indicação de*

Proveniência Regulamentada) and wines carrying the legend 'vinho regional', which allows for a greater flexibility when it comes to non-native grape varieties.

Since the eighties the Portuguese have rightly become aware that they have been sitting on a treasure trove of flavours and textures in what is clearly an ampelographer's – or vine botanist's – dreamland. Touriga Nacional, Baga, Tinto Cão, Tinta Roriz, Tinta Amarela, Jaen, Tinta Miúda, Castelão, Alvarinho, Loureiro, Trajadura, Fernão Pires, Bical and Arinto have all been vinified apart to show what they can do. And Portugal's grape varieties have the most evocative names: dog strangler, red dog, sheep's tail, fly droppings and bastard are just a few translations.

Once again a comparison to Portugal's neighbour is instructive: the grape varieties Garnacha Tinta, Tempranillo and Monastrel account for almost all of Spanish red wine. Portugal shares only one of these: the Tinta Roriz – the Aragonez of the south – is also Spain's Tempranillo. The character is somehow not even the same, probably because of the Spanish love of oak (particularly American oak) which gives so many of their wines a pronounced smell of caramel and marks them down as Spanish before you even lift them to your lips. Portugal's wealth of cultivars puts it in a magnificent position now that the world has voiced its impatience with the endless streams of Cabernet Sauvignon and Chardonnay – varieties which are now beginning to look about as exotic as baked beans or potato crisps.

Virtually every Portuguese winemaker now wants to try his hand at varietal wines. The most popular is Touriga Nacional, but there are plenty of bottlings which isolate Roriz, Jaen, Alfrocheiro Preto, Tinto Cão or Tinta Francesa; not to mention a range of foreign cultivars stretching from the banal Cabernet and Chardonnay to Pinot Noir and Syrah. In general separating and individually vinifying these cultivars is doing much good: it is teaching the Portuguese what they mean and what sort of flavours and effects they can expect from them. In the long term, however, I am certain that the best wine is a blend. Very few grape varieties give complexity on their own, they need foils to provide backing and relief. Touriga Nacional may be a goodish all-rounder, but it can hardly match up to the subtleties derived from a great blend of grapes from a venerable, old vineyard. I feel certain that we will see fewer varietal wines in a decade's time, once oenologists have finished their experiments and have seen where all strengths and weaknesses lie.

Another factor contributing to Portugal's individuality is its climate. Just to the north of Portugal, Spanish Galicia beyond Santiago de Compostella is tremendously wet (so wet, in fact, that vines can't grow) but in general the humidity of northern Portugal is noteworthy. It is the factor responsible for the characteristic wines of the Minho, those ultra-refreshing vinhos verdes grown on trellises or trained up trees to give them a little acid bite, and in the past bottled with some carbonic gas from the malolactic fermentation to make them tickle the tongue.

The Douro is a pocket of Mediterranean climate tucked behind the Serra do Marão, while the Dão, grown high up on its granite rocks, boasts an acidity only rarely found in red wines. Once the source of bulk wines destined for Portugal's empire, Bairrada and the Ribatejo are now vinous playgrounds. Bairrada tries to perfect its native Baga while in the Ribatejo winemakers have planted a number of foreign cultivars to see how they fare in Portuguese soil. The Setúbal Peninsula not only offers powerful reds, but lovely Moscatels; while to the south there is the Alentejo with its rich, silky red wines; and everywhere else, from the Algarve upwards there are even greater things in store.

In another respect Portuguese wines were always different to those of the rest of Europe. They were exceptional in that there was a focus on brands. Possibly the incentive here came from the powerful port wine trade; possibly the brands prospered because of the need for large quantities of reliable wines to slake the thirsts of Portuguese colonialists for whom regional demarcations were of little relevance as they had quit their native land generations before. Wines were made up from consignments of grapes brought in from different regions and assembled in the Ribatejo, Bairrada, Palmela or Vila Nova de Gaia. The dependence on, and to some extent the dependability of some of these brands, impeded the development of demarcated regions when the rest of Europe was already fixed on the qualities of their Rioja, Rheingaus, Bordeaux and Barolo.

Since the eighties, however, with Portugal's entry into the European Union, the country has been brought increasingly into line with the rest of a continent that perceives a branded wine as something cheap and of poor quality. The middle-class consumer wants to see a wine with a home and a landscape dotted with vines. In recent years even Portuguese consumers – increasingly divorced from the lands which bore their parents and grandparents – have decided the quinta or estate wine represents the

best. The writing seems to be on the wall, yet, and this is a sign of the obduracy of the branded mentality, many of these quintas are in fact nothing of the sort: just more brands posing as estate wines.

Some of the traditional brands are proving hardy too, however, especially when there has never been any dispute about their quality; and in the circumstances this is hardly something that one should rue. One of these is that wine Johnnie Graham first recommended to me: J.M. da Fonseca's Periquita. This has long since expanded beyond the narrow purlieus of the plot that gave it its name. Another example of a wine where the precise location of the vineyard is – I suspect intentionally – obscured is the prestigious Barca Velha, a wine which bears certain similarities to Australia's Grange and which many still believe to be Portugal's best.

One wonders how long these brands can last or whether they will have to become more specific about *terroir* in the future. Some argue that Portugal should take the Australian route, where brands are still perceived as a quality alternative to estate wines and make up the vast bulk of production; but Australia is increasingly alone. The rest of the world is united in the idea that good wine means estate wine, and with time Australians too might well begin to insist more on wines created in the vineyard, rather than the lab, however good the results.

Giles MacDonogh

London 2001

the history of
Portuguese wine

History is vital to the understanding of Portuguese wines, it demonstrates precisely how and when the country took its highly individual path. The precise period of the first plantings is disputed, but it seems unquestionable that small quantities of wine were made from the Bronze Age onwards. Indeed, there have been archaeological finds in the Douro which prove as much. The Greeks traded off the Algarve coast, and their coins have even been found as far north as the banks of the Douro. Whether or not they had a hand in planting wines in Portugal, the Greek method of fermenting grapes in giant terracotta pots or amphorae has proved remarkably tenacious in the Alentejo and the Algarve. It was the Carthaginians from their home in north Africa who, schooled in winemaking by the Phoenicians, who were the first to create a colony on the Peninsula in

about 1,000 BC, long before the Roman province of Lusitania, but we do not know if they planted vines on Iberia's western seaboard.

After the defeat of Carthage in the Punic Wars, the Romans settled on the north bank of the Tagus at Olisipo, the present Lisbon. The substantial remains of the temple of Diana in Évora give ample evidence of the degree of their settlement south of the Tagus. Digs also provide indications of Roman cultivation of the vine in Portugal from 218 BC onwards, possibly to provide wine for a permanently thirsty Italy. Evidence has been found that vines were planted in the Douro too.

The Barbarian invasions may have interrupted winemaking, but they did not put a stop to it. Germanic tribes now settled in the north of the country. The Suevi, or Swabians, and the Visigoths had no distaste for wine and a Visigothic code dating from the seventh century clearly alludes to it. The Arabs were a greater menace. They arrived after 711 and even if their stay in the northern Minho lasted a mere few decades they remained a presence for centuries in the Alentejo and Algarve. Naturally, as Moslems they gave no encouragement to wine even if they allowed their Christian helots to carry on drinking it freely enough. Certain monastic institutions, such as the abbey at Lorvão near Coimbra, continued tending their vines unimpeded and there were pockets of vines in the Alentejo and the Estremadura. The Church was responsible for keeping the vine alive at that time and in return wine became a Christian weapon; drinking it, an affirmation of faith. A cup of wine liberated you from your alien, teetotal lord.

Evicting the Moor provoked a bacchic celebration. From the time of the *Reconquista* – which finished in 1249 – planting vines and drinking wine took on an extra special significance as did the consumption of pork. Religious orders played a very important role in all this, particularly the Benedictines and their austere reformed wing, the Cistercians. These monasteries also needed to plant vines to provide wine for Holy Communion; more important still, they needed to finance their own communities. There was work to do: the Arabs had enjoyed some success in suppressing wine drinking by encouraging conversions, especially in the deep south.

Portugal was gradually reconquered from the kingdom of Leon in northern Spain and its first rulers remained vassals to its monarchs. In 1095 the king of Leon had assumed direct rule over the Portuguese. His illegitimate daughter, Teresa, married Henry of Burgundy, who established the first county of Portucale. On 6 April 1129 Portugal declared its independence under their son Dom Afonso Henriques. In 1139 he began to style himself 'king' although international recognition didn't come for another forty years.

The first kingdom stretched from Minho to the Mondego rivers. Lisbon fell after a protracted siege in

1147. During the fight, Anglo–Norman mercenaries refreshed themselves with the products of numerous vines around the city. An Englishman, Gilbert of Hastings, became first bishop of Lisbon, establishing a close contact between two of the world's great seafaring nations. Another Englishman, the monk Osbern, was the great chronicler of the *Reconquista*. From 1165– 1169 the battle moved to the Alentejo, leading to the foundation of the see of Évora. The process was not irreversible, however, and between 1171 and 1190, much of the hard won territory was overrun by the Arabs.

The pugnacious, militaristic style of the *Reconquista* was effected by the Papal shock troops of the day, the orders of chivalry. Together with the ecclesiastical orders they were compensated for their labours with large estates all over Portugal, particularly in the Alentejo. These were only released from the hands of the Church and the orders in the nineteenth century; when the Portuguese monarchy found itself bankrupt after the civil war and reverted to the old trick of dissolving the monasteries to restock their depleted coffers.

It was the Benedictines who built the great fortress–like cathedrals you still see in Oporto, Lisbon, Coimbra, Viseu, Guarda and Braga. The Cistercians established the country's two great abbeys at Alcobaça and Santa Cruz in Coimbra. Exceptionally the Benedictines functioned in the towns and cities, while the Cistercians classically established their abbeys in the countryside. Alcobaça with its 360 square miles of land was a phenomenon. The Cistercians promoted scientific agriculture, reading deep in the works of the Roman agronomist Columella to find out how they had cultivated the vine. Centuries later when the Englishman William Beckford visited the monastery he was struck dumb by the size and scale of the kitchen alone. One particularly well-preserved example of a small scale Cistercian abbey is the Convento de Aguiar wine estate near Castelo Rodrigo in the north-east, which is also an excellent little hotel and as far from the madding crowd as anyone could wish.

Portugal established its maritime trade in mid thirteenth century. It was regulated in 1377 by Dom Fernando (1367–83), who also extended the vineyards to the south. Exports begin at this time, and some Douro wine made its way down to Oporto and Gaia on the south bank of the river, which was originally the home of the the city's noisy coopers. Although Portugal had been born of a Spanish rib, there was never any love lost between the two states. In 1385 the new Aviz king João I saw off a Spanish invasion at the Battle of Aljubarrota. Later English architects helped design the great commemorative abbey church of Batalha built near the site. It was not the first instance of Anglo-Portuguese military cooperation – a defensive pact had been signed in 1373, and English ships had had access to Portuguese ports from 1353. When they left it was often Portuguese wine that filled their holds. The alliance was formalised by the Treaty of Windsor signed on 9 May 1386: the Portuguese agreed to support John of Gaunt's claims to the Castilian throne. On 1 November the English duke met the Portuguese king in Ponte de Mouro, near the wine town of Monção where it was decided to cement the pact with nuptials. In 1387 King João married John of Gaunt's 26-year-old daughter Philippa. Henry the Navigator was one of the results.

From his base in Sagres in the Algarve, it was Henry who planned the journeys that opened up the world to Portuguese mariners. The famous era of the discoveries provided a fillip to wine production. Not only was wine required for the sailors who undertook the long and often perilous journeys in their *caravelas* and *naus*, but many of Portugal's new subjects developed a fondness for it, particularly in Africa. Lisbon became the greatest entrepôt in Europe as a result. Camões describes Vasco da Gama giving normally teetotal Mohammedans a little treat:

As mesas manda pôr em continente;
Do licor que Lieu plantado havia
Enchem vasos de vidro, e do que deitam
Os de Faeton queimados nada enjeitam.

He ordered tables to be spread at once
With foaming bowls of Bacchus' liquid;
Phaeton's scorched Muslims drank their fill,
Relishing the vintage, spreading goodwill.
Trans. Landeg White

In Portugal's more temperate colonies – such as the Azores – vines were planted. After the seven-year fire which initiated the new territory of Madeira, vineyards were developed before the middle of the fifteenth century and the ensuing wines were admired almost from the outset.

Early Modern Portugal

The enormous take-off of Portuguese trade as a result of its new, burgeoning empire proved the people's undoing. The land was deserted and the population was sucked towards Lisbon and the prospect of easy money. Industry was abandoned and the reliance on the entrepôt trade led to economic collapse. In the meantime the markets had plenty to offer: ivory, 'grains of paradise' (pepper) from the African coast, cinnamon and cardamom from Ceylon, cloves from the Moluccas, mace and nutmeg from the Banda islands, aromatic woods from Timor, and camphor from Borneo. Much of it was re-exported to northern Europe, allowing Portuguese merchants to stow a few casks on board to warm the palates of those inhabitants of what contemporary native poets see as a snow-girt wasteland.

The crisis occurred at the time of the Counter Reformation when the Church achieved absolute power over the state through the Inquisition. The country ground to a standstill with more than a third of the year given over to religious holidays. Intolerance was rampant: and many Jews and 'new

Christians' (that is Jewish and Mohammedan converts, whose loyalty to the Church was deemed questionable) were burned at the stake in gruelling *autos-da-fé*. The elimination of the Jewish colony was a further setback to Portuguese trade, as it had been responsible for a good deal of commerce. The Portuguese attitude to foreigners – especially Protestants – was also unsympathetic.

The penultimate Aviz king, Dom Sebastião, died in 1576; like his tragic ancestor, Dom Fernando, he had tried to take on the Moor on his home ground and was slaughtered in the Magreb. After much wrangling the dynasty was wound up four years later, and the Spanish king, Philip II, took over. There was not much trade carried out during the *dominio filipino*, and no encouragement given to Portuguese merchants. The Invincible Armada included 31 Portuguese ships, however. It was the first time that Portuguese had borne arms against their old ally – England.

In 1640 Dom João IV, duke of Braganza, reluctantly ascended the throne after the revolt of the Portuguese nobles. In reprisal for his allowing Charles I's nephew Prince Rupert to operate his fleet from the Tagus, and for supporting the Stuart cause, Richard Cromwell forced Portugal to sign the Treaty of Westminster in 1654. It stipulated that Britain be allowed to trade with the Portuguese colonies and that Britons might practise their religion on Portuguese soil, even if Protestants as yet enjoyed no diplomatic protection and had to bury their dead in the sands by night. It cannot have been clear at the time what great advantage the British would eventually derive from this new commercial treaty. Only after 1700 did it become apparent that the British would receive a large part of the riches being grubbed up in the mines of Brazil, where gold had been discovered six years before.

The Treaty was confirmed at the restoration of the English monarchy in 1660. Portugal made a further present to the new king in the form of Catherine of Braganza, who arrived in Falmouth in April 1662 as the bride to the new King Charles II. She brought Tangiers and Bombay with her in her dowry. In 1668 the Spanish finally recognized Portuguese independence but retained Ceuta, Portugal's last colony in North Africa. There were compensations: foreign politics were increasingly deciding English drinking norms: close relations with Portugal meant more and more Portuguese wines flooding the market from 1678 onwards, to the detriment of the traditional English tipple, Bordeaux claret.

A British 'factory', or merchant community in Oporto was first mentioned in 1666 and firmly established in 1678 when the bulk of its business shifted from Brazilian sugar to Portuguese wine. In 1682 an Anglican pastor was sent out to look after the colony's spiritual needs. There were other British factories at Lisbon, Faro, Coimbra and Viana de Castelo. This transformation of English drinking habits, with ever more Portuguese wine taking the place of French formed the subject matter of at least six poems by the barrister cum poetaster Richard Ames, who went out to visit London's inns on a fruitless *Search after Claret* in 1691.

> ... we went first to the Vine
> To see from those grapes we could press claret wine
> But the master it seems was an ill–pickled youth,
> And assur'd us his Vine was of Portugal growth.

The letter books of the Madeira merchant William Bolton written at the end of the seventeenth century reveal just how dependent Portugal was on its overseas trade by the eighteenth. The island was supplied from anywhere other than Lisbon. In exchange for wine shipped to the West Indies, New York, Boston, England and Ireland, South America, Saint Helena, Madagasca, India and Java, Bolton received cargoes of food, manufactured goods (including sash windows) and wheat. Madeira could not hope to provide the butter and cheese it needed. This came from Ireland, Newfoundland cod (incidentally still available from the pretty covered market in Funchal) was delivered from across the Atlantic, as was whale oil and timber – from Boston and New York – rice and maize – from Carolina and Virginia. Sugar was shipped from the West Indies. Woollens, silk, cotton, furniture, pewter and plate came from London.

Madeira wine had yet to evolve into that which we know today. The island still produced sizeable quantities of non-fortified dry wines: ordinary reds and whites, Verdelhos and dark, staining brews from the Negra Mole grape which as 'Tent', had been popular in England since Shakespeare's day. The ancestors of fortified Madeiras were late-picked Malvasia ('Malmsey') and Vidonia wines – but as yet unfortified. Adding brandy occurred for the first time during the War of the Spanish Succession (1701–1714). That way it was hoped they might last until the end of the conflict.

Portugal had yet to admit defeat as far as commerce was concerned. It was still to have its own, Colbert-style, reforming finance minister in the conde d'Ericeira. He advocated a far-sighted mercantilism in an attempt to kick-start Portuguese manufactures. Silk worms were bred in the Amoreiras to the west of Lisbon, in a bid to beat Lyons (Europe's great manufacturing centre) at its own game. Maize was planted north of the Douro, and corn bread or *broa* became the rule in the Minho at this time. The Pragmatical Decrees, which obliged the native population to wear the simplest clothes, were thought to be aimed at excluding British cloth and promoting Portuguese fabrics.

The Methuen Treaty

This brief economic experiment came to an end with the new century, and the centre of European navigation passed from the Tagus to the Thames. This was bad for the Portuguese economy as a whole but decidedly good for native vine growers. Port wine was first exported at the end of the seventeenth century, but its eventual adoption as 'the Englishman's wine' was due to the English Trade (better known as the Methuen) Treaty of 1703: a pact which maintained Portugal in a form of economic vassalage for a century and a half, but which none the less guaranteed the Portuguese nation, only recently ripped from the claws of Spain.

Sir Paul Methuen was the British Ambassador to Lisbon. In exchange for support in the War of the Spanish Succession Britain won valuable concessions in the Portuguese markets which further facilitated well-established relations now that British cloth sales were slumping in northern Europe. The Portuguese had won a considerable coup in being able to supplant all those other nations which had hoped to dump their wines on the thirsty British market. The Treaty wiped out native looms that had been doing reasonably well and it would later be blamed for stunting the growth of all Portuguese industry (there was a small expansion over the next hundred years). Brazilian gold probably played a greater role, however. Between 1,000 and 3,000 tons entered Lisbon in the first half of the eighteenth century. Much of it was used in *talha,* or the elaborate baroque decoration of eighteenth-century Portuguese churches. It found its way to Britain too, in specially adapted ships.

The period was not entirely negative, however: few are. Many great palaces were constructed using architectural ideas culled from Italy. One of the most famous of these is Mateus, near Vila Real, which has figured on the label of the famous *rosé* in its bulgy, Germanic *Bocksbeutel* for nearly sixty years. The story goes that Fernando van Zeller Guedes offered the proprietor of the estate a percentage of every bottle sold, but he rejected the deal, saying that the taste for sweet *rosé* would not last, and took a paltry lump sum instead.

The Methuen Treaty changed the face of British drinking and restarted the Portuguese economy in the process. From 1678–1687, imports of Portuguese wine averaged just 632 *pipas*, equivalent to 550 litre casks. A century later they had risen to over 40,000 casks per annum. From the diary of John Hervey, first earl of Bristol, it is clear that Portuguese wine became a commonplace in Britain in the first years of the eighteenth century. A great consumer of first growth claret, champagne, burgundy and hermitage, Bristol made his initial purchase of Portuguese wine in 1710. For the Whigs to drink Portuguese wine was to support the anti-French cause. France, after all, was playing host to the Stuart Pretender. There were economic reasons besides, as Daniel Defoe forcefully pointed out in his pamphlet 'Trade with France, Italy and Spain' of 1713: Britain was at a trading disadvantage with France. The Whig Dean Swift (who was made chaplain in Lisbon in 1702, but never took

up his post) was no exception. In February 1713 he conceded to Stella 'I love white Portugal wine better than claret, champagne or burgundy. I have a sad vulgar appetite.' Only Tories and Jacobites – the latter in specially designed glasses which contained a drop of liquid inside a bubble in the stems – continued to drink expensive claret. The glasses allowed them to toast the king 'over the water', namely in France.

Those who knew Portugal were less certain of the advantage the Treaty had brought to English consumers. William Colbatch had been chaplain in Lisbon just before the signature of the Commercial Treaty. He called the Portuguese 'a people who cannot be insensible to the great advantage that our trade brings to their country; for we furnish them with our woollen manufactures and feed them in a great measure with our fish from Newfoundland, and in exchange for these commodities, we rid the country of their wines (and that at excessive rates) which all of the wiser and better sort among them think much better parted with at any rate, than kept at home.'

Methuen also jumped on the bandwagon himself. He had his own vineyard at his quinta outside Lisbon and sent consignments of wine back to Britain where 'Methuen' was a byword for red Lisbon in the first half of the century. Besides his own brews, Methuen had his favourites: Barra Barra from Santarem and *palhete*, which was possibly a claret-like confection, made from a mix of black and green grapes.

As the century wore on, however, it was port from

the Douro which stole the hearts of the English public. From 1720 onwards it was laced with ever greater additions of raw brandy, much to their delight. Addison's *Spectator* gives a fine example in 'honest Will Fennel, the West Saxon'. Fennell was trying to compute how much liquor had passed his lips these last twenty years: 'twenty three hogsheads of October [ale], four tuns of port [ie 4,800 75cl bottles], half a kilderkin of small beer, nineteen barrels of cider and three glasses of champagne, besides which he had assisted at four hundred bowls of punch, not to mention sips, drams and whets without number.'

The treaty was considered a scandal in certain quarters from the first. Writers before and after Adam Smith have never ceased to point out that Portugal had renounced all prospect of industrial development, and the British in return were overrun with Portuguese wine – and, more importantly, Brazilian gold. During the eighteenth century, some were moved to complain that not enough of the latter was forthcoming especially when the great minister Pombal sought to clamp down on the illegal export of bullion and began to prosecute British gold smugglers in the ordinary courts. Mercator's' *Letters on Portugal* of 1754 point out that a great deal more Portuguese gold needed to find its way to London if the trade were to be worthwhile. The Portuguese took in cloth, armaments, manufactures, metals and coal from England, and butter, salt beef and salted fish from Ireland. From Newfoundland and Nova Scotia came the vital dried cod. In exchange, lamented Mercator, all the Portuguese had to offer was wine. The British took Pombal's clampdown seriously, and sent Lord Tyrawley as ambassador to Lisbon to parley with the court. He even threatened war, although in his heart, he had little sympathy for the pampered merchants, dismissing the whole business as 'a pother about nothing'.

As it was the British prime minister, Pitt, was up to his ears in the Seven Years' War and had no time to see to the claims of outraged merchants in Portugal. Pombal was able to punish whomsoever he pleased. There was evidence, however, that the English were getting their own way – *and* the precious Brazilian gold. In *From London to Genoa* of 1770, Joseph Baretti was shown the secret compartments built into the ships which traded with Portugal. 'I need not tell you that the Portuguese (considering king and people together) are very rich in gold and jewels. Their riches however, are not the product of Portugal, but of their ultramarine settlements: and I have often heard it affirmed with confidence, that from Brazil alone they draw yearly above two millions sterling. As to Portugal itself, its products are but scanty and its manufactures inconsiderable. The only things that it yields in very great plenty, are oranges, lemons and wine. Of these the English buy up large quantities; but still the balance of trade rises high in their favour, as the Portuguese get from them many articles both for home and their settlements abroad. Therefore the surplus due to England is paid by Portugal in gold; and this gold goes every week into the holes in the cabin.' Baretti did not think, however, that the trade would come to an end 'as long as [England's] inhabitants are fond of the bowl and the bottle...'

Forty years on, in April 1811 the French politician M. de Puymaurin was moved to protest in his pamphlet *De la Fabrication des vins en Angleterre*. Portugal continued to exert a stranglehold on the British market. In 1792, for example, 26,938 tuns of Portuguese wine entered Britain at a value of £667,184; compared to 1,617 tuns of French wine at a value of £40,152. In 1833 Cyrus Redding also thundered against the Treaty and its effects 'which disgraced the good sense of the British government, and ensured the worst wine in Portugal for the British market... under the specious pretence of encouraging our woollen manufactures.'

The Marquês de Pombal

Sebastião José de Carvalho e Mello, the future conde de Oeiras and marquês de Pombal, entered government in 1750 with Dom José. As a diplomat he had served in London and Vienna and married an Austrian who had contacts with Maria Theresa's court. He had had ample chance to admire central European enlightened despotism during his ambassadorship to Vienna. In 1755 central Portugal was hit by the most destructive earthquake in modern European history. Pombal ordered the rebuilding of Lisbon, imposing dour architectural uniformity on the new *quartiers*. He was highly influenced by what he had experienced in Britain, and wanted to see Portugal's mercantile fortunes revived. In the same year as the earthquake which destroyed Lisbon, he received a delegation of Douro landowners who were upset by the British merchants' threat not to buy their wine that year, because, they said, the farmers were in the habit of adulterating it.

Although he in no way objected to the trade as enshrined in the Methuen Treaty, the landowners' complaints gave him the excuse he was looking for: to curb the power of the overmighty merchants who had been squeezing the growers over prices. As a contemporary put it, the objective was 'to hurt them in such a way they cannot scream.' In 1756 he licensed the Real Companhia or Companhia Geral de Agricultura das Vinhas do Alto Douro, partly at least, to 'restrain the unbounded greediness of the English merchants' and stop them from adulterating the wines with pepper, sugar, elderberries and to establish a fair price. It was not just the English who were meant to suffer: the growers of the Dão and Bairrada were doubtless peeved at being pushed out of the area privileged for port production. And for miles around peasants were forced to pull up their profitable elders, with which they coloured their weedier wines.

The owners of the new company were a group of interested Douro farmers, men who had the ear of the minister. On the suggestion of a friar, João de

Mansilla, whose family owned vines in the area, the whole wine-producing region of the Douro was to be demarcated, although the statute contained some notorious inclusions and omissions when it was published in 1761. As one recent historian has put it, 'shrewd economics [were] tempered with venal corruption'. One notorious instance of the latter was the Minister's own estate at Oeiras on the Tagus, some hundreds of miles south of the region, which was allowed to despatch its wine to Vila Nova, to enhance family fortunes.

The English trade reacted badly. It disliked the privileges accorded to the newly formed company, which enjoyed a monopoly on the sale of brandy, and in supplying the taverns of Oporto. The British are thought to have encouraged disgruntled coopers and innkeepers in what has come to be known as the Drunkards' Revolt of Ash Wednesday (February 23) 1757. The Oporto mob seized a sympathetic judge from his sickbed and marched him through the streets of the city before sacking the house of the director of Pombal's wine company. Pombal responded ferociously: he sent a squadron of cavalry and two infantry regiments to put down the riots and 478 people were subsequently tried. Thirteen men and one woman were hanged, their limbs exposed on spikes around the city. The judge was of their number.

Once again, not everyone in Britain sympathized with the loud complaints of the English traders in Oporto. The author of the *Memoirs of the Rt Hon*

Viscount Cherrington, Richard Miller, was in the service of the Portuguese Crown. He visited the factory house as they were throwing a lavish ball to celebrate one of the early victories of Frederick the Great in the Seven Years' War. He found them boorish – 'a set of traders and wine merchants, the utmost extent of whose knowledge never went farther than the art of dextrously imposing upon each other, or upon their correspondents in England, and in keeping clear and mechanical accounts of debtor and creditor.'

William Dalrymple, who visited Oporto in the 1770s, was not won over either. He enjoyed feasting with the merchants at the factory house:

'The only thing I disliked among them was their supercilious treatment of the Portuguese from whom they derive their wealth and opulence. They complained heavily of the exclusive privilege of the wine trade, granted to the Portuguese company, which, from all I could find, appeared rather a disadvantage to the company than to Great Britain; for from the principle, that a rivalship in commerce is of advantage to the consumer, the London market has been supplied with better wine since the establishment of this company, and the commodities of England are still exported as before...'

Dalrymple was another who thought port an overrated drink: 'It is surprising, that any nation that has the least pretence to refinement, should so long persist in drinking such an infernal liquor as the wine sent from this place to the English market; in its genuine state, it is agreeable, but to please the palates of our boreal friends, such a quantity of spirits is incorporated with it, that it is rendered poisonous and destructive to those who use it.'

There were other wines from the Lisbon area such as Charneco (which is commemorated by a rare grape variety in California) and Carcavelos, which came from the hills close to Pombal's palace in Oeiras. Ames mentioned the latter at the beginning of the century, and the traveller Richard Croker found it 'miserably bad' in 1799; on the other hand he was impressed by what he drank at Williams' English Hotel in Lisbon: 'Excellent wines, in the greatest variety, are found here, port only excepted: this favourite beverage of the English nation has no honour in its own country.'

The Peninsular Wars

Napoleon's tentacles spread out over Europe after 1806. Portugal fell foul of the Corsican by its refusal to adhere to his ban on trade with Britain and French troops were despatched into the Peninsula. Spain took advantage of the attack to annex several villages east of the River Guadiana. They should have been returned in 1814, but never were. The loss of the town of Olivença, south of Badajoz, still rankles today.

At the approach of the French Marshal Junot in 1807, the king and 10,000 courtiers and hangers-on fled to Brazil under British escort. The British Army commanded by Sir Arthur Wellesley, later duke of Wellington, landed at Figueira da Foz and defeated the French at the Battles of Roliça and Vimeiro. In the Douro, Portuguese soldiers took advantage of the steep slopes to establish positions in the vineyards which permitted them to fire down on the invading French armies. The shameful convention of Sintra of August 1808 concluded peace, but allowed the French to return under British escort with their booty. There was outrage throughout Britain and Lord Byron gave voice to his anger in *Childe Harold*. Portugal none the less benefited from the war. It became an 'economic lung', re-exporting British goods to Britain's Continental enemies.

The French returned in 1809 when Marshal Soult occupied the north of Portugal. Wellesley also came back and drove him out; according to one famous story, literally capturing Soult's dinner as it was laid out in the Factory House in Oporto, and sitting down with his officers to eat it. In September 1810 Wellington – as he now was – and his fellow countryman Beresford beat Masséna at Bussaco. In the British armies was the future Lieutenant-General Sir William Warre, a scion of one of the British trading families in Oporto. In his letters home he found the time to grumble about the continuation of the 'infamous Wine Company' and its restrictive practices. He was evidently the man who could be relied upon to furnish his commanding officer with a pipe of port. It was not until May 1813 that the last Frenchman left Portuguese soil. By then 100,000 Portuguese were dead and trade and commerce had come to a stand-still.

The Nineteenth Century

The war was over, but Portugal was still in turmoil. Politically it seethed. An increasingly unpopular Marshal Beresford had been left in charge while the king languished in Brazil. In 1820 a successful revolution broke out against the absent crown – Portugal was to have its constitution and 'Cortes', or legislative assembly. In 1821 Dom João VI was summoned back after fourteen years in Brazil and swore an oath to the new constitution. Dom Pedro, his son, however, refused to return. A month later he was declared Emperor of Brazil, while another son, Dom Miguel, raised an army against the Cortes and the constitution. Dom João responded by abolishing the latter. In 1826, however, at the death of Dom João, Pedro refused to accept the crown and proposed his seven-year-old daughter Maria da Gloria as queen. She was to marry Dom Miguel, her uncle, but Dom Miguel's refusal to accept any legal limitations to his power led to Dom Pedro's return and a long-drawn-out civil war.

Constitutional Pedroites faced reactionary Miguelites. Fighting on the liberal side were the writers Almeida Garrett (of partly Irish origin) and the historian Alexandre Herculano. From 1832–1833 the city of Oporto was defended by an international brigade of cockneys and Glaswegians. The port companies naturally took measures to protect their interests, but with only limited success. A chapel owned by the British port company, Grahams, was inscribed with the legend 'propriedade Inglesa' in the vain hope that would do the trick. The siege lasted eighteen months, with the Miguelites blowing up or setting fire to a number of port wine lodges in Gaia. Some 27,000 tuns of port ran into the Douro, turning the river a muddy red. One witness to this was Joseph James Forrester, a talented and far–seeing British merchant who was later ennobled by the Portuguese king. The war came finally to an end when Miguel was defeated and banished, and for the next three quarters of a century Portugal functioned as a constitutional monarchy.

The civil war had been destructive. Trade and industry had been nullified, the government was bankrupt. One of the first actions of the new regime was to abolish the company created by Pombal in the Douro, which Henry Vizetelly (1880, No pais do vinho do Porto) had been quick to characterize as 'absurd'. It was reinstated ten years later, but shorn of the arbitrary powers granted to it by Pombal. In 1834 all church lands were confiscated. These amounted to roughly a third of all property in Portugal. Their sale created a new landed middle class among the purchasers. Many of the larger wine estates we know today owe their origin to this act of regal theft. One of these is the Englishman Piers Gallie's delightful Quinta do Convento da Franqueira in the Minho, another is the Alentejo's most recherché wine, 'Pera-Manca', which comes from a Jesuit property built in the shadow of an old charterhouse or cartuxa.

The Methuen Treaty, which bound Britain to Portugal, was increasingly unpopular in both countries. Borrow was moved by his cold reception in Elvas to complain of a 'treaty of commerce' which had obliged the British to drink '...coarse and filthy wines, which no other nation cares to taste.' No less a voice than that of Adam Smith was added to the clamour against a treaty: 'by which we obtained the exclusive privilege of supplying the Portuguese markets with woollens; but the Portuguese would not have had the power of giving effect to the Treaty, or of supplying us with the equivalents for our woollens, had we not given them the monopoly of the British market for wine. The Treaty was thus obviously productive of a double mischief. It was injurious to the Portuguese, by narrowing their market for woollens, and attracting too great a proportion of their scanty capital to the production of wine; and it was injurious to the British, by obliging our government to impose heavy, discriminating duties on the wines of France and other countries, which compelled us to buy much worse liquor at a much higher price, at the same time that it stimulated the French, Spaniards, etc to retaliate on our commerce by excluding several of our most valuable commodities from their markets.'

The Methuen Treaty was eventually scrapped by an agreement between the British foreign secretary Lord Palmerston and the duke of Palmela in 1842. Its passing heralded a brief period of free–trade in wine. In 1860 Britain and France signed the famous free-trade or Cobden-Chevalier Treaty by which it was hoped to wean the common man off gin and onto table wine. Grocers' shops were able to sell wine by the bottle for the first time. The snobs scoffed at 'grocers' claret'. Five years later the Royal Company lost its exclusive privileges in Oporto. All port houses became equal before the bar. Port prospered, but elsewhere Portuguese wine exports to Britain very quickly slipped away to a position of about half those brought in from France, and slightly lower than Spain.

Relations between Britain and Portugal worsened due to colonial rivalry. They nearly came to blows over Africa: Britain's desire to link north to south collided with Portugal's to unite east and west. In 1897 the British signed another Treaty of Windsor, this time with Imperial Germany. The name must have stung, especially when the Portuguese learned the nature of the pact: Portugal's colonies were to revert to Germany in the event of the Portuguese state suffering financial difficulties. In Oporto they changed the name of the Rua Nova dos Inglezes (the new street of the English) to the Rua Nova dos Ladrões (the new street of thieves).

This mutual disaffection showed up in the wine. It might have been the moment to wean the English onto the better natural wines, which were still respected at the time, such as Colares or Bucelas. Port was being condemned in many quarters. The wine merchant T.G. Shaw, for example, writing in 1863, stated that 'port is losing its caste, seldom seen on the tables of the higher classes; and we know that when anything in this country has become vulgar, its fate is sealed.' There was already a feeling that Britain might have made a mistake to encourage port producers so much. Writing thirty years before in his *History and Description of Modern Wines*, Cyrus Redding criticized the Methuen Treaty for promoting the 'brandied wines of Portugal, at the expense of those of a worthier character.' It was Forrester's argument too. Until he went under in the Cachão Rapids, the baron fought tirelessly to cease adulterating and lower the alcoholic content of port. Ideally, he thought, port should have the strength of burgundy – an allusion perhaps to the idea that the grapes of the Douro such as Tinta Roriz were thought to have arrived with the Burgundian kings. He was fighting a losing battle, one of his contemporaries described a brandy free port as 'an abominable drink'. As the nineteenth century went on, the strength of port increased.

Elsewhere, Portugal became increasingly a producer of bulk wines. There was great demand in the Portuguese-speaking world, as no Portuguese colony could provide for its own drinking needs. Along the banks of the Tagus, in Vila Nova, or in the Bairrada region, huge wineries were built, often with more Brazilian gold, with the expressed purpose of making wines for export to Angola, Goa, Timor or Rio. Sadly the wines were too crudely made at the time to have a more general appeal. Fortified wines were regulated, but not table wines, and the absence of workable cooperatives meant wine of very variable quality. They were only good for the hard–nosed farmers who laboured under the scorching sun of the tropics.

Despite the hopeful predictions of jealous colonialists who coveted it for themselves, the Portuguese was the last of the great European empires to collapse, only being finally wound up after the Revolution of 25 April 1974. At that point bottlers who could not find a market among Portugal's many large expatriate communities were forced to the wall.

The Twentieth Century

The second half of the nineteenth century was characterised by further political instability. This ultimately resulted in the declaration of the Republic. On 2 February 1908 both Dom Carlos and his eldest son, Luis Filipe, were assassinated in the Terreiro do Paço in Lisbon. The double murder led to chaos. Manuel II succeeded but ruled for just 30 months. During that brief swansong of the Portuguese royal family, the dictator João Franco extended the demarcated areas in Portugal which were to become the basis for its DOCs at the far end of the century. Statutes were signed protecting Colares, Carcavelos, Moscatel de Setúbal, Dão and the vinho verde country of the Minho. On 3 October 1910 revolution erupted again, however, and Manuel left to go into exile on board the inevitable British warship.

The first republic carried on the work for a while and similar laws were issued to protect both Bucelas and Madeira on the eve of the Great War. Shorn of its monarchy, Portugal was none the less careful to honour commitments to its old ally. In 1916 the seizure of some German vessels led to a declaration of war. The Portuguese Army fought alongside the British on the Western Front, its little force ruptured in the German Spring Offensive of 1918. The unrest in the country continued after the war. A spate of assassinations led to a military dictatorship from 1926–1933. It was followed by the rather more famous Estado Novo dictatorship of Antonio de Oliveira Salazar, the professor of economics at Coimbra and minister of Finance. Salazar brought in a new constitution in 1933 and occupied the post of prime minister from 1926–1968. He was succeeded by Marcelo Caetano, professor of administrative law.

Salazar's measures were felt in every area of Portuguese life, not least in agriculture. He encouraged the 'interior' colonies to relieve overpopulated parts of the country, and shifted the centre of wine production to the area between the Douro and the Tagus. The Alentejo was reserved for grain production, as in Roman times. He also created a number of regulatory bodies to govern production and exports as well as the *selos de garantia* which supposedly ensured the quality of the wine in bottle. Salazar's biggest legacy to wine, however, has been the many regional cooperative cellars. The first of these, in Muge in the Ribatejo, was created as far back as 1935, but most were founded twenty to thirty years later. The cooperatives were Salazar's pride and joy, and even now some of them are at the forefront of quality winemaking in Portugal. Sadly, however, in some regions they were granted the power to stifle almost all opposition which further retarded the development of estate wines.

Salazar was cautious in his foreign policy. He supported Franco, but gave the British the run of the Azores in 1943, while continuing to supply the Germans with wolfram. Portuguese fascism was eventually brought down by a revolt provoked by the strain of long-drawn-out colonial wars and unhappy junior officers who were passed over for promotion in the armed forces. The Revolution of 25 April 1974 was led by a group of army captains. There was a short period of lunacy when it looked as if a good many businesses would be nationalised and some of the larger private fortunes appropriated. Indeed, two port firms, Borges & Irmão and Royal Oporto, were briefly purloined by the state. The big estates in the Alentejo were occupied and there was some talk of nationalising foreign-owned farms in the Douro. There is a story that one German farm was menaced in this way, and that the then German Chancellor, Helmut Schmidt, telephoned Lisbon to say that for every farm they nationalised he would send home 100,000 Portuguese *Gastarbeiter*. The threat of land appropriation ceased. In general, it was a mild, bloodless coup and within a few years the country had turned to the series of centre-left ministries – occasionally interrupted by

the odd centre–right administrations – which continue to this day. A new constitution published in 1989 finally buried the rhetoric of 1974. Portugal had well and truly calmed down.

Despite an overweaning pride in the cooperative he created, Salazar's era witnessed the birth of some of Portugal's most successful wine companies. Sogrape was founded in 1942, while the rest of Europe was at one another's throats. Its business was mostly based on the highly successful Mateus rosé brand until the eighties, when it spread out into the regions and started making up market wines in the Dão and the Douro. In the meantime it has acquired the port house of Ferreira and with it Barca Velha and a number of top unfortified wines.

More important as far as the improvement of quality in Portuguese wines, has been the creation of a system of regional appellations and DOCs. The process was accelerated after 1986, when Portugal joined the European Community – or Union, as it has since become. That has allowed Portugal to escape from the bulk mentality which had led to the planting of productive cultivars all over the country and focus once again on tradition and quality. The transformation of the wine business mirrors the general desire to see Portugal move forward as fast as possible. As the former prime minister Cavaco Silva put it, 'Portugal needs to do in ten or twenty years what other countries achieved in a century.' It looks set to succeed. The future now looks rosier than it has for a very long time.

principal grape varieties

whites

Alvarinho is Portugal's most media-friendly white wine grape. It is the same as the highly prized Albariño of Spanish Galicia. Its origins are obscure, but many find in it a resemblance to the noble Riesling of the Rhine, Mosel and Danube. It does best in the drier parts of the northern Minho, and unlike the other vinho verde grapes it improves with age. Some growers now ferment it in oak, with mixed results. There have also been plantings outside the Minho, notably in the Estremadura, where José Neiva successfully blends it with Chardonnay.

Antão Vaz is a popular thick-skinned green grape, apparently indigenous to the southern Alentejo where there are some 174 ha planted. It yields well, ages well and has both flavour and aroma.

Arinto is another grape variety with two personalities: as **Padernã** it is a useful source of acidity in vinho verde. It is a late ripener and makes rather weightier wines in sunny Bucelas, so much so that certain growers ferment it in oak and treat it as something like a Chardonnay substitute. It is generally thought of as one of the best grapes for white wine. There are 81 ha in the Alentejo where it is believed not only to provide acidity but also complexity. It goes by a variety of names, one of them being **Pé de Perdiz Branco**, or 'white partridge foot'. Many of the local names point to a grape of Spanish – possibly Galician – origin. **Arinto do Dão** is not the same grape, it is a synonym for **Assario**, a

variety which crops up both in the Dão and the Alentejo.

Avesso is a popular cultivar in the Douro Litoral region of vinho verde. It tends to be a mite rounder than the usual varieties.

Azal Branco is a white vinho verde grape grown around Amarante and Penafiel.

Batoca is also used in vinho verde.

Bical is a promising grape in central Portugal where it is the mainstay of the whites from the excellent Casa da Saima. José Neiva makes a fine pure Bical, one of just two in the country, he says. In the Dão it is called **Borrado das Moscas** or 'fly droppings', an allusion to the size of the grapes. It is sensitive to diseases. When blended with **Maria Gomes** it makes a harmonious white Bairrada.

Boal. In the Douro this is a synonym for the French **Semillon**.

Cercial is a sharp but aromatic white wine variety in the Dão and the Douro. Its thin skins make it sickly. It needs to be harvested before the rains. It should not be confused with its homonym on Madeira.

Códiga. White variety popular in the Douro.

Crato Branco is the workhorse white wine grape in the Algarve. It tends to make strong, heady whites.

Encruzado takes its name from the cross-like form of the first shoots. It is highly valued in the Dão, where it is often vinified in oak, with good results.

Esgana Cão is the famous 'dog strangler'. So sharp, they say, that not even a dog would eat it. It is actually Madeira's **Sercial**, but on the mainland it has no great distinction.

Fernão Pires is the most commonly planted white wine grape in the Ribatejo, where it was burned for brandy. It has qualities of its own, adapts well, makes well balanced refreshing whites and has a pleasant grapefruit-like taste. Its disadvantage is a comparative lack of acidity. It needs to be brought in early. It is called **Maria Gomes** in Bairrada.

Gouveia is a white variety popular in the Douro.

Jampal is a green grape found in the Estremadura and the Ribatejo.

Loureiro. This is one of the most important grape varieties for white vinho verde, where it provides the fresh, floral aromas found in the best of them. The scent is not long-lasting, however, and it tends to need a friend, generally **Trajadura**.

Malvasia is apparently all things to all men. The **M. Corada** or **M. Fina** are synonyms for **Vital**. It has nothing to do with the more aromatic sorts of grape known by this name elsewhere in Europe, or indeed on Madeira.

Manteúdo is a dull, Alentejo white; it produces

alcohol but little else of interest.

Maria Gomes is Bairrada's name for **Fernão Pires**.

Moscatel de Setúbal. This is the big berry, Alexandrian Muscat which is used to make the great sweet wines on the Peninsula.

Olho de Lebre. 'Hare's eye' is a fairly common-or-garden green grape, the same as **Malvasia Rei**.

Padeiro Branco is thought to be the same as **Ugni Blanc** or **Trebbiano**. The name is used in the Minho.

Perrum is the increasingly favoured white grape in the Alentejo, where there are nearly 200 ha planted. It is believed that it might have hailed from Andalucia. It is small and thick-skinned and well-suited to the hot sun.

Rabo de Ovelha. This is the same as **Rabigato**. A very widely planted variety in Portugal: there are 1329 ha in the Alentejo alone. It is a decent all-rounder. In the Alentejo it needs to be picked early to retain its acidity.

Rabigato. The 'cat's tail' is the same as the 'ewe's tail' or Rabo d'Ovelha. They have funny cats in Portugal.

Roupeiro goes by as many names as the town drab. In the Alentejo – where it is the most widely planted green grape – it is also sometimes called **Alva** and in the Dão, **Siria**, while it masquerades as **Códega** in the Douro. It does well in the high Beiras where it makes the crisp white wines which should bring fame to the region. It is a good cropper and aromatic, reminding

tasters of tropical fruits, but in the Alentejo it needs to be picked early to prevent the wines from being flabby.

Talia. This is probably a corruption of 'Italia' and is the **Trebbiano** or **Ugni Blanc**. It was almost certainly imported for base wines for brandy in the Ribatejo.

Tamarez is common in southern and central Portugal.

Tamarez d'Azeitão is the same as **Trincadeira das Pratas**. It behaves capriciously.

Trajadura is one of the most popular grapes for white vinho verde, and provides the necessary back-up for the more lyrical **Loureiro**.

Viosinho makes fresh white wines in central and northern Portugal.

Vital is the workhorse white.

reds

Alfrocheiro Preto is one of the black grapes which lends colour, acidity and individuality to Dão wines. It is not thought to be local in origin, not even Portuguese in fact. It is gaining in popularity these days. It also makes a showing in the Alentejo. Sometimes known as **Pé do Rato** or 'rat's foot'. It tends to rot in rich soil.

Alicante Bouschet. This pariah grape in France is now recognized as being one of the best parts of a blend in the Alentejo and in the Ribatejo, although there are still pockets of it as far north as the Douro. A *teinturier*, it was developed in the mid nineteenth century for its deep, blue-black colour. In the

Alentejo, however, it offers much more besides, including a haunting blackberry scent. It is at its best at the Herdade de Mouchão or the old wines from the Quinta do Carmo. The 1987 Carmo *garrafeira*, for example, was an eye-opener.

Aragonez is the Alentejo's name for the **Tinta Roriz** which is the Tempranillo of Spain. There are nearly 600 ha planted in Portugal's southern province and it is gaining in popularity.

Azal Tinto is an astringent grape used for red vinho verde.

Baga. The mainstay of Bairrada's red wines. It is an abundant but late ripener and Baga can be as tough as old boots or as rustic as a dung heap in a poor year or in the hands of an inexpert winemaker. When handled well its result can be glorious, and it exudes a wonderfully rich blackberry scent. It does best on limestone. It is sometimes found in the Ribatejo (called **Poeirinha** or the 'little dusty one') or in the northern reaches of the Estremadura.

Bastardo. 'Bastard' has been known in Britain since Shakespeare's time; indeed Prince Hal refers to 'brown bastard' at least twice in *Henry IV Part I*. Thought to be identical to the **Trousseau** in the formerly Spanish Franche-Comté region of France, it is now on the wane in the Dão and Douro – pity really, it would be a perfect gift for a supermarket marketing man. The style of the wines is described as 'claret-like'. It ages quickly, but yields are low, which must be why there is so little of it about.

Borraçal is a variety used in red vinho verde.

Camarate is a stocking filler in the Estremadura, thought to be the same as **Moreto** and **Castelão Nacional**.

Castelão is the new EU approved name for a grape

which goes under the names of **Castelão Francês**, **João de Santarém** (in the Ribatejo), **Periquita** (in the Sétúbal Peninsula and the Alentejo). It is one of the very best black grape varieties in southern Portugal, acting rather like the Grenache Noir in southern French blends. Like Grenache it is not deeply coloured, but it provides alcohol and aromas. Mixed with **Trincadeira** it forms a stable partnership in the Ribatejo. In the Alentejo the duo becomes a trinity with the addition of **Tinta Roriz** or **Aragonez**. There are as many as 2,078 ha planted here. Young it is supposed to remind tasters of redcurrants. It can be quite gamey with age. In Palmela it is generally used simply by itself. In Bairrada it can be too luxuriant to be really useful.

Espadeiro Tinto is one of the better black grapes which go to make red vinho verde and no relation of the Palmela grape of that name, which is in reality **Trincadeira**.

Jaen is the **Tinta Mencilla** of north-east Spain. Pilgrims are believed to have brought it back after walking to Compostela. It has a short vegetative cycle, which makes it ideal for the higher parts of Dão, such as Gouveia, where the soil is porous, granite sand. In Bairrada it makes wines with low acidity but good aromas.

Marufo is probably a synonym for the undistinguished **Mourisco Tinto** which is used principally for port. Also known as **Olho de Rei** or the 'king's eye'.

Moreto. An also-ran black grape in the Alentejo, where it has played a role for centuries. It produces large crops but gives little alcohol. Used only in blends. In Bairrada they speak highly of it in and around Cantanhede and Coimbra.

Mortágua. A synonym for **Castelão** or **Touriga Nacional**, depending where it is planted.

Moscatel Roxo. There are tiny amounts of red Muscat grown on the Peninsula, and both J.M. da Fonseca and JP make wines from it.

Português Azul. A grape which is gaining a renewed reputation in the Douro. It is much despised in France, where it used to be planted in Gaillac, and in Germany and Austria, where as **Blauer Portugieser** or **Portugieser** it makes very ordinary red wine.

Ramisco. The grape which dominates in the few remaining plots of vines in Colares. J.P. Ramos uses it to make a wine elsewhere in the Estremadura.
Rufete is a Douro variety believed to be the same as the **Tinta Pinheira** in the Dão.

Sousão is an underrated port grape which might be the same as the Minho's **Vinhão**. It does well in the Douro where it is increasingly highly prized for port. It was widely planted in California in the years before Prohibition when fortified wines were the main vocation of Napa winemakers.

Tinta Amarela. Sometimes known as the **Rabo d'Ovelha Tinto**, this quality Douro grape tends to be despised for its sickliness. It is a good provider of aromas.
Tinta Barroca. One of the favoured five in port production, it is also used in red Douro table wines.
Tinta Caiada is also known as **Monvedro** in Oeste,

Carcajolo and **Tinta Lameira**. Generally appreciated for its robust health, it should taste of prunes and provide colour. As yet there is but little.
Tinto Cão was called the 'dog' because of its poor yields and truculent behaviour. It is one of the best grape varieties in central and northern Portugal and is increasingly vinified on its own.
Tinta Miúda. This is Rioja's **Graciano**, a small black berry which provides concentrated juice.
Tinta Negra Mole is the Algarve's stock in trade for red wines. It tends to produce rather pale, sinewy wines, although they improve with age. There is some dispute as to whether it is the same grape that bears the name on Madeira.
Tinta Pinheira is a bit of a Cinderella among Portuguese black grapes. It is relatively highly thought of in Bairrada, but it does not age well.
Tinta Roriz. Also known as **Aragonez**, this is the Spanish **Tempranillo** and provides silky, fruity wines which remind me of raspberries, but other tasters think more of plums. In Portugal they do not tend to be clobbered with quite so much American oak as they get on the Meseta. Popular everywhere, it furnishes colour and complexity and ages with grace. In the Alentejo it has a tendency to shrivel if picked too late.
Touriga Francesa is one of the big five in the Douro, and one which is considered interesting on its own. It has been championed by Peter Bright. The wines are dark and tannic and are often marked by a

mineral character, accompanied at times by the smell of ripe grapefruit.

Touriga Nacional is the top black grape for port production, and as such it has been planted all over the world by countries interested in making a stab at port. Although it was probably born elsewhere, for the past century it has been associated chiefly with the Douro. In the past twenty years its reputation has been transformed by the view that it is also Portugal's most important table wine grape.

Now it has burst out of the narrow confines of northern Portugal and has become something of a vinous cynosure; there have been attempts to plant it in every region from the Algarve to the Minho. In the last few years there has even been interest from Spain! A producer in Priorato has admitted planting Touriga Nacional.

It was long believed to be related to the Burgundian Pinot Noir, but this has now been disproved by DNA tests on the grape. It almost certainly originated in the Dão region, possibly in the village of Tourigo.

Although Touriga Nacional was always blended it is currently fashionable to vinify Touriga Nacional as a monocepage for table wine. Certain estates have built their reputation on this: Quinta dos Roques in the Dão, for example, or Douro table wines as Calém's Lagar de Sá, Ferreira's Quinta da Leda, or the Quinta do Crasto.

Touriga Nacional has many things going for it,

not least its generally healthy condition and resistance to fungal attack. Young Touriga wines are marked by the smell of black fruits: blackberries, elderberries, sloes, as well as pine needles, gum cistus (the Douro *esteva*) sometimes even rosemary.

Professor Loureiro, who makes the wine at Quinta dos Roques, suggests Tronçais oak marries best with Touriga. In Dão, the grape's probable birthplace, it was more likely to be chestnut.

Trincadeira. Currently seen as one of Portugal's very best, Trincadeira is a popular grape variety for adding colour, body and structure to wines in the Alentejo – where there are more than 2,000 ha - and the Ribatejo. It is meant to taste of plums, but also of pepper and herbs, becoming jammy with age. It is now to believed to be the perfect stablemate for **Castelão**. It is possibly the same as the Douro's **Tinta Amarela** and is also a synonym for **Espadeiro**, **Mortágua** and the Algarve's **Crato Preto**. It has to be treated with care in the Alentejo, however, where the fierce sun can lead it to shrivel up. That doesn't stop growers from planting it: at the fashionable Tapada de Chaves estate, the red wine is 60% Trincadeira.

Vinhão is one of the best and most flavoursome grapes used for vinho verde, above all on granite sand soils.

river minho

chaves •

valpaços • miranda do douro •

braga • **trás-os-montes**

vinho verde

rios do minho

porto • river douro • régua • **douro**
• lamego

• varosa
• encostas
da nave

castelo rodrigo •
pinhel •

lafões • • viseu

bairrada **dão**

coimbra •

beiras

estremadura

• covilhã
• fundão

leiria •
alcobaça •

• tomar river tagus

• encostas d'aire

obidos •
santarém • • chamusca **portalegre** •

torres
vedras • • almeirim
• cartaxo
alenquer • • coruche
arruda •
colares • bucelas • **ribatejo** **borba** •
lisbon •
carcavelos • • redondo
palmela • évora •
setubal •
arrabida reguengos • • granja
• amareleja
• vidigueira
• moura

**terras
do
sado**

alentejo

madeira

funchal •

graciosa

biscoitos •
pico **terceira**

algarve

lagos • • portimão tavira •
faro •

Portugal's
wine regions

Since Portugal joined the European Union in 1986 a large number of new wine regions have been officially recognised. There are now four tiers to Portugal's wine legislation.

The first level, **Denominação de Origem Controlada (DOC)**, includes established designations of origin such as Vinho Verde, Dão, Bairrada, Colares, Bucelas, Setúbal and Carcavelos.

The second tier of newer wine regions goes under the heading of **Indicação de Proveniência Regulamentada (IPR)**. Some examples of IPRs are Chaves and Lafões.

Grape varieties, maximum permitted yields and ageing requirements are rigorously controlled at both levels.

The title **Vinho Regional** covers a series of larger wine regions and permits greater flexibility in terms of grape varieties and ageing. There are eight Vinhos Regionais: Minho, Trás-os-Montes, Beiras, Estremadura, Ribatejo, Alentejo, Terras do Sado and Algarve.

Wines that fall outside the DOC, IPR or Vinho Regional requirements are classified as Vinho de Mesa (Table Wine)

The Minho

Portugal's northernmost wine region is also its wettest. The humidity of the Minho has given rise to an individual form of wine over the centuries: red and white vinho verde (green wine), so called because it is best drunk whilst the wine retains its fresh, youthful character. This sharp, refreshing wine used to be made solely from high trained vines which the locals sent up to the tops of trees or propped up on pergolas in order to preserve precious space for other crops below. It was a cheerful wine, drunk foaming straight from the cask in half pint mugs; it was the heart and soul of the *tasca* or pub.

That wine has changed a little. Vinho verde now comes in bottles and foams less, but it is generally cleaner and fresher than it was in the past, and a little more serious. Still principally a summer wine, it is now no hardship drinking it in the colder months as well. Few vinhos verdes are bottled with a vintage date on the label as the wine is assumed to be from the most recent harvest.

The Minho has other faces. Where the region touches the Douro Valley the weather is hotter and drier, and the wines have more alcohol and greater depth of flavour; and there is Alvarinho which makes a claim to being Portugal's greatest white wine. The grapes are grown in arid pockets on the Spanish border. It has more alcohol than vinho verde and a capacity for maturation. A good Alvarinho exudes the aromas of fruits and flowers but is supported by a steely acid backbone.

Trás-os-Montes and Douro

The Douro has been associated with the 'Englishman's wine' (port) for three centuries and it has only been in the past fifteen or twenty years that the unfortified red wines of this ravishing valley have begun to create an identity for themselves. Everyone is agreed that the Douro has the potential to make the best red wines in the country, but there are several schools of thought as to how to perceive the wines, and until recently the port producers have been resistant to the idea of allotting decent grapes for red and white table wines, and therefore diminishing the quantities available for port. Douro producers can only make top table wines when they agree to allocate the best grapes.

There are two DOCs, one for port and one for the non-fortified wines of the Douro. Added to this are three recently created IPRs: Chaves, Planalto Mirandês and Valpaços. The regional appellation, Trás-os-Montes (meaning Behind the Mountains), provides an opportunity for growers to use foreign cultivars on soils that are mainly granite-based.

Beiras, Bairrada and Dão

Beiras is a house with many mansions covering much of central Portugal. It is divided into three sections: Beira Litoral by the sea, Beira Alta up in the mountains and the Terras do Sicó on the plains. In the highlands of Dão are produced some of Portugal's greatest red wines, relatively high acidity providing great length of finish in brews made from indigenous grapes such as Touriga Nacional and Alfrocheiro Preto. In Bairrada the Baga grape is also capable of

making wines of excellent quality. Like Dão, Bairrada contains some of Portugal's great individualists, and increasing number of growers are learning from their success. It is hoped that with time the two newest DOCs will start to gell too: with altitudes up to 600 metres, Beira Interior would seem most interesting for white wines.

There are four DOCs: Dão, Bairrada, Beira Interior and Távora-Varosa; plus one IPR in Lafões.

Estremadura

The Estremadura is a large and still largely inchoate region hugging the sea to the north of Lisbon. Sometimes known colloquially as the Oeste in reference to its location on the Atlantic west coast. Only Alenquer lies to the east of a range of hills which tend to break the back of the more humid weather and allow growers to make bigger, stronger wines as a result.

It is an area for specialities: vinho' leve is a light white wine consumed in the summer months, the regional equivalent of vinho verde. Down on the coast there are three surviving historical wines: the port-like Carcavelos, Colares – for which the vines are planted directly in the Atlantic sands to the north of Cascais – and Bucelas, a serious white wine under threat from Lisbon's sprawling suburbs.

Where some regions have opted for a single appellation with regional subdivisions, the Estremadura has gone the whole hog and created a

couple of handfuls of DOCs, some of which lack definition for the time being. The older, established DOCs are Colares, Bucelas and Carcavelos – the latter has a tiny production; then come the new regions, formerly IPRs: Lourinhã (for brandy only), Torres Vedras, Arruda, Alenquer, Óbidos, Encostas de Aire and Alcobaça.

Ribatejo

As its name implies, the Ribatejo embraces the vines which lie on either side of the Tagus up river from Lisbon. Historically this was chiefly a source for bulk, branded wines which went to slake the thirst of parched colonialists in Africa, Brazil and the East. Latterly much of it was used to fuel Portugal's armed forces until the Revolution put an end to Portugal's ancient empire.

The comparatively unsophisticated wines made in the Ribatejo in the past tend to colour people's attitudes even today, when a good many excellent estates have come to the fore making powerful red and white wines. In general the weightier wines will be made in the poorer soils away from the alluvium which proved such a boon to the more commercially minded ventures of the past.

There is just one DOC covering the Ribatejo, with six subdivisions: Almeirim, Cartaxo, Chamusca, Coruche, Santarém and Tomar. The regional appellation allows for a freer use of foreign cultivars.

Terras do Sado and Setúbal Peninsula

Since the middle of the nineteenth century, the Setúbal Peninsula has been best known for its sweet, fortified Muscat wines, but red wines also flourish in the arid, sandy soils of the region which juts out like a spur into the Atlantic. One variety in particular, the Periquita or Castelão has brought fame to the wine town of Azeitão which lies at the centre of the region, tucked in behind the national park.

Azeitão, and the Peninsula in general, are dominated by two highly successful firms: J.M. da Fonseca and J.P. Vinhos. These tend to obscure a growing number of excellent small producers and reliable cooperatives, such as that at Pegões.

In recent years there has been a degree of successful experimentation with other grape varieties, not all of them of Portuguese origin. These experimental wines carry the regional label: Terras do Sado.

Setúbal is the DOC for the sweet wines, Palmela its counterpart for unfortified dry wines.

Alentejo

The hot, spacious, rocky Alentejo, which covers almost a third of continental Portugal, has been a discovery of the past twenty-five years. In Salazar's time its vocation was to produce cereals: it was Portugal's bread basket. Vines were few and far between, a few rows here and there, or an ancient vineyard attached to a noble demesne. Things have blossomed since the constraints were lifted at the Revolution and few would have the temerity to deny the fact that the Alentejo makes some of Portugal's suavest and most prestigious red wines as well as some interesting whites – now that equipment is available for cold-temperature fermentation.

In complete contrast to the northern regions the

Alentejo is divided into large estates, some of which are many hundreds of hectares in size. There were formerly a number of separate DOCs for the Alentejo, but in 1995 a general appellation was created and the single DOC now has eight subdivisions which figure on labels under the word Alentejo: Portalegre, Borba, Redondo, Reguengos, Évora, Moura, Granja-Amareleja and Vidigueira.

The region also produces a large proportion of the world's cork.

Algarve

In the past generation tourism and wine have collided head on in the Algarve. The sun and sea have attracted millions of people to Portugal's southernmost beaches, and the result has been a seemingly unbroken line of hotels constructed along the shoreline, interspersed with golf clubs and other amenities thought proper for the tourists' needs. The peasants and fishermen who used to eke out a frugal living under these blue skies have now deserted their fields and boats to seek more profitable, less arduous work in hotels and restaurants. Some of the vineyards have been deserted, others have been sold to make way for more hotels and more golf courses. Only two of the cooperatives at the heart of the four DOCs are functioning correctly at present, but there are signs that salvation is at hand in the form of a number of private estates owned by rich individuals who want to have a wine of their own, and are no longer interested in sending their grapes to the cooperative.

Once this movement gets under way it will be good news for the reputation of Algarve wine. Up until now the region has been notable for some powerful, aromatic whites from Lagoa and some more or less rustic red wines. Some decent Muscat wines are also traditional to the region, but it would be difficult to argue that there was no room for improvement.

DOCs: Lagos, Portimão, Lagoa and Tavira.

The Islands

Wine is still made on Portugal's remaining island territories: Madeira and the Azores. Most of the former falls outside the scope of this book, but the Symington family – which has a controlling interest in the Madeira Wine Company – makes a fresh rosé wine from Tinta Negra Mole grapes which can come as a relief to visitors to the island, after an uninterrupted diet of fortified wines – most of them sweet.

Most of the wines made in the Azores archipelago are also fortified and bear a slight resemblance to sweet sherry: Biscoitos comes from Terceira, while Pico hails from the island of the same name. The only unfortified wine from the Azores is the delightfully named Graciosa, which also has a slightly sherry-like, oxidised style.

IPRs: Biscoitos, Pico, Graciosa.

the minho

The DOC is divided into five sub-regions: Monção, including Melgaço; Lima e Braga, including Ponte da Barca, Viana do Castelo, Arcos de Valdevez, Barcelos and Guimarães; Basto; Penafiel; and Amarante. There is some agitation to create a new zone on the Douro, given the very different climatic conditions there.

Maximum yields are 80 hls/ha, and the minimum alcohol is 9% for whites and 8.5% for reds.

For red wines the recommended varieties are Borraçal, Espadeiro and Vinhão, except in Monção, where Pedral and Brancelho are favoured, and the mountainous Basto where they approve Padeiro Basto and red Rabo de Ovelha. For whites Monção favours the classic three: Alvarinho, Loureiro and Trajadura; Lima e Braga omits Alvarinho and adds Pedernã; Basto advocates Pedernã, Azal Branco and Barroca; Penafiel, Azal Branco, Loureiro and Pedernã; and Amarante, Azal Branco and Pedernã.

Given the low alcohol content of the grapes, Minho wines lend themselves to the production of both sparkling wine and brandy.

In 1998-1999 the region produced 397,550 hls of white and 205,120 hls of red vinho verde, as well as 1,244 hls of white and 1,117 hls of red regional wine.

Almost the whole of northern Portugal, from the Mondego River upwards, is one great granite plateau. In the Minho region between the Douro and the border with Spanish Galicia the granite is occasionally interspersed with ancient crystallines and pockets of Silurian schists and pierced by thermal springs. It can rise quite high, with grapes being grown at 700 or 800 metres. Rivers such as the Lima, Tâmega, Cávado and Homem cut deep furrows in the rock, bringing more water to a region already famous for rain. Apart from a two-monthly lull in July and August, it can be guaranteed to rain here on and off all the year round. The Minho can be fiercely hot in the summer months, however, and remarkably arid. As the locals put it, 'in August, the hills run dry; in September, the wells run dry; in October, everything runs dry.' It is the moment to broach a bottle.

We should not exaggerate, however; vinho verde country has little in common with the land which produces port. Although they touch, the Minho is climatically very distinct from the Upper Douro. The one is Atlantic, the other Mediterranean.

Vinho verde is one of Portugal's great claims to fame – a speciality. It is called 'green' wine because it is 'immature', made from underripe grapes and

- the land of vinho verde

not destined for long conservation. Its weakness is also its strength: with a light prickle, a refreshing acidity and low alcohol, it is one of the most refreshing wines I know.

Everything is granite here. From pre-historic effigies of pigs to the posts supporting the vine trellises, to the walls isolating fields and vineyards, granite is everywhere you look, surfacing in the middle of the thin soil and turning it into impenetrable rock. To the unschooled eye the granite looks much the same, but there is *old* granite (we are talking relatively here) and *new* granite. Wines made from grapes grown on old rock have more aroma. The newer the bedrock, the more fruit and weight to the wine.

It is fertile for all that. Here is the greatest density of population in rural Portugal – indeed at 216 per square km, as great as anywhere in Europe. They work the land. There are over 100,000 farms in the region, and of these 90% possess vines. There are over 150 bottlers, 22 cooperatives and about 30 large companies trading in the vinous products of the Minho's soils. All farmers appear to use every inch of that precious soil to grow a bewildering cornucopia of edibles and drinkables. Ideally the Minho is self-sufficient; the farmers practise a form of autarky which does not require them to shop elsewhere. It has been suggested that these farming techniques came from the Visigoths, who in turn learned them from the Romans. The Romans didn't settle here happily, however: they preferred Évora. The Minho they found too wet.

The Visigoths adapted to the climate better. Their presence is recorded in so many non-Latin place names in the region: Adaufé, Redufe and Merufe, for example, are instances of Germanic names; whereas the Latin influence reappears in Vila, Vilarinho or Paço. The Visigoths and their descendants did not get round to drinking wine in the Minho until later. They liked cider, and their tastes may have had some bearing on the sort of wine which evolved in the region after the end of the first millennium.

Monção's wines were the first to gain an international reputation, and they were shipped to Britain before port, as we know it, ever existed. Already by the sixteenth century people were calling the wines from the River Minho the best in the land, and Camões alludes to them in *Os Lusiadas:*

Entre os braços do ulmeiro está a jucunda
Vide, c' uns cachos roxos e outros verdes...

Vines threaded the boughs of the elm
With hanging clusters, purple and green...
Trans. Landeg White

The wines were shipped from the port of Viana Cabeça do Lima, now Viana do Castelo; but Vila Nova de Gaia soon eclipsed Viana, and port wine Monção.

The region between the Douro and Minho was demarcated early. The first decree dates back to 1908 and the monarchy. This was further enhanced in 1929. In 1953 Salazar's government laid down the law on what grape varieties might be used and two years later he launched the cooperative movement which was one of his chief claims to fame.

The overcrowding led to emigration from the sixties onwards. There was simply not enough land to nurture all the Minho's children. They went to Brazil, Canada, the United States, they also went to France and Germany. Every year in August they return to show off their flashy new cars and their newfound wealth. They build retirement homes – often in execrable taste – by the sides of the main roads, and they marry their children off to other Portuguese emigrants in elaborate ceremonies which go on for days on end. The whole month of August is a cacophony of firework displays. Huge *morteiro* missiles are sent up at tremendous risk to life and limb and the roads are permanently clogged up with hooting cars with their telltale snippets of gauze attached to the radio aerials; an indication of a forthcoming wedding.

The Portuguese who stayed behind tell jokes about the emigrants, and mock the curious language they speak which often combines French and Portuguese, but for the time being these millions of voluntary exiles are fiercely loyal to their country, and they eat Portuguese food at home. More importantly, they continue to drink Portuguese wine.

The wines from the different parts of the Minho region express themselves in different ways. Monção, Lima, Braga, Basto, Amarante and Penafiel all possess subtly different *terroirs*. These are reflected in the grape varieties which predominate. These have now been tried and tested and the best ones figure among the recommended sorts. This approach was made necessary by the sheer number of cultivars that exist in the region; some 65 in all.

Now it is much clearer than ever before. The drier, hotter area on the River Minho around Monção and Melgaço is ideally suited to Portugal's best white grape, Alvarinho, but Monção also fares well with Pedral and Brancelho for its reds. Near the Lima and the Cávado, the Loureiro has found its *pays d'élection*. Basto is a rugged, mountainous region on the western side of the peaks that separate the Minho from the dusty, arid area known as Trás-os-Montes or 'Beyond the Mountains'. Red sorts such as Rabo de Ovelha and Azal Tinto excel here. Down on the Douro the favoured grapes change once again: Avesso, Azal and Pedernã for the whites; Azal, Borraçal and Vinhão for the reds.

The most productive subregion is Braga, with 15,000 ha of plantable land. This is followed by Penafiel and Amarante with 10,000 ha apiece. Ponte de Lima is the smallest in terms of the amount of wine it makes, but it has the most individual growers: over 6,000 with an average of just 0.4 ha.

The methods of training vines are changing fast. In the old days the Minhoto would generally send them up some tall tree – generally a poplar, elm, linden, cherry or chestnut: it was called the *vinha do enforcado* or 'hanging man vine'. This was the method advocated by the Romans, which is still employed in the Italian Campania and in the pergolas used to make Lambrusco wines in the Po Valley. Roman writers such as Columella, Cato and Virgil may well have inspired the Visigoths who settled here. The national poet Camões also mentions it as a distinguishing feature of the Minho. Tree-training meant saving space to be used for other crops; it also provided windbreaks.

There are other traditional training methods besides. The vines can be festooned from trees, hanging from one to another, or set up on *arejões* in the schisty soils of the Terras do Basto or in the Tâmega Valley, that is attached to wires connecting two trees. Arbours are created for vines; or a *bardo* or fence is made using those celebrated granite posts. As the word would imply, a *cruzeta* includes a transverse beam to the fence allowing for more luxuriant foliage. This is a speciality of the Cávado Valley. If many of these old methods are disappearing, the trellises or *ramadas* are still a common sight. They have the added usefulness of providing shade in summer. On a large estate such as Aveleda, for example, they offer cool walkways protected from the sun. These arbours are ideal places to take shelter and enjoy a picnic of some freshly grilled sardines and a bottle of cold, slightly sparkling white wine. Locals use them for more profane purposes too: to listen to a game of football, to play cards or to take a well earned siesta after tending the vines.

The traditional vinification of the wines required a short malo-lactic fermentation which released some carbonic gas. The trick was to capture this, for it provided that refreshing prickle which was the charm of vinho verde. Sixty days after the harvest, the thirsty locals broached the cask. That was vinho verde at its best. It continued good until the end of the year, although by January the fruit was in decline. That youthful charm had a downside, however, for the rest of the year traditionalists were reduced to drinking a wine that was often dull and flat.

Vinho Verde

There is a lot of vinho verde. Currently there are 30,000 ha under vine, which is more than half the total hectarage of vines in Austria or Chile. Recent legislation has altered much of the spirit of the drink: the wine sold traditionally from cask in the *tascas* may no longer be called vinho verde even if, ironically, this is was what the wine was all about: when it 'punned and quibbled' in these old casks the locals referred to it as 'the champagne of the poor'.

There is now much more care spent in isolating the proper grape varieties for the wine. In the classic, damp regions, the key cultivars are Loureiro and Trajadura. Loureiro provides something of that spring flowers and lemon blossom character that is almost the hallmark of good vinho verde, but these aromas are not long lasting, and the fruit can fade after six months in bottle. The Trajadura has greater staying power and provides length. Another grape variety which is useful for body is Pedernã. Avesso tends to be high in acid, which makes it useful in the warmer stretches of the region, near the Douro, while Azal Branco makes crisp wines in the southern production centres of Amarante and Penafiel.

There have been considerable changes to the way vinho verde is grown and the way that vines are trained. Trees are very rarely used now, and fewer and fewer grapes are picked from the hedgerows which surround the compact properties of the Minho. In general the tendency is to plant on wires in dedicated vineyards. Inevitably this will reshape the wine. The more sap the grape receives, the more serious will be the stuff in the bottle: less of a summer thirst-quencher, more a wine to be savoured over a good meal.

Quality has certainly improved. You only have to taste some of the new wave vinhos verdes to know that. I am thinking now of wines such as Solouro, delicately exuding an aroma of lemon and acacia blossoms with a hint of grapefuit on the palate. This is a wine which is more than merely refreshing. Or the very serious Casa de Sezim, where the winemaker avoids the malo-lactic fermentation to lend it as much life giving acidity as possible – the perfect summer wine.

Another model, new-wave vinho verde comes from the Quinta Villa Beatriz in Santo Emilião. The nose is melon-like, but there is a classic malic sourness there too coupled with prodigious length.

Casa de Laraias is made from Azal Branco, creating a rather exotic wine in this instance, with the scent of passion fruit. Gilvaz from Quinta do Lago was less complex, having the smell of ripe apples. It is made principally from Avesso. Borges' 'single quinta' Quinta de Simaens, has a textbook sweet lemon nose with a sour finish. Similar in its flavour profile is the Quinta de Ameal.

Barcelos is classic vinho verde country: humidity and granite rock. The Quinta do Convento da Franqueira is here, the substantial remains of a Franciscan friary built around a holy well in the middle of the sixteenth century. It was bought by the Englishman Captain Brian Gallie RN, in 1961, and locally it is known as the 'Englishman's Quinta'. The captain's son, Piers Gallie, now vinifies the grapes from nine hectares of vines, mostly Loureiro and Trajadura, but with a tiny amount of Azal too, from which he makes a zippy, lavender-scented wine with some nice little nuances of peaches, apricots and honey.

I sat out with Gallie in the cloister surrounded by his various dogs, while he pointed out how much the cards are stacked against the vinho verde producers.

Nature is not entirely kind: the damp climate means frequent sprays to stop the grapes from getting mildew. Each time he disinfects his vineyards, it costs him £1,000; money which, he says, he finds hard to recoup. White wines are currently out of fashion in Portugal and there is less vinho verde drunk in the smart resorts such as Cascais or Estoril, or in the Algarve, than there was in the past. On the other hand, this depressed situation is not likely to last long, especially when there are few wines as refreshing as vinho verde to drink in a hot climate.

I learned this on my first ever trip to Portugal. It was a hot summer in 1980 and I often had recourse to a bottle of vinho verde with my fish at dinner. The biggest seller in those days was Gatão, which came in a Germanic *Bocksbeutel* with a label showing an image of Puss-in-Boots. Another I liked at the time was the Casal Garcia, which had a rather more dignified abstract, blue label, more reminiscent of a Portuguese tile, or *azulejo*.

Casal Garcia is one of several brands made by the Quinta da Aveleda, a 135 hectare domaine in Penafiel, which is particularly well represented on export markets – indeed, Casal Garcia sells six million bottles a year worldwide. The owners are the Guedes family, cousins of those who control that other important Portuguese wine company, Sogrape. It is a model estate with its farm buildings and one of the most ravishing parks in the north of Portugal. This was conceived by Manuel Pedro Guedes more than a century ago. There is an ornamental lake or two with bits of mediaeval masonry from Henry the Navigator's old house in Oporto set up on the island in the middle. The ruin is protected by a couple of bad tempered black swans, which have been known to nip the legs of tourists. The white swans are clearly frightened of them too and live elsewhere. Only the boss, António Guedes, seems to be able to discipline them.

Of course there are vines too. Some of these are still trained on traditional *ramadas,* which, as I have said, have the advantage of providing shady walks when the sun is up, but for the most part, more modern methods have pride of place.

The centre of the estate is the family home of the many cousins who live scattered round the country, but who can book themselves in at different times of the year. It is preserved as an Edwardian gem, filled with wonderful artefacts and possessing a delightful chapel. You eat in a dining room with a stained glass screen illustrating the coats of arms of the various empires which thrived in 1914: Hohenzollerns, Habsburgs, Romanoffs. Most of these families have since been deposed, but the Guedes family is still enthroned at Aveleda.

The range has expanded at the Quinta. There are now some successful varietal wines: Trajadura with a mineral-like, grapefruit smell; Loureiro with a classic aroma of spring flowers, but far less acidity; a refreshing blend of the two called Grinalda; and Aveleda, which adds a little Pedernã and has a rather denser fruit.

Wines labelled Quinta da Aveleda' include a little bought in Alvarinho. All these wines are dry, but Aveleda (as opposed to Quinta da Aveleda) and Casal Garcia are only half so – Aveleda is the sweeter of the two. They are quite frothy and need to be drunk well-chilled as a summer drink. Quinta d'Aguieira is a new acquisition in the Bairrada, where the wines are made under the supervision of Denis Dubourdieu of the University of Bordeaux – the so called *pape des blancs*. Not for nothing is one of the whites fermented in new oak like an upmarket white Bordeaux. Another is made from Bical and has a really intense taste of grapefruit. There is a red version made from Touriga Nacional and Cabernet Sauvignon, and Charamba – a Douro wine. This is a blend of Tinta Roriz and Touriga Nacional. It is made in the hot-country style with a nose of dried herbs, an excellent food wine. There is also a ripe, fruity Bairrada wine.

Over towards the Douro the wines enjoy much more sun and are less often doused in rain. There is naturally a lot more sugar in the berries by harvest time. Around Mesão Frio there is a patch which is not granite. Naturally the wines are very different from here. The burning desire in these parts is to see a new appellation created which highlights the special qualities of the wines. They have more fruit and alcohol, for example. One of the leading lights in this campaign is Champalimaud from Quinta do Côtto. His Paço de Teixeiró is a case in point. It has a creamy, malic character and has obviously rubbed shoulders with new oak. Its alcoholic strength is a prodigious 13%. It should be clear from this that the Champalimaud wine is a very long way from classic vinho verde.

Another Minho estate which has difficulty in accommodating itself within the rather narrower definitions of vinho verde, is the Quinta da Covela, which occupies an 18 hectare amphitheatrical site looking south across the Douro, just off the delightful old Régua to Oporto road. It is a very

attractive domaine which centres on a ruined sixteenth-century chapel. The slopes are steep and the owner of the estate, Nuno Araújo, equips visitors with cattle prods so they don't slip over and fall. Everywhere, it seems, natural springs bubble up providing all the moisture you could need in a dry part of the Minho. The area is peppered with estates. In the old days British merchants would have come up here looking for wines to turn into port, not light, frothy whites.

Araújo has elected to plant what *he* thinks will do best in that crumbly granite shale soil. He talked to his cousin, João Nicolau da Almeida, who pointed out that his was not vinho verde land. He then planted fifteen different varieties to see what would do best. The experimental period is drawing to an end. Now he concentrates on Gewürztraminer, Chardonnay and Avesso for his whites; and Touriga Nacional, Cabernet Sauvignon, Cabernet Franc and Merlot for his reds. With the help of his oenologist nephew Rui he makes three white wines and red and a rosé.

I tasted the fresh, sappy Avesso 'Campo Novo' after a swim in Araújo's pool. It was the ideal wine, with its high acidity and honey and apple bouquet. The rest were served with a lunch designed to honour the nineteenth-century writer Eça de Queiroz who lived at a neighbouring quinta.

Avesso is always the backbone, but Araújo uses foreign cultivars in the main wine, the Quinta da

Covela. Avesso is paired with Chardonnay to make wines which are both smoky and appley in their youth, but which develop complexity and richer fruit with age. The Avesso naturally provides a little useful acidity. There is an oak fermented version of the wine, which has a predictable vanilla–creaminess to it.

I was impressed by the Quinta da Covela red. The bouquet was a lovely reminiscence of red, summer fruits, and there was a serious tannic grip on the palate leading one to suppose that it would age extremely well. A most unusual wine for a region typecast as a producer of light, fizzy whites.

Red, Sparkling Wines and Brandy

The red was always the favourite vinho verde of the mere locals. In the past it was the overwhelming majority of vinho verde produced, but in recent years it has sunk to some 40% of the whole. Red vinho verde was made in tanks with submersible caps so that the maximum amount of colour could be extracted in the shortest possible time. Minhotos drank it out of little white ceramic cups – like those you still see in Galicia to the north – in order to admire the livid garnet hue. When an old-fashioned minhoto was impressed by the colour he would exclaim 'It paints well!' as he watched the wine tint the sides of his cup. He had another peep to judge the tears: 'It cries well!', he shouted, and called for another bottle.

Red vinho verde went well with the local foods, particularly salt cod, but its rustic reputation was against it. As the Portuguese grew more sophisticated, they wanted to know less and less about it, until a point was reached when most people in the wine trade were unaware that it existed. After a sharp decline in the quantity of red

vinho verde produced, it has rallied a little lately, as the Portuguese, like so many other people in the world, have accepted the cheerful findings of various wine-loving doctors and scientists, who have put it about that red wine is good for your heart, and prevents you from catching various wasting diseases.

The principal grape used is the Espadeiro Tinto, which reminds the British authority on Portuguese wines, Richard Mayson, of a light Pinot Noir. Others favour the Vinhão, which provides that vital colour. With better vinification these wines are less sour, or plain acid than they were in the past. In those days their significance was purely local. Now you meet quite serious red vinhos verdes, such as that from the Casa da Vila Boa, made by the Albuquerque de V. Lencastre family, descendants of England's John of Gaunt. This is a proper red, with a taste of sour cherries.

The cooperative in the pretty town of Ponte da Barca on the River Lima is the great specialist in red vinho verde. It was built in 1968, yet another vinous institution which owes its birth to Salazar. Until 1977 it bottled everything in five litre flagons for an essentially local market. On top of that it sold – and still sells – casks. These may not call themselves vinho verde now, but have to use the regional appellation. You can actually bring back your keg if you like, and have it filled up with the cheaper wine at the coop. Naturally this is not the wine it is most proud of. That now comes in 75 cl bottles. The reputation of its wines means that its bottles travel far and wide throughout Portugal.

Still fifty percent of its wines are white, but as its oenologist points out, there is a topsoil of gravelly sand here, and that is much better suited to red wines. There is nothing wrong with the whites, mind you: they are made from a blend of Loureiro, Trajadura and Pedernã and have a light, apricot-like bouquet and a little refreshing spritz. The top white is called Terras da Nóbrega. This is made from 100% Loureiro. It is a very pretty, floral vinho verde, with a lovely appley flavour.

The coop is happiest with its reds. The basic blend takes in Vinhão, Borraçal and Espadeiro. There is a pronounced cherry fruit, with a hint of almonds. It is very slowly fermented in order to leach out all the garnet colour in the grape and then they add back the press wine. For the elect the wine is the Terras de Nóbrega. It has a light mousse and smells strongly of sour cherries and blackberries. As I sipped from my cup at lunch, my neighbour reached across and muttered compassionately 'When God sends food as good as this, he sends wine to match.'

One way of putting the waning sparkle back into vinho verdes, is to vinify them as proper fizzy wines,

either in tank, or by using the champagne method. There are good reasons for exploring this particular route: the alcohol is naturally low, which means that the strength does not rise too high once the second fermentation has taken place. Another factor which recommends Minho musts to sparkling wines is the high acidity, which makes wines of this sort both refreshing, and a good, hunger-provoking aperitif.

For obvious reasons too, vinho verde makes some of the best brandy in Portugal. The same factors obtain: the wine is low in alcohol and high in acidity – just like the base wines for cognac. The most famous, and expensive, is Quinta da Aveleda's Adega Velha with its lovely incense smell, but there are plenty of others, some of them made from pure Alvarinho, like the Aguardente Velha from Monção, which smells of spiced oranges. Most of the cooperatives have a good, aged product; the 15-year-old VSOP from Ponte da Barca is a case in point. The Conde de Carreira is something rather special. It is over fifty years old; again, it is rather spicy, and naturally rather woody too.

Alvarinho

Up on the Spanish border there are two centres of Alvarinho production: Monção and Melgaço. In the opinion of many, these are the regions producing Portugal's best whites. The *terroir* is different to the part of the Minho dedicated to vinho verde. In Monção grapes are grown to some extent on pebbles, beside the River Minho which forms the border here; whereas the latter comes from rocky soils. The result, they say, is that Monção wines are softer, and the Melgaços are more acidic. The two sub-regions share a hotter, drier climate than the rest of the Minho, making wines with more body and alcohol which lack the sourness characteristic of vinho verde. In the summer the vines actually suffer stress from lack of moisture.

There is more Alvarinho in Melgaço. Eighty percent of the vineyards are planted with Portugal's favourite green grape, as opposed to 60% in Monção, where there is a lot of Trajadura and red varieties.

Monção wines were frequently compared to white burgundy in the past. Unlike the normal wines of the Minho, they were always perceived as *maduros* – capable of ageing. These were among the first, with those of Viana to be shipped to England. The grape variety here is the counterpart to the Galician Alvariño which has become so fashionable among rich Madrileños. Many think the Alvarinho came from elsewhere, and it is often suggested that it is related to the Central European Riesling, sharing something of that grape's nobility, as well as its steely acidity.

An impressive wine is the pure Alvarinho Portal do Fidalgo – made by Anselmo Mendes – with its rich, ripe, plummy fruit. Some winemakers are beginning to ferment Alvarinho in new oak, and the Portal do Fidalgo's old vine cuvée, Vinha Antiga, has the creaminess you would expect from this treatment. I am not sure, personally, whether it does not detract from the lovely bouquet.

The same approach had been used at Muros do Melgaço, where the creaminess betrays the oak barrel fermentation. There is enough fruit, however, to break through and the wine is nicely balanced. I tasted through a range of Melgaço wines with Mendes, who is a big cheese here, when he is not busy making wine in the Douro or the Dão. Solheiro has an almost meaty nose, like the very pleasant smell of fresh foie gras, but there is a more conventional smell of apricots besides. Q.M. stands for Quintas do Melgaço; it is the wine from the local promotional bureau. This is another one of Anselmo's wines, nicely measured and long. I was surprised by the residual sugar, however; at 6.5 it was quite high. Another is Dom Salvador, which also has a faint meatiness about it allied to the flavour of a conference pear. It has an attractive, juicy finish.

Dona Paterna smells like fresh orange juice. There is a little lemon peel tang on the palate, nice length and a powerful finish. At 12.5 % alcohol it is a long way from a standard vinho verde. The Encostas de Paderne has a strong, almost farmyard-like aroma, with substantial cut and thrust.

Touquinheiras returns to the fruit-bowl: oranges, with a little smokiness. It is long and creamy.

I admired an older wine from Carrolo. It had developed a certain complexity, a demonstration that you need to lay Alvarinho down for a year or two. Good too was the Encostas dos Castelos. The bigger, more commercial operations have picked up on Alvarinho too. The cooperative in Monção makes the popular and reliable Deu la Deu ('God given'). Another popular example from Monção is Muralhas, while the Palácio da Brejoeira seems to enjoy the admirable position of being wanted by every half-way smart wine list in the country. This is well merited: it was here that Alvarinho's merits were first perceived in the seventies. It is a ravishing property, easily seen from the road, and it makes itself 'worthy of a detour', by having a small museum. Aveleda in Penafiel is another large concern which makes a good one: it smells of stewed apricots.

The hype surrounding Alvarinho can have its disadvantages. Not all the wines from the region are pure Alvarinho, by any means, and they are none the worse for being blends. Take Varanda do Conde from Monção, for example, where a lemon and fresh flowers bouquet is created by the addition of Trajadura. Indeed, Alvarinho has become the cynosure of the whole Minho region, so that many people no longer think too hard about vinho verde, and the delicious, light-hearted wines which have slaked the thirsts of the northern Portuguese for the best part of a thousand years.

In 1998-1999 were produced 16,380 hls of white and 59,706 hls of red Douro wine. Yields are fixed at a maximum for reds and whites of 55 hls/ha. The minimum alcoholic strength is 11%. Recommended white varieties are Donzelinho Branco, Esgana Cão, Folgazão, Gouveio, Malvasia Fina, Rabigato and Viosinho. For red wine they are Bastardo, Mourisco Tinto, Periquita, Rufete, Tinta Amarela, Tinta da Barca, Tinta Barroca, Tinta Francisca, Tinta Roriz, Tinto Cão, Touriga Francesa and Touriga Nacional.

Two out of the three new IPRs in Trás-os-Montes – Chaves and Planalto Mirandês – declared no production whatsoever. The third region, Valpaços, made 868 hls of white and 1,227 hls of red. Trás-os-Montes also provided 7,100 hls of white and 25,148 hls of red regional wine. The Regional wine of Trás-os-Montes allows Douro producers, for example, to make wines using a broader palate of grapes: Gewürztraminer, Sauvignon Blanc, Semillon, Cabernet Franc and Sauvignon, Merlot and Pinot Noir are all possible.

Chaves is a region up to now better known for ham than wine. Maximum yields for reds and whites are 55 hls/ha. White wines may use Boal, Gouveia, Malvasia Fina or Códiga; reds: Bastardo, Tinta Carvalha and Trincadeira Preta.

Valpaços has the same minima as Chaves, but Fernão Pires rather than Boal is recommended for whites and adds Tinta Roriz, Cornifesto, Marufo, Touriga Francesa and Touriga Nacional to the palate of reds.

Planalto Mirandês is also minimum 11%; the whites are preferably made from Gouveio, Malvasia Fina, Rabigato and Viosinho; the reds from Bastardo, Marufo, Trincadeira and Tourigas Francesa and Nacional.

The remote and mountainous Douro, with its steep incised terraces descending to fast-flowing streams, its sparse, solid, whitewashed quintas surrounded by vineyards, orange and olive groves, is the loveliest wine region in the world. The rock – soil is a misnomer here – must have always looked promising to a man who wanted to make good wine: pre-Cambrian schist and crystalline rock from a time pre-dating most living organisms is occasionally penetrated by granite. The friable schist is particularly important: when the strata are formed vertically the roots of the plants can travel down the fissures in search of scarce and precious moisture.

trás-os-m

This ability to nourish the vine roots on rock alone is important in a region when there is next to no topsoil. What there is comes rich in potash, high in nitrates and phosphates. Planting is obviously a nightmare, and for centuries now Douro farmers have been skilled in the use of explosives, which is often the only way in.

Although it touches on the Minho Region with its high rainfall, the Douro's climate is wholly Mediterranean. It is shielded from the Atlantic by the Serras do Marão and Montemuro, which rise to 4,700 and 4,600 feet respectively and force the clouds to drop their loads before travelling east. Rain tends only to penetrate in the winter months. If there has not been a healthy downpour in January the Douro farmer will complain for the rest of the year.

It is very hot. In August the temperatures are unbearable, frequently surpassing 100 F and few people connected with the trade venture into the Valley at this time. They return in September when it's cooler, and it is time to pick the grapes. Winters can be rude. Frosts, virtually unknown in the Minho, are common here, and it is wet in the spring. I have travelled to an Upper Douro quinta at Easter when we have had to light a blazing fire to dry out our clothes, warming up a couple of bottles in the process, before warming ourselves up with the contents.

In the old days *socalcos* or terraces were built of smooth, ashlared stone, like the walls of some magnificent castle complete with neat little stone staircases. Such terraces are now considered too costly to work. Vertical terracing or *vinhas ao alto* made their appearance in the seventies, at about the same time as the new horizontal strips or *patamares* were introduced. The up and down terraces were the brain child of João Nicolau de Almeida, who was doubtless influenced by what he had seen in the Mosel and the Rheingau region of Germany. The horizontal terraces were created by bulldozers and allow access to tractors, yet they are anything but beautiful, and in contrast to the noble old constructions, look like some crude, Aztec earthwork. Anyone who wants to see the original terraces flanked by all the later experiments should go to Ferreira's Quinta da Boa Vista: the old estate of Baron Forrester has been preserved as a museum of Douro viticulture.

Nobody knows how many different grape varieties grow in the Douro Valley. The phylloxera blight which

ontes and douro

exterminated almost all of Europe's vines in the last quarter of the nineteenth century must have killed off a good many species, but many were replanted. In the 1970s João Nicolau de Almeida was also the man who whittled down the 88 he was able to study to isolate five varieties which he thought contributed the most to the red wines of the Valley: Touriga Nacional, Tinta Roriz, Touriga Francesa, Tinto Cão and Tinta Barroca. As Ramos Pinto was beginning a massive replanting programme at the time, vines were planted in vertical rows as in the Rheingau or the Mosel. Once the old stone walls were down, Ramos Pinto committed itself to using the same five in the firm's new vineyards. The new broom went farther than that: the World Bank enshrined de Almeida's findings in the conditions it made for loans, thereby imposing a certain orthodoxy on the Valley.

Over the next twenty years almost all the major firms in Gaia restructured their terraces, replanting the vines at the same time using the fabulous five and thereby whittling down the number of cultivars found between Régua and the Spanish Frontier. By the end of the nineties, however, there was a slight change of heart. David Baverstock, who occasionally emerges from his Alentejo base to advise the Bergquists at Quinta de la Rosa – and was previously employed as a consultant at Quinta do Crasto – began to doubt the sagacity of replanting hundred-year-old vineyards which had always given fruit of excellent quality. For some people, at least, the vineyard, rather than the grape variety had become the key to excellence.

Another controversial subject is oak. Port never required new oak. The original barrels were brought in from the Baltic, which explains the Portuguese word for the wood: *memel*; now growers seeking some of those vanillin tastes that go down so well with consumers, have begun buying in oak barrels from France and America, as well as using a little native oak. Given the temperatures reached during the summer months in the Douro, it is fair to say that a little oak goes a long way, and there is a considerable danger of drying out the wine by leaving it for too long in cask: 'Douro bake' or maderisation is an occupational hazard in the Valley. One estate has produced a delicious Douro red by spurning wood altogether: Francisco Olazabal, a grandson of the pioneer of Douro wines, Fernando de

Almeida, makes the wines at the Quinta de Valado (the wine is confusingly spelled Vallado). They are matured in stainless steel, then stored in specially converted 'Lollobrigidas', the big, allegedly breast-shaped, cement-coated tanks you see all over the Douro.

Centuries of contact with the British trade have transformed the quintas from working farms to comfortable houses with guest rooms. Spode china, Wilton carpets and dog-eared copies of *Country Life, Punch* and the *Literary Review* create an impression of Englishness which sits bizarrely with the intense sun and heat outside. Servants, often from Spanish Galicia, are the rule. The cooking is Portuguese, but the service Anglo-Saxon. Somewhere at the back is generally a

huge kitchen hung with gleaming copper pans where the food is prepared on spits and embers in a way that has changed little since the eighteenth century. The Douro Valley boasts some of the best preserved historic kitchens anywhere on earth.

The only problem about the Douro is access. Even now the trains travel slowly through the magnificent scenery and the roads are hazardous, but both have improved immensely these last twenty years. Three centuries ago the area was extremely remote and the steepness of the ravines made cultivating the vines difficult. When Pombal's new region was mapped out for the first time in 1761, the principal area for quality grapes was the more undulating Baixo Corgo or Lower Douro, with a few patches up river in what is called the Cima Corgo, chiefly at the mouths of the Corgo, Torto and Pinhão rivers. Now that transport has improved, the merchants can shop farther afield in the Douro Superior. Some of the best grapes grown in the Valley today come from right up against the Spanish Frontier.

For many centuries, the wines from the Lower Corgo were known as Lamego wines, after the little bishopric on the south side of the Douro Valley which is now associated with sparkling white wines. From the late middle ages, Lamego wines were being shipped down river to Oporto. The prescient Jesuits knew, apparently, how good Douro wines could be and were the first to ship them abroad. As Britain's trade with Portugal took off in the second half of the seventeenth century, however, Anglo-Saxon merchants made increasing numbers of forays into the valley and came back with wine for the British market. Those pioneers were the Beazleys, Job and Peter. They initiated what was to become the port-wine trade, which is still flourishing, more than three centuries later.

Towards the end of the eighteenth century engineers made the Douro navigable right up to the Spanish Frontier, by removing the 'great slabs of rock' and boulders which rendered the Cachão Rapids all the more treacherous. This opened up a further stretch of the Douro to planting. Joseph James Forrester also contributed to the expansion of the vineyards when he published his famous map of the Douro Valley, something which is inevitably hung up in a prominent place when you visit the offices of one of the port companies in Gaia. Ironically he was claimed by the Cachão Rapids after a heavy lunch with the woman who was rumoured to be his mistress, Dona Antónia Ferreira. He sank, weighed down, it is thought, by the quantity of gold in his pockets. She remained buoyant as a result of her voluminous skirts and crinolines. Another victim was the cook who had been responsible for the extra weight on board. He was sorely missed, as he had a dab hand in the kitchen. Forrester's body was never found.

Does The Douro Mean Port?

Port held sway over the hearts and minds of Whig England for a century at least. By the nineteenth century, however, there were increasing numbers of dissenters, many of them wondered why they couldn't drink unfortified wines from the Douro Valley. The great enemy of port, the journalist and author of a *History and Description of Modern Wines,* Cyrus Redding entered a plea for Douro table wine as early as 1833. He asked 'why Englishmen should not have the benefit of the best wines of the Cima do Douro in a pure state, without adventitious mixtures, no rational answer can be given.'

In the last quarter of the nineteenth century the port houses were buying up the quintas in the Douro Valley with the same mania that nation states had been acquiring African colonies in the quarter century which preceded it. The big houses in Vila Nova de Gaia wanted to seize control of the sources of the best grapes -- a further step towards the elimination of good table wines in the Valley. It was at this time, however, that the artist and journalist Henry Vizetelly visited the Douro and noted that the ordinary wine of the Quinta do Noval possessed the characteristics of Bordeaux and Burgundy, all at once.

The English in Oporto had already become the butts of jibes and jokes. Colonial rivalry and the end of Portugal's favoured trading status had given way to some barbed comments by the end of the century. Some of these surfaced in Ramalho Ortigão and Eça de Queiroz's *As Farpas* of 1885, which focussed on the menial status of the Portuguese agents and farmers in the Douro Valley when they came into contact with the

English traders of the port . The generally Régua-based agent had to follow him about like an equerry, carrying his bags, which contained 'a pair of socks, his carpet slippers, his nightshirt, a razor blade, some Windsor soap, the last issue of *Punch* and a cork screw.' What Ramalho Ortigão resented most, it seemed, was the condescension of the British trader towards his countrymen: 'It is a race... finer, more beautiful, more intellectual, and more noble than you. He is Portuguese. His family in the sixteenth century, when your ancestors... were as barbarous as Mexican Indians, were illustrious all over the world for intelligence, courage, science, commerce, letters and the arts. You are both decadent,' said Ortigão finishing his tirade, 'he from three centuries of Jesuit education, you from insular egotism and mercantile interests.'

It seems that virtually all Portugal's best late nineteenth-century writers had something caustic to say about port: Camillo Castelo Branco, for example, wrote an essay entitled *O vinho do Porto – Processo de uma bestialidade ingleza* in which the novelist referred to the 'killer wine... adulterated with ingredients to please the Englishman, but corrosive.'

Table Wines from Vila Nova de Gaia

The revival of that wine which English merchants castigated as 'abominable' in the nineteenth century, has owed a great deal to the European Union and the limits it has set on the production of port. In the past,

Douro table wine was *consumo,* with some notable exceptions, not much more than rough plonk. The reasons for this were simple: before refrigeration and air-conditioned wineries it was hard to make a stable red wine in the baking Douro Valley. The best grapes were also creamed off to make port, the only Douro wine with a reputation, and a market to match.

Now all port houses are obliged to make some table wine, which they can either sell off or market themselves. The official *beneficio* only licenses a quantity of three hectolitres a hectare to be made into port, all that is left over *must* be made into table wine. On average that means about two hectolitres, and many Douro estates don't want to make port these days, and they sell their *beneficios* to others. Most people have now seen the sense in making and marketing table wine. Among the last to resist this development were the two 'English' port houses, Taylors and Symingtons. Now the latter has started making table wine. Taylor Fonseca has so far shown no desire to follow suit.

Another important factor in the development of Douro table wines has been the right of quintas to trade directly with the outside world. Wine no longer needs to come down to Vila Nova de Gaia before it makes its way in the world.

The first Douro table wine to turn heads was Barca Velha. The history of the wine exhibits some striking parallels with Grange Hermitage, Australia's most famous – and expensive – red wine. Barca Velha was the invention of Fernando Nicolau de Almeida, an oenologist working with the company Ferreira. He had an aversion to tawny port, and while he laboured in the furnace of the Douro Valley, the only beverage he could abide was vintage port. Then he cracked.

Like Max Schubert, the winemaker from Penfolds' – the Australian company which produces Grange – Almeida visited Bordeaux just after the war and returned to the Quinta do Vale do Meão with a bee in his bonnet. He wanted to make something of the sort in the Douro Valley. That he succeeded is proof of a certain tenacity – and genius. Like Schubert again, he didn't have the grapes and he didn't have the climate. By deft use of blocks of ice, however, he was able to bring down the temperatures in the vats, and by buying in grapes grown at the highest altitudes – 305 metres or 1,000 feet – he was able to inject a little life-giving acidity into his wine. French oak casks were bought, and the wine was lodged in them for twelve to eighteen months. Nothing was corrected, there was no scientific intervention beyond a dozen egg whites or so. In 1952 Barca Velha was born.

Classic Barca Velha is a wine like the 1983, full of fruit, but with a filigree acidity which comes and goes in waves across the tongue. Unlike Grange, until recently Barca Velha remained quite a claret-like wine. One is still struck by the well-heeled elegance of the 1991. It is not a wine that shouts about itself. Again, unlike Grange, it exhibits a little aristocratic breeding. That wine was made by José Maria Soares Franco, who took over the winemaking when de Almeida retired in 1987.

Stylistically, however, Soares Franco admits that he still adheres to the views of his predecessor. I tasted a potential Barca Velha from 1997, it was another pair of socks: bigger, bolder, less claret-like; the fruit was huge. The claret style was well and truly buried.

Barca Velha has moved too. It is now made at the Quinta da Leda, up against the Spanish frontier, and the owners of Vale do Meão are keen to make their own wine from the grapes on the property. Soares Franco defends the decision to move. The previous location was too hot, the potential alcohol in the wine often hit 16 degrees. Leda has terraces at high altitude which allows Soares Franco to achieve the balance he seeks. With what is left over he has made a Quinta da Leda since 1997, a really splendid wine which will take the world by storm.

Officially, the second wine of Barca Velha is the Reserva Ferreirinha, which occupies a position analogous to the 'single quinta' ports which surface in a 'non-declared' year. This is also a blockbuster wine. It can be more instantly appealing than the Barca Velha in that it is not created for such a long innings. It is very stylish, especially when it is ten years old or more; when it gives off a heady smell of dark chocolate and blackcurrants and lingers for a full minute on the tongue.

Barca Velha is just made in great years. To date only twelve vintages have been released. For a long time it ploughed a lonely furrow. There were no rivals to its crown. It was Portugal's rarest, most expensive wine, and in the opinion of many, the best too. Now there are many good, even excellent table wines made from Douro grapes. Almeida's son, João, was the creator of Duas Quintas, and the fabulous Duas Quintas Reserva for Ramos Pinto. Like Barca Velha it turns its back on the hot country style which would normally assume to be that dictated by the region, taking the fruit from two properties - the Quintas do Bom Retiro and da Ervamoira and turning it into a wine of wonderful suavity and elegance.

The best place to find a range of wine such as Barca Velha or Duas Quintas is in Vila Nova de Gaia, because they are put together by the same men and women who make the household names of port wine. A Gaia tasting room is an experience in itself. In 1981 I watched the team at Cockburns making up a simple wine for the boardroom. I looked around mystified by all the little bottles marked with undecipherable hieroglyphs arranged on the shelves. The chief taster was clearly annoyed that he could not put his hand on some vital ingredient among the scores of samples around the room. 'I know,' he bleated, spitting a thin stream of liquid out of the side of his mouth into the spitoon, 'top it up with white!' Then we went off to lunch.

I remembered that occasion as I stood in the tasting room at Ferreira, with its superb view of the quay of Oporto opposite and the maze of houses which climb up the steep hill towards the cluster of cathedral and the bishop's palace which wholly

dominates the great, grey city. There were some interesting objects around: long dead brands of port emblazoned with pictures of fox hunting in full swing, but not just port. One crudely manufactured bottle contained the remains of a *garrafeira* from the 1840s. Proof that table wines were always made, but generally played down in the English houses.

That was in the old days. There is a new spirit in the Gaia lodges. From Ferreira I went up the hill to the Symingtons, who make Dow's, Warre's, Graham's and a host of lesser brands, as well as the greatest of the single quinta ports, Vesúvio.

Peter Symington pointed at the samples of the the new vintage. There must have been nearly a hundred glasses there, filled with the juice of vines from the best possible sites. He was wondering whether they were good enough to make a 'declaration' for that year. Then his son Charles brought in three bottles: Symingtons' new venture, table wine.

The Symingtons have been planning to make table wines for years, but every time they make some progress they pull back from the brink of the abyss. Then in 1997 and 1998 the decisions were taken, largely, I think, because Charles Symington had set his heart on making it. He did his training in Rioja, and is no stranger to wines of this sort.

The 1998 vintage was too poor and too rare to consider taking anything away from the ports which are the bread and butter of the company. Charles had to wait until 1999. Then he could use the firm's new facility at Quinta do Sol, on the south bank of the Douro between Régua and Pinhão. Here an air-conditioned underground cellar had been dug out which would allow him to age the bottles there. As Peter Symington puts it, the process for making table wine is wholly different from that which creates port.

It needs different equipment. Too many Douro Quintas are making table wine by adapting the fortified winemaking process.

The only wine to be released so far is Altano, the name of which commemorates a hot wind. It is soft and fruity, a rival to a wine like Esteva. I tasted two more wines: one a reserve wine aged in American oak – another legacy from Charles's Rioja days. The fruit for this comes from the top Symington quintas, such as Bonfim and Malvedos, and there must have been a little tug of war between Peter and Charles. It is a much more serious tannic wine, made principally from Touriga Francesa and Tinta Roriz.

The third wine is 'Chryseia', the Greek for gold, which plays on the name of the Douro. This is made in partnership with Bruno Prats, the former owner of Cos d'Estournel and other growths in Bordeaux: his know-

how combined with their grapes. Prats sold his estates to the insurance company Axa, so he has time on his hands. It has superb fruit, but it was a long way off being released when I tasted it. With Chryseia the Symingtons are tilting at the top wines of the Douro Valley, indeed, all Portugal.

Royal Oporto is the heir to Pombal's Companhia Geral, which found its way into the Real Companhia Vinicola do Norte when that was provided with a royal charter by Dom Luis. A generation ago it had huge interests in northern Portugal, but now that Pedro Silva Reis has taken over from his father he has restructured the business, stripping it back to its Douro core.

He is also much more interested in table wines than many heads of houses. To that end he has taken on Jerry Luper, a veteran Napa Valley winemaker, to rethink the range and improve quality across the board. Luper is an authority on the use of small oak. He is no stranger to Portugal. He has been around for years, and used to make some of the more highly rated wines in the centre of the country. Luper has not only reformed the table wines, from 1996 he has reformed the ports. The difference now is noteworthy. Luper makes the wines. In charge of the vines is Luis Carvalho, who has been in his way, as influential as Luper.

Luper, Silva Reis and I went up to look at the Quinta das Carvalhas, the stunning property above Pinhão which occupies an ox bow in the river, and looks down on the Douro and its tributary, the Torto. It is

particularly steep, and huge, flaky schists lie scattered over the earth. Many of the vines are old, and they have decided not to pull them up and abide by the fabulous five. Instead they are trying to keep them, sometimes propagating them by *provignage*: burying the growth from the old vine until it takes root. There is a risk of phylloxera that way, but it is a risk they are prepared to take.

There is a little museum of grape varieties here: Malvasia Preta, Bastardo, Rufete, Alicante Bouschet and Português Azul, to name only a few of the rarer ones. These go into some of the company's best table wines.

The whites come from the higher altitudes of Casal de Granja above the Quinta do Noval. Evel is made from a combination of Códiga, Viosinho, Gouveia and Sercial and a hefty slug of Moscatel to give it some interesting top notes. They have also planted Gewürztraminer, Arinto and Fernão Pires.

The other white celebrates the famous granite prehistoric pig of Murça. There is nothing swinish about it. Thirty percent is barrel fermented. It is considerably richer than Evel. Luper has created a range of varietal wines which go out under the Porca de Murça label: a ripe and ready Tinta Roriz; a plummy Tinta Barroca; and a more mineral, spicy Touriga Francesa.

The successful red Evel brand was created in 1926. It is currently aged in old oak casks and smells nicely of ripe figs. The reds from the Quinta dos Aciprestes come from low-lying, north-facing vines in Tua in the Upper Douro. This is a much richer, plummier wine, and one of the better wines in the Royal Oporto stable.

The ravishing Quinta do Cidrô, with its formal French gardens, was once the property of the marquês de Soveral, ambassador to the Court of Saint James's and a close friend of King Edward VII. Real Companhia Velha bought the place in 1972. Here Luper makes another varietal range, but one which is aged in *barriques*. The Touriga Nacional is really lovely. It smells of cherry pie. There is also a Tinta Roriz and a buttery Touriga Francesa. The Cabernet Sauvignon has to call itself Trás-os-Montes wine.

There are two reserves: the Porca de Murça and the Evel Grande Escolha. The latter – made with 40% Touriga Nacional from the Upper Douro – has a huge bouquet of baked plums, it is very rich and built to last. It is clearly year in year out one of the best red wines in the Douro Valley.

Other wines, particularly Dirk van der Niepoort's

Redoma and the Quinta do Côtto, have some of that Russian leather smell which is generally the hallmark of hot country wines. Niepoort's best reds to date are Battuta, and his more burgandy-like Charme. The 1990 Battuta was quite monumental. Niepoort has also been the first producer to make a truly remarkable white wine in the cooler climes of the valley, and one which exhibits some of the characteristics of great white burgundy.

Wines from the Valley

Other very fine wines have also emerged in the Valley where the owners of estates have taken the decision to produce port only in certain years, in limited quantities, or to sell just a part of their harvest in order to finance their table wine making. The Quintas do Côtto, do Crasto and La Rosa are good examples of the former, while Gui Serôdio Borges with her enormous, black wines at Vinha do Fôjo, is of the latter. The Grande Escolha ('Grand Selection') from Quinta do Côtto is one of the Douro's very best wines. Made not far from the pretty old town of Mesão Frio, it demonstrates the potential of those early Douro wines, for this is probably about as far as the Beazleys were prepared to venture. The first vintage was made as early as 1980, making it one of the pioneers of Douro table wines. Like Barca Velha, Grande Escolha is only made in the very best years. It is a big, leathery wine that reeks of heat.

Crasto is a magnificent property perched high above the north bank of the Douro, midway between Régua and Pinhão. It is owned by a branch of the same Roquette family which has the huge Esporão estate in the Alentejo. The wines are conceived in a juicy, slightly new world style, and the *reserva* packs a prodigious whack of alcohol, but there is no denying the beauty of them. The best wines come from two old plots of promiscuous vines: Ponte and Maria Teresa. These might contain anything up to fifty different varieties of grape. A few years back they would have been ripped up to plant the mighty handful. Now they are lovingly preserved.

Quinta de la Rosa is an old Feuerheerd property. In the old days the grapes were sold to make port, but for the past fifteen or so years, the Bergquists have decided to go it alone. They make a little port and olive oil, but concentrate on their remarkably well distributed table wines. The estate is advised by David Baverstock, and they are currently making experiments to find out what might be the appropriate wood for their reserve wines. Now even the best whites are partly fermented in oak. I met David Baverstock there once. He was moved to pronounce on the potential of Douro table wine: 'It can rate as the best wine in the world – certainly the best in Portugal,' he said, but at the same time he stressed the need for the right varieties, altitudes, low yields and good vineyards. The old problem came up: if there were no port there would be a lot more quality grapes to play with.

La Rosa is an excellent and wholly dependable Douro wine, full of plum and raspberry fruit tastes.

They also make a single variety Tinta Roriz, where the oak appears to add a dash of cream to the fruit.

Gui Borges' Fôjo has achieved great notoriety in a very short time. A sometime pupil of Dirk Niepoort's, she used to consult Dominic Morris, David Baverstock's Douro assistant, until she felt she had learned as much as she needed to know. Her approach is still slightly nervous, she seems rarely certain whether she has achieved exactly what she wanted. As such her wines are, like Niepoort's, both artistic and pragmatic. They are massively conceived and equally gigantically priced. A recent press release emitted by her British importer focussed on the fact that hers were the most expensive Portuguese table wines on the market – at least £10 more than Barca Velha!

Besides Ramos Pinto and Niepoort, many of the port houses are now making very good table wines. Cockburns' Tuella is a reliable standby. It is made by its consultant, Jim Reader, at the winery in Vila Nova de Foz-Côa, using mostly the classic Douro grapes. In the past, one the best Douro wines was Sandeman's Quinta do Confradeiro near Sabrosa, but in an entangled series of events, the multi-national drinks company Seagrams sold off the land to its former accountant, Eugenio Branco. To make matters as confusing as possible, the estate is now called Quinta do Portal. The wines are now made with advice from the Bordelais Pascal Châtonnet, a partner of Michel Rolland. They are rather more extractive and oaky than they were in the Sandeman days.

Sandeman has hung on to the name 'Confradeiro', and under this label it makes some fine red Douro wines, but not, perhaps, the equals of the old *quinta* wines. Quinta do Noval markets two table wines. A light, fruity, every day wine with a hot country taste called Corucho and the rather more serious and refined wine from the van Zeller property, the Quinta do Roriz.

Producers such as Domingos Alves de Sousa at the Quintas da Gaivosa and do Vale da Raposa near Régua, have concentrated entirely on table wines. He also makes a series of varietal wines with the assistance of his oenologist cum motoring winemaker, Anselmo Mendes: Touriga Nacional, Tinta Roriz and Tinto Cão. The 'red dog' is probably the most successful of these.

Five more Douro wines deserve a mention here. They are the up-and-coming Quinta da Capela; and the Quinta de Covelos near Régua where the Portuguese press have greeted Anselmo Mendes' wines by storm. The suave, plummy reserve wine is particularly recommended. The Quinta Seara d'Ordens is built in a rather more leathery, hot-country style; while Dorna Velha from the Quinta do Silval makes an exciting single varietal Tinta Barroca. The Vinha das Castas from the Quinta das Castas in S. Marta de Penaguião reeks of brown sugar and blackcurrants. It is a long, chewy wine.

The owners of Dona Antónia Ferreira's company, Sogrape, have some highly creditable Douro table wines on offer. Esteva takes its name from the pungent gum cistus plant, which grows all over the hillsides and terraces of the Douro and the perfume of which is supposed to be a feature of Douro wines, fortified and unfortified. It is a decent red wine for every day, highly popular in Portugal and has generally sold out long before the new vintage is released.

The Ferreira wines are made at the Quinta do Seixo, a huge, ultra-modern installation looking across the Douro to Pinhão. Recently the decision has been made to hang on to the old vines here too. Among other things they go to make some of the best of the company's Douro 'brands', such as Callabriga, which is given some sweeter, more modern appeal through the use of American oak casks. Vinha Grande is another of Ferreira's new departures, which combines Seixo fruit with some of the leftovers from Barca Velha and Reserva Ferreirinha. It is aged in old Barca Velha casks.

The Ferreira family itself have sold off most of their properties in the Douro. One of the last to go was the splendid Quinta do Vesúvio in the Upper Douro, where the Symingtons now make their best single quinta port. When the notary called on all the former owners to sign the deal, more than fifty Ferreiras appeared. One estate which is still in family hands after seven generations, however, is the Quinta do Valado on the River Corgo, which used to be one of the most go-ahead port farms in the region. The port was naturally sold to Ferreira.

In 1993, however, the current owners of the estate, together with another descendant of Dona Antónia (Francisco Olazabal, the estate's winemaker), decided to make a table wine and retain the farm's production for themselves. There are now 64 ha of vines in production, with two-thirds of them old. The red and white wines made today are made entirely in stainless steel, but it is hoped to make a reserve wine soon, and this will be aged in oak.

There are also a certain number of good value, unpretentious wines made from Douro grapes, such as DFJ's Patamar (see p111). It is a big wine, combining Touriga Francesa and Tinta Roriz. Peter Bright makes Douro reds in at least two locations, buying up fruit and renting office space, so to speak. One serious Douro which goes into the British supermarket chains is made at the Symingtons' spanking new Quinta do Sol. At the Quinta dos Frades he makes Torcular entirely in *lagares* using Touriga Francesa and Tinta Roriz. From the same site comes TFN (Tourigas Francesa and Nacional) which is fermented in barrel: 'Barca Velha at half the price,' he calls it. In truth it is a great deal less than half the price.

The Beiras region contains three sub-regions: Beira Litoral, by the coast, Beira Alta, in the highlands and Terras de Sicó south of Coimbra. The minimum alcoholic content is 10%. There are some forty grape varieties permitted for the regional whites, and roughly the same amount for the reds. Most Beiras regional wines are dealt with in the sections covering the DOCs: Dão, Bairrada and Beira Interior. They are, after all, often experimental wines which use varieties which are not included in the official recommendations and have no right to the DOC. Some good wines, however, are made outside the main demarcated regions, and they may only use the regional appellation.

In the - as yet small – fourth DOC of the Beiras, Távora-Varosa made 5,508 hls of white and 4,389 hls of red in 1998; and in the IPR Lafões 385 hls of white and no red. 23,476 hls of white wine and 47,967 hls of red were declared as Beiras regional wine.

Távora Varosa touches on the southern part of the Douro Valley near Lamego and Tarouca. Maximum yields are 60 hls/ha for whites and 55 for reds. In Lamego sparkling wine is a speciality, and the DOC now permits red sparklers to be made. The recommended varieties for whites include Bical, Cerceal, Chardonnay, Fernão Pires, Folgazão, Gouveio, Malvasia Fina (which should climb to 30%), Malvasia Rei, Rabo de Ovelha, Siria and Viosinho.

For reds it is recommended to use Arvelhão, Tinta Roriz, Bastardo, Malvasia Preta, Marufo, Castelão, Rufete, Tinta da Barca, Touriga Francesa, Touriga Nacional, Trincadeira Preta and Vinhão.

In the IPR Lafões along the Vouga Valley yields are naturally more relaxed: 65 hls/ha for whites and 60 hls/ha for reds. So far only white wines have been made. Arinto, Cerceal, Dona Branca, Esgana Cão and Rabo de Ovelha are the favoured grapes.

Production in the DOC Távora Varosa remains small and the wines are not seen much outside the region. The co-operative in Távora makes a Dão-like Terras do Demo as well as some nice, floral whites. There are also good white and sparkling wines from Murganheira in Tarouca.

Beiras is a region in the making, and the smaller DOCs and IPR have yet to define themselves, except in one or two places, which will doubtless earn some statute of their own before too long. Where the Beiras touches on Bairrada, DFJ has earned a well-justified reputation for its excellent Bical which it sells under

beiras, l

its Bela Fonte label. The oenologist José Neiva claims it is one of two pure Bicals made in Portugal. They have a leathery Jaen too and a great bruiser of a wine made from the Touriga Francesa grape, which is rarely seen outside Douro blends. They are labelled 'Tinto' Jaen and 'Tinto' Touriga Francesa.

airrada and dão

One or two quality Baga-wielding estates lie outside the demarcated Bairrada region in the all encompassing Beiras regional appellation. The Quinta de Foz de Arouce is owned by Filipe Osório who happens to be João Ramos's father-in-law, so it should come as no surprise to see that Ramos is involved with the vinification. The latest news is that Ramos has advised a considerable amount of replanting on the property, and the quaint old vat house I visited has had to make way for more up-to-date equipment.

The Osórios live in a charming house in the village of Lousã. He is a passionate huntsman, and shares with his son-in-law a mania for shooting woodcock. This bird, he says, goes best with his remarkably svelte Baga wines.

Dão

Dão is divided into seven sub-regions: Alva, Besteiros, Castendo, Serra da Estrela, Silgueiros, Azurara and Terras de Senhorim. Maximum yields are 80 hls/ha for whites, 60 for reds and 80 for sparkling wines. For white wines the law recommends Barcelo, Bical, Cerceal, Encruzado, Malvasia Fina, Rabo de Ovelha, Terrantez, Uva Cão and Verdelho.

For reds they recommend Alfrocheiro Preto, Alvarelhão, Tinta Roriz, Bastardo, Jaen, Rufete, Tinto Cão, Touriga Nacional and Trincadeira Preta.

In 1998-1999 Dão declared 18,810 hls of DOC white and 79,981 hls of red.

Dão is made in a demarcated enclave between the Dão and Mondego rivers. The region touches the slopes of the Estrela and other mountain outcrops of the *meseta* appear in the form of Açor and Lousã. It is a high altitude wine. Grapes ripen on thin soils on granite rock ranging in altitude between 200 and 1,900 metres. This explains a red wine with a particularly pronounced acidity which can be spectacularly long on the palate.

Although the climate appears rude, the growing season is long, and there are five months of every year which are virtually guaranteed frost-free. Like the Minho, rainfall is high, but it is also highly seasonal, and the region sees virtually no precipitation during the summer months, when the grapes are ripening on the vines.

It is often very cold at the time of the harvest. Old *lagares* were equipped with an open space so that embers could be put under them to heat the musts and set the fermentation in motion. Traditionally the wine was run off into chestnut casks, but these days they use oak, and the chestnut, where it exists, is reserved for *aguardente* or *bagaceira*.

Dão is part of the large area known as the Beira; it abounds in standing stones probably deposited by ice age glaciers. Some of them look perilous. Dão is also famous for its prehistoric dolmens: strange tripods often capped by a huge boulder, looking like some great, stone stool.

The Romans knew the region, and it was they who probably first fortified the hilltop at Viseu, the pretty regional capital, with its fine, massy cathedral and renaissance bishop's palace. Small quantities of wine would have been produced here from then onwards, but there was enough by the mid thirteenth century for the locals to petition the king to stop the import of wine into Viseu: they had enough of their own.

Dão lived well by hiding its light under a bushel. Grapes went elsewhere; to the Douro and even as far as Bordeaux. In the last quarter of the nineteenth century Dão was wasted by phylloxera much as the rest of Europe. At that time the majority of black grapes planted were almost certainly Touriga Nacional (Tourigo is a village in the Dão). Sadly for the locals, they did not replant Portugal's most prestigious black grape, which did not take to the new rootstock being offered from America. By the time Dão was demarcated, the wines had lost much of what had made them special a generation before.

The period of Dão's mediocrity persisted for most of the century. In 1943 the Estado Novo created ten cooperatives which even now vinify nearly half the wine of the region. It has only been in recent years

that the region has seen an increase in the amount of Touriga Nacional available. This has largely coincided with the desire to create 'estate' or *quinta* wines in the early nineties. Their rise has also encouraged the cooperatives to enforce a greater selection when it comes to the grapes brought in by small-scale farmers.

Recent Progress

In 1987 I went out to help a friend who had a small estate in the Dão and about seven hectares of vines to pick. I remember my enthusiasm when I saw the clusters of grapes which were already beginning to shrivel from the fierce sun, and thought of the dense,

concentrated wines I was going to make. Then I was woken in the night by the sound of torrential rain. It continued to pour down for a week, during which time the fragile berries burst and rot set in.

During our many enforced idle hours we went to see what was going on elsewhere. We visited some of the cooperatives. It was an undeniably bad year. I recall the bunches of white grapes carelessly strewn among the blacks and the lack of any policy for rewarding people who had done their work well and produced grapes with impressive levels of sugar. All this has changed today. Under the beady eyes of the local *Comissão*, growers now must be a lot more careful.

The *Comissão* or CVR has the job of policing the region. Growers can consult them if they like, and they also lay down the law as regards the DOC. They make up batches of the Dão yeast and oblige all local growers to use it. It is popular elsewhere: as QD (Quintas do Dão) 145, it is employed for a good many wines around the world.

I visited the CVR again recently. In its main reception room it has a magnificent series of tiles depicting scenes from the viticultural year in the local *alleluia* blue and made in around 1900. It will soon be moving into the sixteenth-century bishop's palace next to the cathedral, and these lovely *azulejos* are due to come with it.

Of course, the *Comissão* is not the only organisation on hand to offer advice in this way, and there are quite a number of highly rated oenologists working in the region. It comes as no surprise to see Anselmo Mendes crop up again here, where he works for Borges & Irmão. He is also looking to buy his own small estate in the Dão. His choice is an interesting one: he makes wine in the Douro and the Minho as well, but his heart, it seems is here. Another who advises two top domaines is Professor Virgílio Loureiro. He is behind the wines at the Quinta de Cabriz and those from the Quintas dos Roques and das Maias.

Dão is changing like the rest of Portugal. Over towards Tazém you see many abandoned terraces or *mortuários*. Here the growers took their grapes to the cooperatives in the past, and earned a little pin money at harvest time. The vines were interspersed with olives. This sort of agriculture is now on the wane. Here, as elsewere, farmers have begun to specialise. It is the same story all over Portugal. As the Australian Peter Bright puts it: 'The one hectare estate is finished.'

Whites

'The wine I was trying to make in 1987 was white. I remember I had my eyes on the Moscatel grapes, which I thought would spice it up a bit, but found the pickers generally munched on those for their lunch, leaving me precious few to play with. Eating was a problem with those pickers, unofficially led – and distracted – as they were, by a raunchy girl in hotpants whose many pranks led to frequent despairing cries of 'Ai Silvina!' As many of the bunches were affected by grey rot I issued a simple test: 'If it's good enough to eat it's good enough to pick!', but I had to stop this when I realised that the remaining usable grapes were all going down the throats of the harvesters.'

White Dão has less reputation than red, but it can be very good. The grapes favoured these days are Encruzado, Assarío, Borrado das Moscas (or fly droppings, the evocative local name for Bical) and Cerceal. Some growers use a little 'Malvasia', which – to make matters more complicated – is the local name for Arinto. This is the case, for example, at the Quinta do Pereiro. More popular these days is Encruzado. It gives a good balance of sugar and acid and takes well to oak. Sogrape, for example, makes a version fermented in new oak, which has nice, apricot and greengage fruit. Its Duque de Viseu is also partly oak-fermented Encruzado.

Dão whites don't actually always need oak: at the Quinta do Corujão, for example, the white is 100% Encruzado which makes a fresh, apricot-scented, simple wine. The white Quinta da Turquide is 90% Encruzado topped up with Fernão Pires. It has a good, citrus taste and a fine acidity. It goes nicely with shellfish.

Some of the most remarkable whites are those produced by the Dão Sul company which controls 38 ha of land and built itself a modern cellar in 1998. The wines are bottled under the Quinta de Cabriz label. It is a great believer in oak, both French and Portuguese. The latter comes from the forests of Trás-os-Montes in the north. Not all the wines are oaky, however. There is a very successful blend of Bical and Cerceal, the latter providing the acid and the former the alcohol. I found it almost reminiscent of the northern Rhone grape, Viognier. The straight Encruzado is very floral, a frank expression of the grape. Then there is a tribute to the winemaker, 'Virgílio Loureiro', which is made up of four local whites. It also makes a Champagne-method sparkling wine by blending Bical and Arinto. When it has had a few years in bottle it can be quite impressive, with a pleasant old wine character.

Sogrape has experimented with late picked Encruzado, including some affected by noble rot brought on by the autumnal mists in December. It is currently sitting on the first release of this wine: just 2,500 litres have been bottled.

Reds

They will tell you in the region that the Touriga Nacional, Portugal's number one native black grape, comes from the Dão; indeed, there is a village in these parts called Tourigo, where the cultivar is supposed to have taken its first steps. Vasco Magalhães, at Sogrape, calls it the 'calling card' of the Dão. There was lots of it about before phylloxera struck at the end of the nineteenth century, but it was not replanted at the time. Touriga is good, but there are many other varieties besides, and some of these contribute magnificently to the individuality of Dão wines. Tinta Roriz is also favoured, but it can overcrop and will only make interesting wine when the plants keep their offerings down to under three kilos. One of the most individual local varieties is Jaen. Another is Alfrocheiro Preto which produces lots of wine and lots of acid, especially when it is grown at altitude.

The summers being cool and dry, the grapes ripen properly and in peace. There is no need to chaptalize by adding sugar to the musts, and there is certainly no reason to acidify either. It is a region which still has considerable promise and from which we probably have yet to see the best. In many ways it resembles the Spanish region of Ribera del Duero: both grow grapes at high altitude, and both make excellent red wines with a pronounced acidic bite.

Old-fashioned Dão is quite an austere wine, with its high acidity and restrained fruitiness. I was reminded of this by the wines I tasted from the big firm of Caves Aliança. The reserve wine made from Jaen, Alfrocheiro and Tinta Roriz was riper on the nose, but very stripped down on the palate. The Particular is made in limited quantities from 60-year-old Touriga and Jaen vines. Blackberries sprung to mind. With the older cuvées a forest floor smell, like good burgundy creeps in too. It can also be quite wild and leathery. The wines from the Quinta da Turquide are like this. That rather hard, muscular style is also present in the reds from Penalva do Castelo, such as the Quinta da Murqueira.

One of the estates I visited back in 1987 was the Casa de Santar, the loveliest country house in the region. You park your car by a great rococo fountain covered with *azulejos* emblazoned with the arms of the family which created the estate. The present lord of the manor is called Pedro de Vasconcelos e Sousa. He possesses a dream kitchen complete with a fountain under a catafalque where the local maidens come to drink water in July. In theory at least, they will be guaranteed marriage within the year. There is an early twentieth-century stove under a baldachin. The pots and pans are ancient too. Sadly, the cooking is now done somewhere else, and this dream kitchen is only for show.

In the sixteenth-century chapel there is granite painted to look like marble and contemporary *azulejos* in blue, yellow and green from the Spanish period or *dominio filipino*. The green came from Spain. It went severely out of fashion after 1640. There is a squint for the ladies of the house, rather like the purdah screen in Indian palaces. In another part of the house is a coach museum.

The wines are interesting too. There are 120 ha of vines grown on a 400 metre high plateau. On my first visit they were working with the port house of Calém, which marketed the wine for them. That arrangement has come to an end, and they now have a joint venture with a company in Colombia, which allowed them to rebuild their press house. The vines are over 35 years old and giving really good juice.

We tasted them in an outbuilding beyond the formal gardens. Its main feature is a glorious eighteenth-century horseshoe arch. The present owners of the estate are much taken with oak. They use American wood for their second label wine and French oak from Séguin Moreau for the reserve wines. They send up samples of the wine to France and then they receive the best advice on the proper wood for their needs. Some of the white goes through *bâtonnage,* where the lees are stirred up in the casks to make the wine creamier and richer. The oaking is not too extreme.

The reds are made from Touriga, Tinta Roriz, Alfrocheiro Preto and Jaen. They are very sound.

Naturally the reserve wines are the most concentrated. The estate also markets an excellent ewe's milk cheese. Sheep are never too far away in these high plateaux.

Two estates which have reaped reputations for themselves both in Portugal and abroad are the Quintas da Pellada and Sães. Both are owned by the experimental Alvaro Castro and his family. At Pellada, Castro makes some interesting varietal wines and blends, such as a combination of Jaen and Tinta Roriz, which exudes a creamy blackberry aroma from the *bâtonnage* technique. In this series there is also a straight Tinta Roriz and a Touriga Nacional. The first is a promisingly dense wine which needs time to come round. The latter smells of stewed plums and rather more immediate prettiness. It was that wine which pleased me most.

The Quinta de Sães wines threw off an interesting bouquet of beeswax. Alvaro de Castro has recently bought himself a splendid old ruin in an isolated stretch of countryside visited chiefly by sheep. This he intends to turn into a tasting room, possibly more besides, to attract extra visitors, preferably of the two-legged sort.

Another pair of properties which sets tongues wagging are the Quintas dos Roques and das Maias. Maias used to be owned by a gentleman in the motor trade. It is right up on the Estrela, and at 600 metres, one of the loftiest vineyards in the country. The Jaguar dealer grew bored with his toy and sold it to Manuel Lopes de Oliveira, a retired metallurgist, and his smooth-talking son-in-law Luis Lourenço, a former maths master who met his wife when they were at university together. They went to Professor Virgílio Loureiro, an oenologist who teaches in Lisbon. Lourenço had found his man: most Dão, he says, is spoilt in the vinification. Loureiro knew exactly how to get the best of their high grown fruit. To show his faith in Maias Loureiro has now bought a small stake in the business.

The 40 ha Quinta de Roques is at 400 metres. It is famous for its Portuguese varietal wines. They took the decision at the beginning, being suspicious of the craze for Chardonnay and Cabernet; they thought the wine world was putting all its fruit into one basket and elected to plant Touriga, Tinta Roriz, Alfrocheiro Preto and Jaen instead.

Luis Lourenço is a very fluent spokesman for the top wines of the Dão. He is not worried that Loureiro is also making the wines at Cabriz: 'we need competition,' he told me. 'Only with competition can the wines get better. It is the best wine producing region in Portugal.' He praises the *terroir*, soil and climate, especially the latter, which ensures that seam of acidity so vital to the liveliness of the wine. Nor is there ever a shortage of alcohol. He pointed a finger at the Alentejo at this point: their wines lacked acidity.

The varietal wines come from Roques. There is an exemplary Touriga, and a Tinto Cão. Lourenço jokes about the latter, it was once 'the best Tinto Cão in the world', adding modestly, that it was the only one in

Portugal at the time it was first released. It is Loureiro's favourite. I can see why, it has great length and spiciness with a hint of liquorice.The dog (Cão) was a hard act to follow. The Alfrocheiro Preto we tasted next had trouble keeping up.

There are only small quantities of the varietal wines. In the old days they did a package called *colecção*: buyers received one each of the varietals and a bottle of the blend, a sort of DIY, if you like. Lourenço admits that the sum is greater than its parts, but the monovarietal wines are 'the knowledge': the learning curve.

They are also fond of oak. Barrels are changed every fourth year, a quarter of them being new. When they have finished with the oak it is sold on to the port wine companies in Vila Nova, which do not favour new oak. The casks come from France, Portugal and Russia, but there is a problem with the latter, as supplies can be erratic.There are so many wines on offer that it hard to describe them all. An interesting sparkler turned out to be largely made from black grapes. There is a pink version too: half Alfrocheiro and half Tinta Pinheira. Verdelho, Malvasia Fina and Encruzado are fermented in oak with *bâtonnage*. The Encruzado, with its pineapple fruit, is a great success.

Touriga predominates in the top cuvées at Roques. They are wonderfully structured wines which exude a little gamey smell with time. Naturally the reserve

rather figgy port with nuances of nougat; although the acidity gives it something special. In the future this will be sold as 'vinho fino do Dão'.

The Quinta do Pereiro makes quite oaky reds. The simple wine is Touriga Nacional, Jaen, Alfrocheiro Preto and Tinta Roriz, giving it a frank, black fruit flavour. The reserve wines are made from the same mix. They have impressive staying power. The reds from the Quinta de Cabriz are as good as the whites. There is a weighty, fruity blend of Touriga, Alfrocheiro, Tinta Roriz and Jaen. As well as bottlings of the deconstructed parts: the Alfrocheiro and the Touriga came out best for me. They also make a port-like fortified *licoroso*. This tradition probably goes back to Pombal's time and before.

The Quinta da Fonte do Ouro is the home of Nuno Cancela de Abreu, the guiding light behind the Quinta da Romeira in Bucelas (see p104). In 1991 he decided to develop the small family vineyard near Mortágua in the western part of the Dão region. To make the exercise more worthwhile, however, he joined up with the Vasconcelos family at Casa de Santar, Jim Reader of Cockburn, Miguel Corte-Real and Cristiano van Zeller (the former owner of Quinta do Noval) to buy up some more plots in the region and to make more wine. At Fonte do Ouro he makes a blend of Touriga with Jaen and Tinta Roriz and Trincadeira, as well as a pure Touriga wine. They are aged partly in French oak

wines take longer to come round, but they are the real collectors' items. The blend at Maias is predominantly Jaen. This is the variety that fares best at high altitudes. It tastes strongly of strawberries, toast and honey. They make an interesting wine called Licoroso too, which is 100% Touriga Nacional. It tastes like hogsheads and tend to be a little earthy. The latter is the richer of the two. There are also the wines of the Quinta da Giesta: a white made from Encruzado, Bical and Malvasia Fina and a red made from 30% Touriga Nacional, 20% Jaen, 20% Tinta Pinheira, 20% Bastardo and 10% Merlot. This unconventional Dão blend has to be bottled under the regional Beiras label.

The high acidity of the local red wines was quite evident in the Quinta dos Penassais, made from Touriga Nacional, Tinta Roriz, Alfrocheiro Preto, Jaen and Rufete. The wines are also earthy, with some good redcurrant-like fruit, the *garrafeiras* in particular. There is a very fine pure Touriga with a taste of rich dark fruits. There is also a Touriga, Tinta Roriz, Alfrocheiro and Jaen blend which needs time to come round.

Meia Encosta is the big selling brand made by Borges & Irmão in Vila Nova da Gaia. It retains the services of Anselmo Mendes. Borges has 30 ha in the Dão, half of it planted with Touriga, the rest being made up of Tinta Roriz, Trincadeira, Jaen and Alfrocheiro. The Meia Encosta is clean and reliable, but better are the monovarietal Tourigas and Tinta Rorizes. The Touriga spends six months in French oak, adding a creaminess to the taste of blackberries. Dom Ferraz is DFJ's version. It is curiously highly scented.

Probably the biggest bottler of Dão wines is Sogrape, which operates from its impressive Quinta dos Carvalhais. Sogrape started out with Grão Vasco in 1957, made from fruit it bought in the region. The name commemorated the famous mediaeval master from Viseu, and one of his paintings was illustrated on the label. In the eighties it bought Carvalhais, a 105 ha property with around fifty ha of vines. This is now its production centre for the region, where it processes about three million litres of wine.

It concentrates on Touriga for the reds, then, in order, Tinta Roriz, Alfrocheiro Preto, Jaen and Tinta Pinheira. The whites are largely made from Encruzado, with some Assarío, Verdelho, Bical and Cerceal. A lot of fruit is still being bought in, but Sogrape offers a 40% bonus for the best grapes. This policy is reaping rewards. When I tried my hand at winemaking here, I was told there were more than fifty varieties in the vineyards, including table grape cultivars such as Chasselas. Now the 'recommended' varieties are in the majority and the authorized have declined to 35%.

Sogrape is a great buyer of barrels for its Grão Vasco, Duque de Viseu and Quinta dos Carvalhais. It likes the tight-grained Allier for its top wines. For the lesser wines it uses American and Russian wood.

French oak, for example, is used on the Alfrocheiro Preto wine from the Quinta dos Carvalhais, a very successful brew with a strong aroma of blackberries. The Touriga smells of cassis and is much spicier, with hints of pepper, basil and cinnamon. It has used a little American oak on recent vintages of Touriga, making it taste more like Rioja than some of its earlier wines. There is a reserve wine which is made from fifty-year-old Touriga, Tinta Roriz and Alfrocheiro Preto vines. There are plenty of black fruits on the nose, but on the palate the Alfrocheiro shows its acidic mettle. It is very long: classic Dão.

There are some good little cooperatives in the region, like that in Mangualde, which makes a really nice simple wine from Touriga and Jaen. It is currently carrying out experiments with oak. Nelas makes good, old-fashioned reds, the best being its half century celebration reserve – Meio Século. Tondela makes an excellent white from Bical, a chunky Memórias de Tondela and a very oaky reserve wine.

The cooperative at Vila Nova de Tazem is run by a Lisbon lawyer, Maria Adelaide Cavaleiro Ferreira. There are a thousand members bringing in the produce of just 800 ha, which gives you an idea of the size of the estates. In this part of the Dão there are lots of *mortuários* (literally graveyards) where the terraces have turned up their toes for lack of attention.

The cooperative makes a nice fresh white called Pedra d'Orca (there is a dolmen on the label) from Bical, Encruzado, Cerceal and Malvasia Fina and a red version from Touriga, Jaen, Tinta Roriz and Alfrocheiro, which can be quite gamey. The *garrafeira* has a superb colour and is really leathery. They are proudest of Jaen here, which can be silky and taste of sour cherries. All the wines were clean, good and wholesome. It was evidence, had I needed it, of how far these smaller cooperatives have come on since my brush with Dão in 1987.

Beira Interior

The DOC Beira Interior was created at the end of 1999. It is divided into three sub-regions: Castelo Rodrigo, around the town of that name and Almeida; Cova da Beira near Guarda; and Pinhel in the south. In 1998-1999 the Beira Interior then an IPR, declared 5,824 hls of white wine and 16,151 hls of red.

Yields are fixed at 55 hls/ha for reds and whites. The grape varieties recommended vary. For white wines Castelo Rodrigo favours Malvasia Fina, Siria and Tamarez; Cova da Beira, Alicante Branco, Arinto, Bical, Fonte Cal, Malvasia Fina, Malvasia Rei, Rabo de Ovelha and Siria; in Pinhel, Bical, Cerceal, Fonte Cal, Malvasia Rei, Rabo de Ovelha, Siria and Tamarez.

For red wines the favoured cultivars in Castelo Rodrigo are Castelão, Bastardo, Marufo, Rufete and Touriga Nacional; in Cova da Beira, they add Baga, Moreto, Tinta Carvalha, Trincadeira Preta and Jaen; in Pinhel, Bastardo, Marufo, Rufete and Touriga Nacional are honoured for 80% of the blend.

The landscape is stunning once you leave Viseu and travel up beyond the Guarda Gate. There are great standing stones around Portugal's highest mountain, the Estrela, where even now the odd wolf is seen preying on the sheep who graze there, while they transform the grass and wild herbs into Portugal's greatest cheese – serra. Even at 3,000 feet you will find vines. Borrow described the seemingly tottering rocks in their 'naked horridness, like the ribs of some mighty carcass from which the flesh has been torn.'

It is Portugal's latest demarcated area, and so far most of the wine is produced by five cooperatives and just eight private estates. These days people with as many as 15 ha of vines are encouraged to make their own wines, but there are still locals with 20 ha who take their grapes to the cooperatives. Yields are still quite high, but there are moves to bring them down more substantially, which would surely help to inject a little body into the wine.

It is dry, and growers have a dispensation allowing them to irrigate their vines. Some of the reds can be disappointing. Touriga Nacional does reasonably well, also the Touriga Francesa. There is a little bit of Marufo, Bastardo – which locals compare to Cabernet – and Rufete. These days there is little call for Rufete or Mourisco, as they give little colour at this altitude, and do not age well. There are other, less noble sorts growing in the little plots of the region – they are relegated to the local *consumo*. All the vineyards suffer from the attentions of magpies and wild boars.

The area is most promising for whites, often made from Siria, as the high altitude lends them a good, crisp acidity. This is immediately apparent when you taste the wines of the Convento de Aguiar, a superb former Cistercian abbey near Castelo Rodrigo. It is a large estate with plenty of vines and sheep; the latter make a *serra*-style cheese. There is a crisp rosé, a *blanc de noirs* made from black Marisco grapes, and a refreshing white made from Siria. The wines are made

at the cooperative, which also makes its own fresh, pineapple scented Siria wine. The Convento's reds are light and simple, but perfectly enjoyable wines.

Another estate making zippy whites is the Terras de Cabral. Its reds are also pleasant. Made from Rufete, Jaen and Castelão, they have a good toastiness about them. The Casa do Redondo in

Pinhel makes rather old-fashioned, fleshy whites, but the reds lack colour. Another decent white from Pinhel is made at the Quinta das Boiças. This has a fresh, lively acidity – just what you want from high grown wines.

The cooperative in Fundão in Cova da Beira makes a Praça Velha Garrafeira from Tinta Amarela which is trustworthy.

Almeida Garrett is a descendant of the great early nineteenth-century novelist and political liberal of that name – except it wasn't his name, he borrowed the Almeida from his mother and the Garrett from an Irish grandmother. His descendant has carried on the progressive tradition and specialises in more modern wines made from foreign varietals. The lemony Chardonnay is successful. There is a light, tarry red called Entre Serras made from Jaen, Rufete, Bastardo and Tinta Amarela; as well as a Colheita Seleccionada made from Touriga Nacional, Tinta Barroca and Tinta Roriz. His best red is the 100% Roriz.

The model estate in the Beiras is the 28 ha Quinta

do Cardo, where the wines are made by Nuno de Abreu (see Bucelas p104). The whites, composed of Siria and Arinto, have a real complexity about them and plenty of lemony tang. The pure Siria is very attractive, with aromas reminiscent of apricots and fresh pears. These wines show the region's mettle. The reds like the Tinta Roriz tend to be angular, but they are beautifully made, especially the Touriga Nacional. The best of all is the blend of Tourigas Nacional and Francesa and Tinta Roriz. These wines sell for high prices. That in itself is an indication that the products of this new appellation could become a force to be reckoned with in the not so dim and distant future.

Bairrada Wine and Piglets

In 1998-1999 Bairrada produced 14,303 hls of white and 24,272 hls of red wine. Maximum yields are 55 hls/ha for reds and 70 hls/ha for whites, rosés and sparkling wines. The recommended whites are Arinto, Bical, Cercial, Rabo de Ovelha and Fernão Pires. Together or separately they must make up 85% of the cuvée. For reds Baga is supreme, but also recommended are Camarate, Castelão, Bastardo, Jaen, Alfrocheiro Preto, Touriga Nacional, Trincadeira Preta and Rufete. Baga must equal at least 50%, and the recommended grapes, 85% of the whole. Red wines must be eighteen months old before they are put on the market, sparkling wines nine.

Bairrada, around the ancient university town of Coimbra, is the real heartland of Portugal. The Romans had vines here and it was here, during the dark age of Muslim occupation, that the abbeys of Lorvão and Vacariça kept Roman viticultural traditions alive.

Being close to the Douro was an advantage. After the Methuen Treaty the vineyards of Bairrada expanded while grapes were hurried up to Gaia to be turned into port. This situation continued until the region felt the heavy hand of the marquês de Pombal. He ordered that the vines be uprooted in the interests of preventing fraud and encouraging cereal production instead. Throughout the nineteenth century too, Bairrada's reputation was dogged by its tendency to be used as a substitute, first for Douro base wines, and later – during phylloxera – for a good many deep-coloured French wines.

As elsewhere, land-ownership received a fillip in 1834 when the monasteries were dissolved. Lorvão (now famous only for its 'convent' desserts made from sweetened egg yolks) and the great abbey of Santa Cruz in Coimbra lost its land to a new class of property owners. The region's one big aristocratic estate, the ravishing Solar da Graciosa in Arcos (it makes good wine as well), dates from this time.

The champagne – now 'traditional' – method was introduced into the region by a José Maria Tavares da Silva from 1885, when he was appointed director of the new wine school in Anadia. Together with Lamego, on the south side of the Douro Valley, Bairrada was

eventually to become known as the home of Portuguese sparklers. Bairrada wines had been popular in France during the years when the production of French wines was affected by the phylloxera blight.Once French vineyards began to recover, there was less Bairrada required. One solution was therefore to develop the sparkling wine business. At that time a research establishment was created at Anadia, and the town subsequently developed into the centre of the Bairrada wine trade.

Although the region was demarcated in the last years of the monarchy, until the 1980s Bairrada and bulk went sadly together. Wholesale wine merchants established themselves in the region between the wars and established their 'caves', buying up grapes or wine and ageing it in their cellars like French *négociants éleveurs*. The first was Bernardo Morais, then the Caves Irmãos Unidos (now the Caves São João), Caves de Barracão, Cave Central da Bairrada, Cave Messias, Caves Aliança and Caves Valdarcos. Their stock-in-trade was sparkling wine occasioned by huge demand in the region – where the wine was deemed to go well with the local suckling pig – and elsewhere in Portugal and Brazil where they provided for a taste for cheap fizz, as well as huge amounts of light-bodied red wines for the colonial trade.

Once again the move to create cooperative wineries came during the Salazar years. Cantanhede was founded in 1954, and was swiftly followed by Mealhada, Souselas, Mogofores and Vilarinho do Bairro. The army, fighting colonial wars in Africa, was a major purchaser of Bairrada wines which were shipped in bulk and bottled in Africa. When Portugal lost its colonies in the seventies, the principal thrust of sales was to the emigrant communities abroad. During these years the typicity of the local Baga variety was lost from view. It would be almost impossible to locate a good bottle of red Bairrada wine made before 1970.

A DOC was introduced in 1979, and since 1986 Bairrada has seen a more notable upgrading of its image than practically any other region. Based on one grape variety (Baga) Bairrada growers have demonstrated that they can make red wines as serious as any in Portugal. In this process the new demarcation of the region helped growers to understand the need for higher quality and less bulk. From 1951, Bairrada was included in the Beira Litoral region. Two attempts to create an appellation in 1962 and 1966 failed. It was not until 1981 that the first Bairrada labels appeared on the market. Since then, through the efforts of top growers like Luis Pato and Carlos Almeida e Silva at the Casa de Saima (both, incidentally, children of wholesale wine merchants), Bairrada's reputation has enjoyed a meteoric rise.

One of the first wines from Bairrada to develop something of an international reputation was that bottled and served in the famous palace hotel at Bussaco. The hotel was built in the primeval forest to the east of Coimbra. It had been a favourite monastic retreat, but in September 1810 it saw one of the bloodiest fights of the Peninsular War, when the Anglo-Portuguese armies of Sir Arthur Wellesley – later the duke of Wellington – trounced a French force commanded by Marshal Masséna, at a loss of 4,500 casualties. Half a century later, the palace was a pet project of the king consort, the German husband of Maria II, Ferdinand of Saxe-Coburg and Gotha, who had shown his taste for historicism in architecture when he commissioned the Pena Palace in Sintra.

Ferdinand did not survive to see the building which rose up on top of a high knoll in the middle of the forest. It was to be the greatest of all essays in neo-Manueline architecture, covered in a riot of *azulejos*, within and without, depicting scenes from the writings of the sixteenth-century poet Camões and his older contemporary dramatist, Gil Vicente. Inside the walls were hung with episodes from the glorious days of Portuguese history and the grand staircase lined with suits of armour equipped with luminous red eyes. It was originally intended as a royal palace, but the project was later revised to include a hotel. The royal residence became redundant at the fall of the Portuguese monarchy. Under the guiding hand of a local, Alexandre de Almeida, the building became Portugal's most idiosyncratic hotel. It was also the model for the state-run chain of *pousadas* which was established in 1942 with the opening of São Lourenço in Manteigas in the Serra da Estrela.

Soon after Almeida's arrival, the cellars began to buy in grapes to make a house wine for the hotel adding them to the harvests from the hotel's own vines. Everything in the process was done by hand, and the wines, once pressed and fermented, lodged in casks of oak, chestnut and mahogany under the main building. As the wine could only be drunk *in situ* bottles were recycled. It is still a considerable joy to visit those old-fashioned cellars down by the kitchens and see the bins filled with dusty bottles going back to the vintages between the wars. Those examples of the Reserva Especial do Bussaco have found many apologists over the years, although it seems fair to say that since the quality of Bairrada wines in general have improved, there are fewer and fewer people who give whole-hearted praise to the wines of the hotel.

As we have seen, red wine is Baga in Bairrada. It can be notably tough when it is handled badly, and winemakers have to be careful about oak, which can merely harden it more.

White wines are generally made from Maria Gomes, the local name for the Fernão Pires of the Ribatejo and the Estremadura. I don't know if there is any significance in the sex change: Bairrada whites do not seem significantly more feminine than those from elsewhere. The most interesting green grape is the Bical. A small amount of Arinto is also used.

There are still complaints in the region that the proper soil has yet to be defined. Some authorities maintain that Bairrada comes from *barro* or clay. Others spurn this idea, and say that the word derives from the low Latin *barrium*, or rural district. There is plenty of fertile clay around, however. In too accommodating a soil Baga becomes too exuberant and gives poor quality juice. The better soils of the region are the answer: marl, sand and limestone, as well as increasing the space between the rows. The rootstock most growers use has also come under fire as has the use of oak, even the best Bairrada vignerons, say some, have little idea as to how to handle small oak *barriques*.

The biggest name in Bairrada wines is Luis Pato. He is lucid and literate and his perfectionism coupled with a passion for experiment has hurtled him to the forefront of Portuguese winemaking. He is a controversialist, fond of airing his views in the newspapers. He has recently had a brush with the authorities when they named a man he didn't like to head the local *comissão*. Now he has decided to label all his wines 'Beiras', using the regional appellation, so that they do not need to pass under the nose of the Bairrada authorities.

Luis Pato kicked off as recently as 1980, when he inherited 60 ha of vines from his father. João Pato had begun bottling wine in 1970, with a 1964 red. Until his father's death Luis had been working in ceramics. He has acquired more land since then: he has taken on the wines of his father-in-law around Oiã do Bairro, and now has 24 vineyards chiefly based on limestone soils.

He is proud of the fact that he is not a trained oenologist. Pato is most famous for his knack of taming the wilful Baga. Old vines help. His Vinha Barrosa, for example, is made from 70-year-old vines, giving it an almost Burgundian silkiness and a smell of plums and dark chocolate.

Vinha Pan is made from much younger vines, but it takes to oak better. He has a rarer wine and that is the Quinta do Ribeirinho where he planted the vines directly in the sandy soil in 1998. Here he makes around 100 cases of wine every year in exactly the same way as people did before the arrival of the phylloxera aphis more than a century ago, which forced virtually all European growers to graft their vines onto American rootstock. Pato is quite convinced that the wines were better then.

With Pato there is something new every year and you need to run quickly to catch up with him. Ribeirinho now has a Primeira Escolha label. He has also launched João Pato – a blend of Baga and Cabernet Sauvignon and a new white called Vinha Formal. This is made from 50% low-yielding, old Bical vines grown on clay soils. This, he hopes, will become his Montrachet.

The other star estate in the region is the Casa de Saima, owned by the local doctor, Carlos Almeida e Silva and tended by his wife Graça Maria da Silva Miranda. The third member of the team is the oenologist Rui Alves – who has the reputation for making all the best Bairradas. The 12 ha estate produces tiny amounts of white wines; with just 300 cases they are immediately grabbed up by the trade. You can see why, they are fresh, but have breed and a powerful finish. They are made from Bical, with a little Cerceal. His reds are justifiably famous. The pure Baga wines are notable for their tobacco aromas. The concentration of gamey fruit in the *garrafeira* is legendary. There is something else besides, a hint of aniseed, perhaps. The wine is sold out long before it reaches the market.

Rui Alves is also responsible for the wines of the Quinta das Bágeiras in Fogueira. I know only the 1995 Garrafeira, but that was very fine – quite dry, but with a lovely scent of blackberries and raspberries.

Another man who used to work in tandem with Casa de Saima is Ataí de Costa Martins Semedo at the 25 ha Quinta da Rigodeira. He occupies a spotless cellar out in the woods with stainless steel vats and *lagares*. His white is a blend of Bical and Maria Gomes with a smidgen of Chardonnay. Foreign varietals enter into a Beiras blend of Baga and Merlot which is distinguished by its figgy, spicy fruit.

His best Bairradas are made from 60-70 year old Baga vines. They are superbly deep in colour and reek of black fruits. His *garrafeira* comes from a separate plot called the Quinta da Dôna. Here the Baga vines are anything up to eighty years old. It is a very rich, concentrated wine, but rare: he makes only 2,000 litres in a good year.

There are the inevitable sparkling wines. The basic blend is Maria Gomes with Bical and Chardonnay. The younger wine has all the aggressive bubble you need to deal with a greasy hoglet. The top cuvée, with its redolence of dry marmalade, is a little too mellow for this. It is better on its own as an aperitif.

The 10 ha Quinta do Carvalhinho in Mealhada, is a delightful old house complete with chapel dating back to 1698. The owner, António Afonso Navega, is something of DIY fan and together with a desire to reform the house's interior he likes to fill every available space with bric-a-brac. Much of it comes from churches and monasteries built at a time when most Portuguese were more often on their knees than on their feet.

The press house and vines are at the back of the house, beyond a shady bower created by a 300- year-old wisteria. Here he makes a good sparkling wine from Maria Gomes, Bical and Rabo de Ovelha, but suggests – heretically – that suckling pig is better consumed with a tannic red from pure limestone soils. It is at this point that he introduces his own: intense, tarry, tannic wines with aromas of incense and liquorice. They age particularly well.

Merchants and Cooperatives

In recent years the merchant cellars have reformed their methods, and many of them are making fine Bairrada wines. One good example here is the Caves Primavera, founded in 1947 by the brothers Vital and Lucénio de Almeida. The chief oenologist at this vast, strawberry pink building is Osvaldo Amado. Whites are made from Maria Gomes and Bical, the former providing the bite, the latter, body. One top white (Beiras – as it defies the DOC) includes about a third part of Arinto and is partly fermented in oak.

The top reds fill the Baga out with a little Tinta Pinheira, Castelão, Touriga Nacional and Jaen which provide length and complexity. Beiras provides Amado with the chance to experiment. Baga is combined with half as much Cabernet Sauvignon; again the Cabernet acts as a softener to the sinewy local hero. There is a pure Touriga Nacional in the same range as well as a Beiras Baga with a notable gamey smell and luscious, sweet fruit.

Probably the best of the range is the Bairrada Special Selection, where the Baga has been aged in Allier oak. For the pigs Amado makes some sparklers. The one I liked best was pure Arinto, a big, rounded wine with no *dosage*.

Some of the cooperatives are also notable for the quality of their wines. One which stands out is Cantanhede. Its origins are like all the others in Portugal, except that it was the product of Salazar's dotage, being founded as late as 1974. It is one of the ten biggest in Portugal. The cooperative winery was one of the dictator's hobby horses and many of them still look – physically – as if they have remained in that period. Not so Cantanhede, which has been cunningly brought up to date. One of the cleverest ideas has been to adapt the subterranean vats into a series of small rooms for the storage of the sparkling wines, build round arches and create a visual effect by the use of multi-coloured lights.

Sparkling wine is produced in profusion. Under Antero Silvano's guiding hand it is not to be disdained. The Millennium cuvée was mostly Bical. There is also a rare red sparkler made from Baga – an imitation perhaps of the wines which used to be left in honeymoon suites in Australian hotels in the days before Viagra.

The best whites here are made from pure Bical. They are all, without exception, technically well made wines. Silvano likes to experiment with different oaks and showed me a young wine he had placed in four different casks. The French wood gave the best result, but at a huge cost. The second best was Portuguese.

The Baga wines are very good, perhaps as a result of the predominantly limestone soils of the area. One declassified Bairrada (Beiras) smelled of honey and lavender. The Marquês de Marialva cuvée tends to be approachable and quite soft for Baga. The reserve wine is called Conde de Cantanhede which is beautifully brimming with fruit. Both age well, giving off a few gamey notes after five years or so.

Other cooperatives which produce large quantities of very reliable wine are those in Mealhada (they make the brand Encosta de Mouros), Mogofores, Souselas and Vilarinho do Bairro. Caves noteworthy for their home-grown Bairrada wines are Aliança, Borlido, Império, Messias, S. João and Valdarcos. São João's Frei João wines are also made by Rui Alves. They are a little on the earthy side, smelling of wax, sweat and cherries. Sidónio de Sousa is another feather in Alves' cap: the *garrafeira* represents the drier school of Bairrada.

The best of those companies making Bairrada wines based outside the region are Caves Velhas and Dom Teodósio.

The restaurant Meta dos Leitões in Mealhada has its own production of Bairrada, sold on the premises both to consume there and to take away under the Casa do Sarmento label.

There are a few more commercial operations trading in Bairrada wines of which Sogrape's Quintas de Pedralvites and Quinta de Barzomba are among the most important. Together they total 57 ha, and wines from these estates are served on TAP Portuguese Airlines flights. DFJ's Bela Fonte has a Bairrada which reeks of stewed plums. Peter Bright has one in his range too, a notably soft expression of the Baga grape.

Historic Wines at the Gates of Lisbon

The regional appellation contains just one sub-region: Alta Estremadura (Oeste). Minimum alcohol levels are 11%, or 9% for vinho leve. There is a certain liberal spirit in the recommended regional varieties: for whites – Alicante Branco, Almafra, Alvarinho, Antão Vaz, Arinto, Bical, Boal Branco, Boal Espinho, Cerceal Branco, Chardonnay, Diagalves, Esgana Cão, Fernão Pires, Gewürztraminer, Jampal, Malvasia, Moscatel de Setúbal, Rabo de Ovelha, Riesling, Sauvignon Blanc, Seara Nova, Siria, Tália, Tamarez, Trincadeira Branca, Trincadeira das Pratas, Viognier and Vital.

For regional reds there are Alfrocheiro Preto, Alicante Bouschet, Amostrinha, Castelão, Baga, Bastardo, Cabernet Sauvigon, Camarate, Carignan, Cinsault, Grand Noir, Grenache, Merlot, Moreto, Monvedro, Negra Mole, Parreira Matias, Tinta Roriz, Pinot Noir, Tinta Barroca, Tinta Caiada, Tinta Carvalha, Tinta Grossa, Tinta Miúda, Tintinha, Tinto Cão, Touriga Francesa, Touriga Nacional, Trincadeira Preta, Ramisco and Rufete.

For the old DOCs of Bucelas, Carcavelos and Colares it is different. Bucelas has maximum yields of 70 hls/ha and a minimum strength of 10.5%. The wine must be 75% Arinto and may be topped up with Esgana Cão and Rabo de Ovelha. Carcavelos has maximum yields of 55 hls/ha for its fortified wines. The reds are made from Castelão (confusingly called Trincadeira here) and Negra Mole. There is provision for whites too, but no one makes any. In Colares maximum yields are 70hls/ha for whites and 55 for reds. Minimum strength is 10%. Whites must be aged for 9 months before release and reds for 24. The grape varieties recommended are Malvasia Fina for white wines and Ramisco (minimum of 80% for reds).

The DOC Lourinhã is for brandy: they must have 38% by volume and be aged for a minimum of two years. The grape varieties are Alicante Branco, Alvarellão, Boal Espinho, Mariquinhas, Malvasia Rei and Tália and the red Cabinda.

Torres Vedras DOC limits yields to 90 hls/ha for

estremadura

whites and 80 hls/ha for reds. The whites should be made from Arinto, Fernão Pires, Jampal, Rabo de Ovelha, Seara Nova and Vital; the reds from Camarate, Castelão, Tinta Miúda and Trincadeira Preta.

Arruda DOC wines have similar yields. The whites may be made from Arinto, Fernão Pires, Jampal and Vital; the reds from Camarate, Castelão, Preto Martinho and Tinta Miúda.

Alenquer DOC has the same yields and white grapes as Arruda, but favours Castelão for at least 30% of the red blend.

Óbidos allows maximum yields of 90 hls/ha for whites and 70 hls/ha for reds. The white cultivars favoured are same as the other DOCs, but the reds include Bastardo and exclude Preto Martinho.

Encostas d' Aire stipulates maxima of 80 hls/ha for whites and 70 hls/ha for reds. Jampal is omitted from the recommended green grapes and Tamarez joins the team; the reds should be made from Baga (we are near Bairrada here), Castelão and Trincadeira Preta.

Alcobaça's yields and recommended varieties are the same as Encostas d' Aire's.

In 1998-1999 neither Alcobaça nor Lourinhã declared any DOC wine; Óbidos made 2,540 hls of white and 950 hls of red; Alenquer, 3,180 of white and 4,926 of red; Arruda 463 hls of white and 2,130 of red; Torres Vedras 2,994 of white and 3,878 of red; Bucelas 2,411 of white only; Carcavelos 15 hls of red fortified wine; Colares 3 hls of white and 35 of red. In addition to these totals there were 73,324 hls of white regional wine made in the Estremadura, and 67,483 of red.

The Estremadura is a regional appellation covering a broad block of land running up the coast from Lisbon and centring on Torres Vedras, a small town made famous by the duke of Wellington, who held back the French here, bent on taking Lisbon. With its long coastline, the region enjoys a capricious climate and relatively high humidity, although this is in no way to be compared to the Minho. The result is *vinho leve*, a light white or rosé with around 9.5 degrees, which makes a refreshing drink in the summer months.

There are three old DOCs in the Estremadura: Bucelas, Colares, Carcavelos demarcated in 1911; and a number of VQPRDs which have been more recently elevated into DOCs: Encostas d'Aire, Alcobaça, Óbidos, Alenquer, Arruda, Torres Vedras and Lourinhã. Added to these there is the regional, Estremadura appellation which accepts a broader panoply of cultivars.

Where Oporto had vinho verde and port, Lisbon had Bucelas, Colares and Carcavelos – white, red and sweet wines. That these represented the best on offer for sophisticated Lisbon noblemen is clear from Eça de Queiroz's novel *Os Maias* of 1888. The scene actually takes place in Afonso da Maia's country house in the Douro. Old Bucelas was too good for children:

'Bucelas?' murmured a footman over his shoulder.

The steward raised his glass when it had been filled, admired its rich colour in the light, tasted it with the tip of his tongue and winked an eye at Afonso.

'It's our own!'

'The old one', said Afonso. 'Ask Brown – eh, Brown, a good nectar?'

'Magnificent!' exclaimed the tutor with fiery energy.

Carlos stretched his arm across the table and also demanded Bucelas. His reason was that it was a celebration because Vilaça had come. Grandfather would not consent; the lad could have his glass of Colares, as usual, and one only. Carlos folded his arms on the napkin that hung from his neck, astonished at such an injustice! So, not even to toast Vilaça could he have a drop of Bucelas? That was a fine way of receiving guests at the manor!

Colares was always the most famous wine of the Estremadura. Since the twelfth century the vines have been planted ungrafted in the sand dunes to the west of Lisbon. It is in real danger of extinction. In 1979 Dan Stanislawski referred to it as 'perhaps the best wine in Portugal', but pointed out that summer houses had replaced many of the Ramisco vines: 'Colares is now in the hour of its vespers.'

There are not more than 50 ha of Colares today. The land is being eaten away by the sea on one side and the property spivs on the other. Tavares & Rodrigues, the one decent-sized estate, has been abandoned. It used to make wines under the Manuel José Colares label, which I enjoyed on my first visits to Portugal. The rest of the

growers take their grapes to the cooperative where all Colares, red and white is vinified before being sold off to a scant handful of *négociants éleveurs*. The wines stay in cask for years, and not always the cleanest ones, so that they often lack fruit and taste grubby to a modern generation of wine lovers. One firm which always has a few wines that are not bad, is Chitas, at Azenhas do Mar. A visit offers a chance to taste some old Colares, which can be hard to obtain elsewhere.

It is hard to know now whether the disappearance of Colares should be rued or not. It was pretty hard to grow. Planting was literally a nightmare. You had to dig deep into the sand to reach the clay below. If you were not careful the sand collapsed on top of you. Fatal accidents were not unknown.

Another great rarity was the fortified, port-like wine of Carcavelos, where two or three quintas make wine on some 20 ha of land. The Última Reserva from the Quinta

do Barão is a good example. The colour is red amber. It is less sweet and has more bite than the average tawny. Carcavelos owed much of its popularity to Wellington's officers, who indulged liberally while they picketed the lines at Torres Vedras.

It is not all doom and gloom, however. The fortunes of one of the old wines from the Lisbon area, Bucelas, has undergone a small revival and there are now as many as 300 ha of this historic area under vine. The Arinto grapes are grown on alluvial limestone. They produce a white wine which can have the right sappiness to go with the plentiful shellfish and crustaceans found in the capital. There is just one local red, Charneco, now almost legendary; the Quinta da Romeira has restarted production making a white version to boot.

The Quinta da Romeira is the biggest domaine in Bucelas. The estate was formerly part of the lands owned by the counts of Castelo-Melhor. The present concern was started up by the British sugar company Tate & Lyle; it now vinifies the fruit for half the other wines made in the DOC. Since Tate & Lyle sold it, it has joined a group of properties which market their wines together: the Companhia das Quintas. These are the Quinta do Cardo in Beiras, the Quinta da Barca in the Douro and the Herdade de Ferizoa in the Alentejo.

The Bucelas wines have been made by Nuno Cancela de Abreu since the company began trading in 1987. He also vinifies the wines from the Beira Interior and the Dão properties in the group. Arinto, Sercial and Rabo d'Ovelha grapes grow in poor, chalky soil, with a high pH. The nights are notably humid which lends the wines a certain freshness while the Atlantic climate brings in cool breezes which provide the grapes with acidity and aroma.

Romeira's Bucelas is a very attractive, sappy white made entirely from Arinto with a tangy, lemon-like fruit. If the people of Lisbon were to renounce their passion for drinking red wine with fish, this would be the ideal thing to replace it. Indeed, in Eça de Queiroz's novel, *Os Maias*, the banker Cohen drinks Bucelas with his oysters at the Hotel Central. Morgado de Santa Catherina is the barrel-fermented version – more serious and less friendly to oysters and clams – but Abreu does not perform a malolactic fermentation. He does not like Arinto with lactic flavours.

Romeira makes other wines, again some of them are 'branded' products like Calhandriz, where Muscat and

Arinto are blended together with interesting results. The red is made from Tinta Roriz and Camarate. There is also a well-judged, commercial red called Prova Régia, where 80% Touriga Nacional is topped up with Cabernet and Merlot.

There is the usual varietal range too, which includes Chardonnay and Sauvignon Blanc. Fruit is also brought in from Palmela and the Douro to make red *Tradição* wines.

There are five other producers in the DOC. Caves Velhas is the second biggest producer in Bucelas. Francisco Castelo Branco owns the Quinta da Murta. He is an engineer who grew tired of working in Lisbon and sought the good life here in Bucelas. He has no winery and his wines are made at Romeira. They are quite different even if the mainstay is the same: Arinto with a helping of Rabo de Ovelha and Esgana Cão. Arinto is a difficult character to pin down and Murta's wines change from year to year. In a good one they can be fat, almost Chardonnay-like, whereas in a less favoured one they make refreshing, angular wines which would go down best with a fresh crab or rock lobster in a restaurant in Lisbon's Baixa.

White Wines

The basic white cultivar in the coastal parts of the Estremadura is Fernão Pires, a good cropper which ripens early and provides plenty of aroma, is robust and has a relatively high acidity. It grows well on clay loam, but tends to produce coarse wine in sand. The most popular complimentary grape varieties are Arinto and Vital.

It is Fernão Pires which is responsible for most of the *vinho leve*: light, easy drinking white wines of which Mirante is a good example: a bit like vinho verde without the sparkle.

Grand' Arte is a new series of wines conceived by DFJ and the oenologist José Neiva who lives in the region and advises several different estates. He is the J.P. Ramos of central Portugal - or Ramos is the José Neiva of the south. One of his most interesting whites is a combination of Chardonnay and Alvarinho, offering the weight of one and the delicacy of the other. Another fine wine is Ramada or Coreto, made from Fernão Pires, Seara Nova and Vital. This is a real little cornucopia of fruits and flowers: peaches, apricots, and lavender. In Portada the wines are heavily oaked. Vale de Rosas is pure Fernão Pires. It reminded me of Turkish delight.

Cerejeiras is another spin-off from the JP dry muscat which brought so much fame to Peter Bright twenty years ago.

Another estate that rarely disappoints is the Quinta da Abrigada in Alenquer. The very large region of Alenquer (with 9,000 ha it is bigger than the Alentejo)

lies on the far side of a range of hills which break the back of the Atlantic climate. It is generally warmer, sunnier and less capricious on this side of the divide. On Alenquer's clay soils they make white wines from just Arinto and Vital, but the wine is very pleasant, with a nice fruit and flowers bouquet.

Oeste Reds

Towards the north of the region, not far from Portugal's second most exciting mediaeval abbey, Batalha, is Encostas d'Aire. It borders on Bairrada, so it should come as no surprise to find that there is Baga about.

From Torres Vedras comes Fonte das Moças (the fountain of the young women), a go-ahead operation which uses a lot of American oak on its blend of Tinta Roriz and Touriga Nacional.

Among its red varietal wines DFJ's Grand' Arte makes a brave bottling of Alicante Bouschet with a dash of new oak adding a little vanilla to a dark thundering mix of cherry and blackberry tastes. The same team makes a Touriga Francesa which couldn't be more different. It had me thinking of lemon puffs. Portada is quite a tough wine, while the red Vale de Rosas blends Alicante with Castelão to make a really well balanced wine with appealing fruit.

Manta Preta is bathed in new oak, giving a commercial style for those who still want their wines thus. Caladoc is a new grape variety which DFJ is playing with. It is a synthesis of Malbec and Grenache and has an unusual malty perfume.

Alenquer

Again some of the best red wines from the Estremadura come from Alenquer. The Quinta da Abrigada was originally the home of Fernando Álvares Cabral, the son of the man who discovered Brazil. It received a thorough shake-up in the 1755 earthquake, and now only the exterior walls go back to the sixteenth century, and to all extents and purposes it looks more like an eighteenth-century building. The entire vineyard was restructured as early as the 1960s, and now the area under vine has shrunk from 50 to 20 ha.

The whites are sappy and refreshing, but it is the reds which are most famous from this property. The basic red is a blend of Periquita, Tinta Miúda and Alicante Bouschet grown on heavy clay soils. The Alicante gives it a little leathery note, but there is plenty of waxy flavoured fruit here. In 2001 they will be planting Touriga Nacional, Touriga Francesa and Tinta Roriz, so the style is set to change – fundamentally. The nearby Quinta do Carneiro is a light cocktail of Periquita, Trincadeira and Cabernet Sauvignon; an attractive commercial wine. Possibly even nicer is the Tinta Roriz from the same estate which has an intriguing touch of gaminess about it, coupled with some sweet fruit. A Cabernet Sauvignon is wrought in a minty, new-world style.

A hot tip from the region is the Quinta do Carneiro. The lesser wines are labelled Vinha do Carneiro. They include a fine, lingering, Fernão Pires-based white and a Periquita red. Both have plenty of fruit. The white quinta wine is predominantly Bical. It is full and long and smells slightly of honeycomb.

One of the most successful in Alenquer is the Quinta de Pancas where the vines are owned by the Guimarães family, which offers a range of wines - traditional Portuguese blends and single varieties, as well as foreign cultivars: Tinta Roriz, for example, and Cabernet Sauvignon. Another Alenquer wine with star potential is the Quinta da Cortezia. The Tinta Roriz has a biting taste of fresh redcurrants and a whiff of toast; the Touriga Nacional is a wine of more substance and staying power.

Another innovative property - or group of properties – is the Quinta da Boa Vista owned by José Luis Oliveira da Silva, and vinified by José Neiva. Silva is also behind four other estates: Palha Canas, Casa Santos Lima, Quinta da Espiga, and Quinta das Sete Encostas – twenty labels in all, and 150 ha of vines. Sitting down to a working lunch at the property can be quite a challenge, as Silva puts anything over a dozen red wines on the table to try with the food.

Before the reds there were half a dozen whites. These were tasted as a little aperitif on the terrace of his villa, looking out over the wide spaces and the mountains which cut him off from the sea. Quinta da Espiga brings in Sauvignon Blanc to play with a home team composed of Fernão Pires, Vital, Arinto and Seara Nova. A similar desire to add a piquant foreign element is found in the Quinta das Sete Encostas and Palha Canas cuvées, where Chardonnay is set against Fernão

Pires, Arinto and Rabo d'Ovelha. Only with the Casa Santos Lima has he played the varietal card currently so popular in Portugal: Fernão Pires, Chardonnay – half fermented in oak, the rest in tank – and Moscatel. These wines were first marketed in 1996.

Then came lunch: vichyssoise soup, canard à l'orange, serra cheese and nut cake. Silva's biggest selling wine at export is the red Quinta da Espiga, which blends Periquita, Tinta Miúda, Touriga Nacional and Tinta Roriz. It is a big, fruity drop, conceived to be drunk young. The Sete Encostas has a pleasing cherry fruit, and ages well. The Palha Canas adds an element of raspberry fruit to the mix. Then come the varietal wines: a rare, tarry, blackberry-scented Preto Martinho; a sharp, cherry like Tinta Miúda; a Camarate, reminiscent of strawberries; Trincadeira – which put me in mind of raspberries and custard; a quite jammy Castelão; a complex Tinta Roriz; a classic Merlot with a pronounced green pepper taste; a text book Cabernet Sauvignon; a hefty, tannic Touriga Francesa; a rich Touriga Nacional; and Touriz – a blend of the last two, where the Touriga dominates adding its approachable fruit to the weight provided by the Tinta Roriz.

Oliveira da Silva believes that Portugal's varietal wines are part of the learning process: you deconstruct the vineyard in order to learn how the cultivars function in the blend. Then you put them back together again. There is still a lot to do before the Estremadura, in particular can develop a clear identity of its own, even if the Alenquer seems right on target.

The DOC now has the following subregions: Almeirim, Cartaxo, Chamusca, Coruche, Santarém and Tomar. Yields are 8ohls/ha for reds and rosés and 90 hls/ha for whites.

The following are recommended: Castelão and Castelão Nacional, Preto Martinho and Trincadeira Preta. Small amounts of Baga, Bastardo, Cabernet Sauvignon, Moreto, Pinot Noir, Tinta Mole and Tinta Miúda are also authorised. In Almeirim the Baga is favoured for reds, and Grenache is authorized. In Chamusca Camarate is highly prized, while the mix might be complemented by a small amount of the

teinturiers; Alicante Bouschet or Grand Noir; or Touriga Nacional, Baga or Cabernet Sauvignon.

For whites the recommended grapes are Arinto, Fernão Pires, Rabo de Ovelha, Tália and Trincadeira das Pratas. A little Alicante Branco, Boal de Alicante, Cerceal, Chardonnay, Malvasia, Olho de Lebre, Pinot Blanc or Vital may also be used, depending on the individual sub-region of the DOC.

The regional appellation is more liberal again. White wines may contain the foreign cultivars Chardonnay, Gewürztraminer, Pinot Blanc, Riesling, Sauvignon Blanc, Semillon and Viognier; reds, Cabernet Sauvignon, Carignan, Cinsault, Grenache, Merlot, Pinot Noir and Syrah.

In 1998-1999 the Ribatejo produced 11,394 hls of white DOC wine and 15,020 of red; it also produced 59,769 hls of white regional wine and 41,018 hls of red.

As the name implies, the Ribatejo accounts for the vines which grow above the River Tagus. There are four wine routes, including the 'Templars' road which takes visitors through Tomar with its glorious monastery. An opportunity has been wasted here: there should be a place to sample all that is good in the Ribatejo within the complex of historic buildings which crowns the hill, now that the old convent has

ribatejo

finally lost the squaddies who used to toss down the occasional coarse remark to you from an open window above, as you meditated in its ancient cloisters.

There is naturally plenty of history here on the Tagus, a stone's throw from Lisbon and one of the major routes towards the interior of the Iberian peninsula. Santarém is a royal town and its wines had a reputation to match. The citizens were already exporting olive oil and wine before the end of the fourteenth century, and the Avis kings forbade the importation of foreign wines into the region. There was formerly a royal palace in Almeirim; its remains were demolished in 1890. During the last years of the Monarchy there were moves to protect Ribatejo wines by statute.

There are striking similarities between the Ribatejo and the French Languedoc. Both have their flat, easily worked soil – although both have their rather more impressive highlands; one is close to the port of Lisbon, the other was made accessible to the railway in the second half of the nineteenth century, which meant that big, red staining wines could be taken up to the north of France to be lapped up by industrial workers in regions with no vines of their own. The banks of the Tagus were just as accessible: a wide, navigable river meant that the area was developed to provide bulk wines, many of which were exported either to provide solace for the Brazilians - who were unable to make much wine themselves - or to water the throats of Portuguese colonists in Africa and the

Far East. Much of the money was also Brazilian. They built some of the gigantic wineries you still see in the area, many of which are partly ruinous now that the Portuguese Empire is just a memory.

These bulk wines gave the region a bad name. Like the Languedoc there is more than one side to the Ribatejo. There are subtle differences of soil. In the marshy Campo or Leziria lands, for example, the alluvium comes from the quaternary rock which has been broken down by the action of the Tagus. The soil is rich and fertile and also used for growing fruit and vegetables. Higher up, away from the proximity of the flood, is *barro* composed of iron rich clay, sand and limestone. This is more typical terrain for vines and olives. In Almeirim, for example, there are steep terraces above the river. The higher you climb towards Tomar, the soil becomes less alluvial and composed more of heavy clay. Charneca soils on the south bank of the Tagus are actually similar to those in the Alentejo. They are poor and there is a good deal of cork oak grown here. Hot sun means high alcohol.

White wines used to be the thing in the Ribatejo. One reason for this was distilling. From this region came much of the brandy required for halting the fermentations of red wines in the Douro Valley that were destined to become port. Some of the better brandies were considered good enough to ship out to the colonists in Africa and the East, with their tanned, leathery faces, and permanently parched tongues. The rest was happily drunk at home.

The Ribatejo still contains Portugal's largest cooperatives. Many of them are still not entirely geared up to suit the modern world and produce a lot of uncertified wines from grapes which arrive from outside the demarcated region.

The emphasis has naturally changed a lot. Now the region is moving over to reds, but there are quite a lot of green grapes around still, and with the right sort of vinification they can be made into very clean, refreshing white wines. The chief variety used here is the grapefruit-tasting Fernão Pires.

The red wines are generally made from pure Periquita, as they tend to call Castelão here. If anything is seen as the *cépage ameliorateur* (grape variety set to improve the local blend) it is Trincadeira. Foreign black cultivars have also made their appearance, and one of the most successful wines from the Ribatejo today, is the Syrah from the Quinta da Lagoalva.

One of the largest bottlers in the Ribatejo is Dom Teodosio in Rio Maior. It processes around a million litres of Ribatejo wines, and make some 16 million in all. Quite apart from the wine it purchases, it has 140 ha in the region made up of the 100 ha Quinta São João Batista in Tomar, the 33 ha Quinta do Bairro Falcão and the 8 ha Quinta d'Almargem in Cartaxo.

That the wines are all well and cleanly made is demonstrated by a Sevares. This is a frothy, vinho verde type wine. It is cheap and comes in litre bottles, yet, on a hot day on the beach it provides a pleasant, refreshing glass. They make 1.5 million litres of it.

Naturally there are more serious white wines from this stable. Casaleiro is an IPR made from the grapefruity Fernão Pires grape. Again it is light and refreshing, and with an alcohol content of around 11.5, is not a head-banger. More ponderous is the S. João Batista white, made with the same variety, but having far greater length. Another white from the estate is a *blanc de noir* made from Castelão. It is very pale, almost aqueous in colour. Part of the production is used to make a successful sparkling wine.

The red Casaleiro has a striking smoky, fig-like fruit. Its tarriness alluding to the heat of a summer here in the region, where the barometer can easily climb to 40 degrees C. The reserve wine tastes even riper, with its almost porty sweet fruit.

Serradayres is an old brand now become DOC. It is made from Castelão and has an elegance lacking perhaps in the Casaleiro. The flagship red wines are now the three quintas. S. João Batista reminded me of ripe tomatoes, its reserve version of sour cherries. Quinta do Bairro Falcão is a highly individual wine from Cartaxo. It is smoky again, but the fruit had me thinking of peas. The reserve wine was notably tarry. By contrast there was a friendly, sugar-plum quality to the Quinta d'Almargem. The reserve wine adds a little Trincadeira to the Castelão fruit which is the mainstay of the others.

D & F (from *Dino* Ventura and *Fausto* Ferraz) is a

highly successful operation in the British Isles which imports more Portuguese table wine than anyone around. More recently it has created a Portuguese wing called DFJ and moved into production with the help of the oenologist José Neiva Correia (he has provided the J). It makes some highly successful wines all over the centre of Portugal. It even makes an Algarve wine (see p142).

In the old days these wines were made in different wineries, but now a base has been established in a vast complex of buildings complete with a Heath-Robinson-like still house at the Quinta da Fonte Bela in Vila Chã de Ourique near Cartaxo. In places this blackened brick quadrangle with its immense wings stuffed with concrete vats and vast wooden tuns seems to have been modelled on one of the more extreme fantasies represented in Piranesi's *Carceri*. I wandered around with Dino Ventura, the head of operations in London, and José Neiva. Everywhere we went a score of pigeons scattered through the eaves. On the main chimney a stork had built its nest. DFJ has ambitious plans for the buildings. Let us hope it does not eradicate all the atmosphere of the place.

Its basic Ribatejo wine is Segada. The white is pure Fernão Pires, while the red has marginally more Trincadeira than Castelão. Modestly priced, the red Segada is extremely good value for such a flavoursome and aromatic wine. Senda do Vale blends Trincadeira with Cabernet Sauvignon to make a wine which could pass for something from the new world. It does not lack guts.

The Grand'Arte reds also hail from the Ribatejo. There is a pure Alicante Bouschet which is quite blue at the rim, and has a splendid creamy blackberry flavour together with impressive length for what is generally condemned as a short grape variety. Another Grand'Arte is made from Trincadeira. This smells of smoke and liquorice with a hint of blackberries and bacon fat. It is very good for all that.

José Neiva also lends a hand with the wines from the Quinta do Falcão. There is a white made from Fernão Pires with Tamarez and two good reds: the Quinta do Falcão with its confectionery fruit and the splendid Paço dos Falcões, with its huge leathery fruit tempered by a rich taste of blackberries.

In Almeirim I met the familiar figure of Peter Bright. He may have been in Portugal for the best part of twenty-

five years, but he is still every inch an Australian. A comment on his absent moustache provoked an unrepeatable hunk of antipodean ribaldry. A barrel tour is a *sine qua non*, here as in an Australian winery. Bright draws a little wine from some of the casks with a spindly pipette. It is a thorough approach you don't encounter much elsewhere in Europe.

Bright established his reputation at João Pires (later J.P. Vinhos) in the late seventies, by revitalising a number of brands and estates which were marketed by the company. When he began he was still responsible for the wines at Hungerford Hill in New South Wales and used the unproductive Australian winters to tend his Portuguese interests. He denies being the original 'flying winemaker', and cites instances of other Australians who had interests in European wines before him. In none of those cases, however, did the Australians *make* the wine. Bright was making wines in both hemispheres long before the present rash of peripatetics.

He left J.P. in 1993 and now makes wine in both Portugal and Argentina. The style has changed a lot since those early wines made in Palmela and the Alentejo. He is pitching directly at the British supermarket chains now, to some extent giving them what they want. He is not really looking for an estate style, but seeking to make reliable branded products based on international and Portuguese grape varieties.

Bright's Ribatejo operation is based in the Fiuza winery where he operates a joint venture with the owners. It is yet another old business which used to trade with Brazil, it was built with Brazilian money at the end of the last century. The Fiuzas planted 60 ha of French grape varieties in the 1980s, and therefore have proved a boon to Bright's rather more international perception of Portuguese wine.

We looked at some Sauvignon Blanc with some nice tropical fruit flavours and a decent acidity, but he is not happy with it, and intends to graft it over to Trincadeira – the new broom in the Ribatejo. There is a Chardonnay cut in a buttery, international mould. A Cabernet Sauvignon rosé has an identifying blackcurrant leaf character. It is dry, nothing to do with the base wine for Lancers rosé that he used to make for J.P. There are also red wines from both the Merlot and the Cabernet Sauvignon grapes.

He makes a few Ribatejo wines from Portuguese varieties, and is proud to show off a stainless steel *lagar*. The Cartaxo red comes from Trincadeira grapes grown on gravel soils: a rare wine, there are not many that show the mettle of the Trincadeira. It is not the deepest in colour, but it has a highly perfumed bouquet. Fiuza Reserve is a return to the international cultivars and a rich blend of Cabernet and Merlot with a hint of green pepper on the nose.

Despite the pull of history, there are some small to medium sized estates in the Ribatejo as well as one or two concerns which have spurned the branded approach. The heirs to D.Luis de Margaride are two aristocratic brothers who live in an old house surrounded by books and venerable antique furniture in Almeirim, where they are advised by their oenologist João Sardinha Cruz. They have 60 ha of vines and make wines under the Dom Hermano label as well as a range of varietals. The ordinary white is a mix of Trincadeira das Pratas, Talia (Ugni Blanc - possibly from 'Italia') and Vital. It is a wine which develops well in bottle. Also good is their Fernão Pires, which goes way beyond the standard grapefruit character of the grape to make something far richer, more reminiscent of ripe apricots.

A strawberry-scented rosé blends Castelão and Trincadeira, but it is the reds that give the most pleasure here. The standard Dom Hermano is a cocktail of Trincadeira, Castelão and Baga. It is rich and porty and made in an unabashed Portuguese style. The reserve wine is naturally even more concentrated, and there is a *garrafeira* which hints at smoke and violets and conceals huge tannins behind its attractive fruit. Wines such as these are built to last, as the brothers proved by opening another of their best wines from the eighties.

They are excited about their *monocépages* too. They have planted Syrah, Chardonnay, Arinto and Touriga Nacional. None of these has come on stream so far, but I tasted a Cabernet, a waxy Trincadeira and a Castelão recalling fresh raspberries and woodsmoke.

In Tramagal the Falcão Rodrigues, father and son,

have united their two estates: Casal da Coelheira and Terraços do Tejo. Their grapes are grown on the steeper slopes with their sandy soils above the Tagus near Abrantes. With 43 ha planted and 30 ha in production, they are the biggest of the three producers in the region. They possess a squeaky clean old winery which is crammed full of the latest technology and an airy tasting room where they can cope with the travellers who take the local wine route.

Like so many Ribatejo producers, the accent used to be on distillable white varieties, but in recent years they have brought down the percentage of green grapes from 75% to 50%. The whites are made principally from Fernão Pires, but there is also a smidgen of Tamarez and Malvasia.

The whites are good and fresh, with a lively acidity, the Casal da Coelheira having a degree more complexity, even if its Fernão Pires grapefruitiness is fairly irrepressible. The reds from the Terraços do Tejo are made from Castelão and Camarate. They have impressive colour and a simple, blackberry taste. In the Casal da Coelheira there has been a little Alicante Bouschet up to now, lending the wines a blue-black colour and a denser, sweeter fruit. The reserve wine is particularly impressive. Here there are more citrus notes and the ripe sweetness of marmalade.

In recent vintages, however, there has been a move to replace the Alicante by Trincadeira and Cabernet Sauvignon. Time will tell if it become the equals of the older wine.

Size is a feature of Ribatejo estates. The estate buildings at the Quinta do Casal Branco near Almeirim resemble a substantial village, dominated by a huge chimney which formerly evacuated the smoke from the still house, and now serves as a perch for a faithful stork which flies in every winter to nest there once it becomes a bit too nippy across the Oder. The cellars were built in 1817 but it is significant that the estate bottled no wine before 1989. The fruit from what is now 180 ha of vines (120 in production) was either sold off as bulk wine, or distilled to make brandy for the port wine trade.

Another stock in trade was rosé wine. The owners, the Lobo de Vasconcellos family, are closely allied to the Guedes family, who own Sogrape - the makers of

Mateus - and the Quinta da Aveleda in the Minho. José Lobo de Vasconcellos runs the estate these days. He is a keen huntsman and rides to hounds in Portugal. In his stables behind the pretty, turn of the century manor, he has a collection of Lusitano horses, traditionally used for bullfights; lovely, delicate beasts that are clearly his passion when he is not thinking about wine.

Lobo de Vasconcellos is advised by João Ramos for his estate wines. He makes a further range besides called Globus. These are made from bought in grapes. The basic range is called Terra de Lobos. I asked naively if there were a lot of wolves *(lobos)* around, thinking that there might be one or two on the Estrela, but none so close to Lisbon: 'Only in my family!' replied Lobo de Vasconcellos with good humour. The wolf white is mild and supple, largely Fernão Pires, with a little Talia or Ugni Blanc. The red version is pure Castelão made in *lagares*. It sees no oak and has a pleasant raspberry fruitiness to it.

Falcoaria is the estate's DOC. It commemorates an extant dovecote on what was once a royal hunting ground. The white is partly fermented in oak and made from Fernão Pires and Trincadeira das Pratas. The red is made from fruit from 60-year-old Castelão vines with Trincadeira. It smells of brown sugar and strawberries. There is also an impressive Cabernet Sauvignon called Capucho.

The Globus white is an expansive Fernão Pires wine. The red made from Castelão with a little Trincadeira is a bit more leathery. Lobo de Vasconcellos's company Ribatagus aims to guide the growers and to advise them how to get the best out of their vines.

Not far from the Quinta do Casal Branco are the duque de Cadaval's estates at Muge. It is here that Portugal's only Pinot Noir wine to date is made. There is a family link to the famous estates of the Graf von Schönborn in the Rheingau and Franconia, and Cadaval wines are well distributed in Germany.

The Companhia das Lezirias is a vast landholding created by Queen Maria of Portugal. The sale was effected in order to raise cash in a land brought low by civil war. In 1836 it controlled 40,000 ha of land. It was nationalised after the Revolution of 1974, but returned to the private sector in 1989. It now possesses about half of its original extent, but it is still a force to be reckoned with. Wine is just one string to its bow, with vineyards accounting for about 100 ha. The wines are made in a rather isolated winery off the main road on the south bank of the Tagus where they are proud to show you the Algerian technology the company installed in 1935 for making deep coloured red wines under a submersible cap.

The source of the vats is significant. Algeria was widely admired at that time for the dark, staining reds it produced: ideal material, they said, for mixing with rather weedier wines from Europe which lacked alcohol or colour or both. Since the war of independence with France, Algerian wines have become almost a rarity, and their principal role has long since been forgotten.

The whites from here are made from a blend of Fernão Pires and Trincadeira das Pratas. They are good, but even better is the Catapereiro, or 'wild pear' which has a rather muscat-like fruit. The basic red Catapereiro is a mix of Castelão and Alicante. It is dense and brooding, a great leathery blackstrap. The best is naturally the DOC which is made from Castelão, although they are ready to add some Trincadeira. It is blue-black and has a lovely taste of sweet, black cherries.

The Companhia das Lezirias also makes a nutty *mistelle* called Abafado. Sweet wines of this sort used to be quite common in the Ribatejo. They were a useful foil to the usual eggy puddings which here, as everywhere else in Portugal, excite child and adult alike.

The DOC Palmela permits yields on reds and whites of up to 55 hls/ha. The minimum alcohol level for red is a relatively high 12.5, reflecting the heat of the region. For white wines Arinto, Fernão Pires, Moscatel de Bago Miúdo, Moscatel de Setúbal, Moscatel Roxo, Rabo de Ovelha, Siria, Tamarez and Vital are permitted. For the reds Periquita (Castelão) must account for 67% of the grapes, with the permitted addition of Alfrocheiro Preto, Bastardo, Cabernet Sauvignon or Trincadeira Preta.

The DOC Setúbal is for fortified wines made from Muscat grapes. Yields are limited to 70 hls/ha, and only the Setúbal Muscat (Alexandria or gros grains) is permitted for the whites, and only the Roxo is allowed for reds.

The Terras do Sado regional wine treats grape varieties with a broad brush which allows almost everything planted in the region to date – and that includes Viognier, Syrah, Tannat and Zinfandel!

In 1998-1999 Setúbal produced 9,464 hls of white liqueur wine and 355 hls of red; Palmela made 3,551 hls of white and 20,730 hls of unfortified red wine; the Terras do Sado regional wine produced 32,726 hls of white and 79,943 of red.

As Bordeaux is to its hinterland, Setúbal is to the peninsula behind: it is the port through which all wine is supposed to pass. There are no vines around Setúbal, which used to be a fierce bastion of communism with rough streets prowled by sailors, dockers and their traditional accompaniments. The best wine comes from farther north, from between the Tagus and the Sado, the other side of the delightful national park that runs along the coast. They centre on Azeitão, the real wine capital of the region.

The wines are surely ancient, but their reputation goes back no further than the early nineteenth century. The most famous wine of the Peninsula is the Moscatel, but if it is of great antiquity there are no records to prove it. The first reference to Muscat vines growing in these sand and limestone soils also occurs in the nineteenth century when they became rivals to the similar wines produced in the Cape. Borrow visited Pegões at this time: 'In the whole of Portugal,' he noted, 'there is no place of worse reputation.' He dined at the descriptively named Estalagem dos Ladrões – the Thieves' Inn.

There are two main appellations now. The DOC Palmela which takes in the rocky *serras* of Arrábida, Rasca and São Luis rising to 500 metres, and the rather more relaxed IPR Terras do Sado, which is based on the plain beside the river of that name. There has been a certain amount of understandable complaint, however, that neither appellation means much to the

terras do sado and

setúbal peninsula

wine drinking public either at home or abroad. Setúbal had a rather better pedigree.

It tends to be hot on the Peninsula, sub-tropical and Mediterranean, and influenced by the vagaries of the sea, all at once. The soil is sandy, often with a little loam, but there are also outcrops of limestone which tend to be the most promising when it comes to wine.

The bulk of the wine produced on the Peninsula is red, and is made from one grape variety, the Castelão, known here as the Periquita. According to Vasco Garcia, the winemaker at J.P. Vinhos, Periquita owes its phenomenal success to its ability to lie down in the sand. After phylloxera hit the region more than a century ago, the terrified growers replanted all their vines in bug-resistant sand, but only Periquita could stand the drought and prospered.

There are lots of producers of Palmela wines, fifteen of them are the big bottlers; the household names of the Portuguese wine trade, those generalists who tend to stock wines from all the country's

important regions. A basic Periquita from Veritas, the Companhia das Quintas or the Palmela cooperative can be lively and fresh, an excellent everyday wine. Romeira markets quite a number of different Palmela wines. One experiment it has made recently has been to age them in three different oaks: Portuguese (*Nacional*), French (*Francês*) and American (*Americano*). Of the three I definitely preferred the first. The French version I found muted, the American gave off those rather synthetic flavours I associate with white oak. There is a consolation for the producers: Portuguese oak is almost certainly the cheapest solution.

DFJ from the Ribatejo makes some Terras do Sado wines under its Pedras do Monte label. They are naturally pure Castelão, and smell of tarry strawberries. Another - this time rather leathery - DFJ wine is Fonte do Beco. Its Rocha do Monte adds a softer, blackberry note. A very nice wine. Peter Bright still feels at home in a region he helped shape during fourteen years. He now buys the fruit from a plot of 80-year-old Periquita vines to make some predictably chunky wines and reservas.

Most grapes tend to be sold either to the cooperatives, the bottlers, or to the two big merchant houses in Azeitão. There are only twenty producers in the Peninsula bottling their own wine. One 110 ha domaine which started as recently as 1997, is the Casa Ermelinda Freitas in the ultra-sandy soils of Fernando Pó, which now markets a Quinta da Mimosa. This

seems to be a model for the new generation, quite oaky, but stuffed with good, fresh fruit flavours overlain with a creamy, butterscotch character drawn from the cask. There is a second wine called Terras do Pó, which is predictably simpler, but also impressive.

Another star small producer in a region dominated by big bottlers is Hero do Castanheiro made by Artur Oliveira and his daughter Sandra. They also began to bottle their wines in 1997, but like Leonor Freitas at Casa Ermelinda, they still sell off a good many grapes in bulk, every year reserving a larger and larger percentage for their own wine. The best wines taste strongly of American oak, but they are attractive: rich, full and creamy. Another small producer with a big name is Venâncio da Costa Lima. His *garrafeiras* are highly sought after.

In the future we can expect a few more plums of this sort to be pulled out of the cake, but the big companies have made ample provision, and have bought a considerable number of vineyards over the past few years. J.M. da Fonseca, for example, purchased an 480 ha experimental site bordered by old cork oaks at Aljezur in 1989. So far 220 ha have been planted with vines. From here Domingos Soares Franco takes the grapes which he wants to refresh his old brands: not just Portuguese varietals such as Tourigas Nacional and Francesa, and Tintas Barroca, Cão and Roriz, but also Syrah and Tannat; not only Viosinho, Antão Vaz, Arinto, Esgana Cão and Loureiro, but Sauvignon Blanc and Viognier.

Pegos Claros is another estate wine, and a distant outpost of João Portugal Ramos's Estremoz operation. Since the 1999 harvest he has controlled the vines and winery under a long term lease. There is one 50 ha plot of Castelão vines around a pretty, old manor house with another 30 ha about to come on stream. I have come across the wine in Lisbon restaurants. It is rich and deep. One of the best pure Periquita wines.

In Pegões, where Borrow shivered in fear of bandits, things have changed a lot. Salazar made it one of his interior 'colonies', constructing a new village at Vale da Judia with a church in a strange modernistic form surrounded by houses looking like hives. He also been started the local cooperative in 1958, which is is one of the very best around, especially now, as since 1992 it has also been overseen by Ramos and his crew! The cooperative is interesting in that it makes white Palmela wine. The basic blend is constructed from a majority of Fernão Pires, with a dollop of Muscat, and smells a little bit like bathroom soap. It is cut in the same mould as the highly successful wine from J.P. Vinhos. Higher up the scale is the Fontanário de Pegões, made from 100% Fernão Pires. It smells of vine flowers, lilac and acacia blossoms. Vale da Judia is pure Muscat of Alexandria, vinified dry. It makes a good aperitif wine – but is overpowering with food. The most modern white produced by the cooperative is the Adega de Pegões Selected Harvest, made from Chardonnay, Pinot Blanc and Arinto, and mostly fermented in new oak. The Arinto has the virtue of providing it with a good, fresh acidity.

Of course the reds are better known: Adega de Pegões is 100% Periquita aged in tank; it has a fresh, uncomplicated, morello cherry character. A bit of oak is lavished on the Vale da Judia. It is a much bigger wine too. So is the Fontanário de Pegões, where the oaking is far more noticeable. My own favourite is the *garrafeira*. Here age has lent the wine a little of that leather character, backed up by a big, chunky cherry taste, fine, cooling tannins and a powerful finish.

It is the last of the traditional range. There is one more red, however: Adega de Pegões made from Cabernet Sauvignon, Merlot, Touriga Nacional, Alicante Bouschet and Tinta Miúda and aged in new French oak. It is a huge, peppery beast, and rather magnificent in its way.

Azeitão
The Big Olive Oil

Azeitão is the home of the two most famous companies on the Peninsula and two of the most innovative wine producers in Portugal: J.M. da Fonseca and J.P. Vinhos. The name derives from the Portuguese word for olive oil, and it is not hard to imagine that this area used to be as much dominated by olive trees as it is currently swamped by vineyards.

The firm of José Maria da Fonseca started out in 1834 by the eponymous Fonseca, a Coimbra mathematics graduate who was born in Nelas in the Dão in 1804. He achieved swift success with his 'Periquita' brand, which became the first of its sort in Portugal. The name meaning 'little parrot' originates from a plot of vines which was known as the *cova da periquita* or parrot pit which Fonseca acquired in 1846 and planted with Castelão vines from the Ribatejo. Grapes from this site formed the bulk of the wine then, and it naturally coined the local synonym for the Castelão cultivar. 'Periquita' accounted for much of the initial success of the company and Fonseca was decorated by the king in 1857.

Periquita was the second Fonseca brand – Moscatel came first. One of the mainstays of Fonseca's business was Brazil, where the people were particularly keen to mop up his luscious Setúbal muscats. Before the end of his life Fonseca experimented with shipping the fortified muscat across the Atlantic and back. Some casks of this wine are still jealously guarded in the depths of the family cellars.

Between the wars Fonseca exported considerable amounts of Colares to Brazil too. António Soares Franco, who took over in 1917 added other brands to the portfolio: Pasmados and Camarate – for over a century supplied with fruit from the family quinta – to name just two. Fonseca provides an indication of how much 'brands', rather than *terroir* have been the Portuguese solution to marketing wine for more than 150 years.

Soares Franco's son, António Porto Soares Franco, was the man who took the company into the rosé business. In 1937 he created Faísca, Portugal's first rosé brand, and in 1944 the immensely popular brand Lancers. The idea behind the sweet, pink wine came from the Armenian-American Henry Behar. The name derived from Velasquez's *Las Lanzas*.

J.M. da Fonseca has always specialised in brands, but the grapes don't come from outer space. Fonseca has more than 650 ha of vineyards and buys in grapes to make its huge range of wines. The firm is run by António and Domingos Soares Franco. Domingos was educated at America's leading wine school, U.C. Davis, and since he has taken control of the winemaking there have been a number of changes, with quite a few international cultivars sneaking in under the covers of well-known brands. Across the road from the old-world HQ are two huge modern buildings where much of the process is operated by computers. Here they make Lancers, which after a couple of changes of ownership and a few years in the wilderness, has come home to roost here in Azeitão. Just to show that the old is not entirely redundant, there is an impressive museum of *azulejos* surrounding an even more impressive collection of casks in one of the modern cellars.

One of the big changes effected by Domingos is to remove something of the old-fashioned heaviness associated with the whites. BSE (not to be drunk with beef) is a good, fresh wine these days, made entirely in tank. It has changed a lot since its conception in 1959. Pasmados, made from Arinto, Esgana Cão and Viozinho, is crisp and melon-like, with a hint of peach; Camarate is now made from an eclectic collection of Moscatel, Loureiro and Alvarinho, giving it a pronounced floral character; Albis is mostly Moscatel; while Primum adds a whack of Sauvignon Blanc to a blend of Arinto and Encruzado making a good, nervy wine for one grown in such a hot climate.

Domingos loves his experiments, which come under a baffling series of codes. Some like CO, are hard to gauge, others, like DSF, are clearly allusions to the man himself. There are experimental reds and whites, such as his richly fruity Aragonez, trodden, traditionally in *lagares* and matured in Alliers casks; or a Trincadeira smelling of vine peaches; or a jolly good Tinto Cão. More perplexing codes follow: TO1, a blend of Esgana Cão, Pinot Blanc and Chardonnay, is rich and citric, while TO2, with its mixture of Cabernet, Touriga Francesa, Periquita and Trincadeira, leads on a clear, frank, raspberry fruit.

Then there are the red brands such as Primum with its black and red fruits tastes, a blend of Tourigas Nacional and Francesa; or Camarate (the old Palmela Superior, renamed in 1969), an individual wine which seems to exude a hint of pepperoni. It is made from Periquita, Espadeiro (Trincadeira) and a little Cabernet; or red Pasmados which is made in a Portuguese style from Touriga Nacional, Alfrocheiro Preto and Moreto grapes. Periquita is very much back on form. It has a pronounced nutty bouquet, with plenty of blackberry fruit behind. It now contains a small quantity of the locally grown Trincadeira as well as Castelão.

The reserve Periquita is called Clássico, a chunky, strawberry-scented wine which fetches high prices in Portugal. Then come the coded wines from the Peninsula: FSF – made from Tinto Cão, Trincadeira and the south-western French variety, Tannat, and named after António and Domingos's father – I presume a *garrafeira*, and a lovely wine; or CO – a smooth *garrafeira* made from Periquita grown on clay soils; or the rich and luscious RA *garrafeira*, clearly the best of the lot.

Fonseca also vinifies the wines of two estates in the Alentejo (see p133). One is the Morgado do Reguengo near Portalegre, the property of Jorge d'Avillez, whose family have lived there since 1580. Two excellent wines are made there, D'Avillez and a regional wine called Montado. The other is the Casa Agricola José da Sousa Rosado Fernandes, which began bottling as early as the forties. Its Tinto Velho was a legendary wine, some say it is still on form today. There are 60 ha of vines near Reguengos de Monsaraz. The wine is now called José da Sousa and it is made in amphoras in the traditional *alentejano* way. In order to keep the temperature down in hot weather, wet cloths are wrapped round the clay to cool them down. They don't need any more tending than that.

While Fonseca inhabits old world buildings on the main road (opposite an antique shop which does an interesting line in second-hand stills), J.P. Vinhos has an altogether different complexion. The hexagonal, space-age building was constructed for the Portuguese *Readers' Digest*.

The firm was founded by João Pires in 1922. Pires was a bulk trader who died in 1965. He sold out to Fonseca, who sold the company on to António d'Avillez, who moved it into the book store, adapting the building according to his own designs. From that time dates J.P.'s lunge forward into the new technology of winemaking. Stainless steel and temperature control were the new watchwords, banks of vats were constructed in artistic groupings outside the main building, while antiques, and - not to be outdone by their rival – a collection of *azulejos* was installed inside.

In 1982, the firm hired Peter Bright as chief winemaker and entered the bottled wine market with a whole series of brands. Bright was the first Australian to make a real splash in Portugal after his arrival in 1974. He has left the company now, but he is still here, there and everywhere in Portugal, and elsewhere, where he pursues a career as a flying winemaker with interests in Argentina. His position as winemaker has been taken over by Vasco Penha Garcia, who has

maintained the very high standards set by Bright.

J.P. grew so successful that its most profitable branded product, (João Pires) was mopped up by the British-based multinational UDV. J.P. itself was acquired by Joseph Berardo, who has bought vineyards, including the formerly American-owned Bacalhôa. It is still expanding, both on the Setúbal Peninsula and in the Alentejo, where it has a vinification centre in the carpet town of Arraiolos.

It was the combination of Bright's winemaking talents and Avillez's business acumen that made the company what it is today. Not long after the partnership was formed, the world woke up to a number of J.P. wines, like the excellent Alentejo red (see p125) Tinto da Ânfora, or the superb Quinta da Bacalhôa. Today the company has some 500 ha of vines, and like its neighbour in Azeitão, it makes a bewildering number of wines, and all of them at an impressively high standard.

J.P. has recently started making a peachy, *blanc de noirs* sparkling wine from Periquita grapes from the Estremadura perked up with a small amount of Fernão Pires. It is called Loridos. Its stable-mate *blanc de blancs* is made from pure Chardonnay, and has some fat, mango fruit with a refreshing vein of acidity.

One of J.P.'s best sellers was its Branco, made from a doubtless deceptively simple combination of Moscatel and Fernão Pires. I recall this causing a sensation with its huge lemon and lavender bouquet when it was first released in Britain in the eighties.

The firm has become more international in its choice of grapes since then. Oak-fermented Chardonnay has minority presence in Catarina and a majority statement in Cova da Ursa, or 'bear pit'. Despite the name it smells rather nice and toasty - a classic mid-Atlantic Chardonnay.

There are some stunning reds too. Herdade de Santa Marta comes from a promiscuous vineyard near Moura in the Alentejo, a blend of the usual trinity. It is very hot there, and the wine is chunky, with a flavour reminiscent of liquorice and fruit pastilles with plenty of tannic bite. The Tinto da Ânfora is also from the Alentejo. Again the name sows confusion: it is not made in an amphora. It was one of the first Portuguese reds I bought and I have always been an admirer. It seems to have slimmed down over the years, now there is more oak and a more elegant, sinewy style. It is still a splendid wine.

Meia Pipa uses up the leftover Cabernet Sauvignon from Quinta da Bacalhôa and mixes it with local Periquita to make a hunky, honey-scented wine. The Garrafeira is pure Periquita, and spends a year in oak, and several years in bottle prior to release. It is a lovely wine smelling of blackcurrants, the same fruit, which rather more predictably figures in the Cabernet-Merlot Quinta da Bacalhôa, but the Bacalhôa has that Bordeaux elegance together with a little fruit tang. If that were not enough, there is Má Partilha, a big wine, giving off some gamey aromas with age. J.P. continues to experiment with its wines,

and has recently planted some impressively juicy Syrah in local sandy soils.

Moscatel

Moscatel production tends to be dominated by the big two, but the Sivipa in Palmela also makes a reliable amber-coloured liquid. The best of them probably come from the two great houses in Azeitão, where they insist that the brandy used should not be neutral, but of fine character. Fonseca's basic Moscatel is called Alambre, with its pretty bouquet of lemon balm and oranges. With age the Moscatel throws off ever nuttier nuances. A twenty-year-old Alambre smelled more of walnuts and coffee than anything else. Fonseca has wonderful old vintage wines too. After twenty or thirty years they turn the colour of teak and have the consistency of runny honey. One of the best was Trilogia, made for the Millennium – a combination of three vintages: 1965, 1934, and 1900. It reeked of nuts, and tasted of dried figs.

Naturally J.P.'s range of Moscatels is also impressive. The basic wine – with 130 grams of residual sugar – has a pleasing smell of oranges. The next up, the vintage wine, is even sweeter and smells like a Portuguese egg cake with orange cream. There is also a Roxo or purple Moscatel with a bouquet of roses and tangerines – a real treat.

Wine versus Wheat

The Alentejo DOC currently has eight subregions: the granitic, slaty Portalegre; Borba with its red chalk soils containing traces of schist and marble; Redondo where the clay has ever been a boon to potters also possesses granite and quartzite more interesting to winemakers; Vidigueira where soils are also based on granite and slate, but where the vines tend to be planted in brown, Mediterranean earth; the bakingly sunny Reguengos with its white limestone and schist; Moura - again with clay soils; Évora with its sedentary brown earth; and Granja/Amareleja where a Mediterranean climate is dictated by proximity to the Meseta. Here the soils are slate, granite and white limestone called ranhas in local dialect.

alentejo

Yields are limited throughout the region to 60 hls/ha for whites and 55 for reds. Minimum alcoholic content is 11.5 for red and 11% for white.

For red wines the same trinity of grapes is recommended: Aragonez, Trincadeira and Castelão, but there are regional variations: in Portalegre Grand Noir (a cousin of Alicante Bouschet) is allowed; Borba, Redondo, Reguengos, Vidigueira, Granja/Amareleja and Moura all permit Moreto; Redondo, Vidigueira and Moura all favour Alfrocheiro Preto; while Vidigueira alone includes Tinta Grossa among the recommended sorts.

Alicante Bouschet is authorised everywhere but Granja/Amareleja and Moura. In most regions Cabernet Sauvignon is also possible as a minority planting. In some places there are Carignan, Cinsault, Tinta Carvalha and Tinta Caiada.

The recommended whites are chiefly Arinto, Fernão Pires, Siria (Roupeiro), Trincadeira das Pratas (Tamarez), Rabo de Ovelha, Antão Vaz and Perrum; although Portalegre prizes Malvasia Rei (Assario) and Granja/Amareleja has its local Manteudo.

Among the authorised whites are Alicante Branco (Farama or Boal de Alicante) and a number of other oddities or local standbys such as Diagalves and Larião. Moura allows small amounts of Chardonnay, Moscatel de Setúbal and Bical.

The regional wine is not as tolerant as some, although it allows Chardonnay, Sauvignon Blanc, Cabernet Sauvignon, Carignan, Cinsault and Pinot Noir,

as well as a few rare locals such Corropio.

In 1998-1999 the Alentejo produced 53,516 hls of white and 80,181 or red DOC wine; the regional wine production amounted to a further 42,890 hls of white and 60,369 hls of red.

Where most of Portugal is overcrowded, the Alentejo offers space and fresh air. It covers some third of the country but only about 4% of the population lives here, and wine production is as little as 3% of the national whole.

It is a distinctive land, mostly sleek and dotted with single storey farm houses called *montes*. Around them grow forests of cork oak which provide more than half the raw material for natural bottle stoppers the world over. They are flanked by plantations of olive trees which go to make a dark green oil, famous since Roman times. In the towns the whitewashed buildings are daubed with pastel colours at street level. This way the *alentejano* refreshes his individuality annually with a new lick of paint.

The richer soils were always reserved for cereals, the poorer ones for vines and olives. There is a fair amount of rock: granite, quartz and schist. There is also clay, on which vines are also planted, as well as cork oaks and olives.

'The Alemtejo [sic]… is not beautiful and picturesque, like most other parts of Portugal: there are a few hills and mountains, the greater part consists of heaths broken by knolls, and gloomy dingles, and forests of stunted pine; these places are infested with banditti.' (Borrow). The Englishman made an exception when he came to Évora, and the sight of the 'picturesquely beautiful' Serra de Ossa in the distance. He wandered around the old university town and looked at the former Temple of Diana, then partly clad in gothic robes, and converted into a Christian church. It has since been restored.

The Romans liked Évora. They liked the grapes and olives, and the wide, open wheat fields. At Redondo and elsewhere in the region, you see remnants of viticulture reminiscent of Roman times: the odd *dolium*, the Portuguese *talha*: a big, terracotta jar for storage of wine or oil. In a handful of places, wine is still made in giant amphoras equipped with taps at the bottom. The grapes ferment there with the stalks, and the latter act to filter the wine, which is then drawn off below.

The Romans left other souvenirs. In Évora they turn up every time they lay the foundations of a new building: under the Town Hall, for example. There are Roman remains displayed in the mediaeval offices of the Rota do Vinho. Many of their monuments, however, fell victim to their Visigothic or Arab successors. The relatively protracted Muslim period in the history of the Alentejo almost certainly resulted in a hiatus in the development of viticulture. It was not until the thirteenth century that the Arabs left, and

the long war of attrition had removed all confidence in perennial crops, such as grapes and olives, in favour of annuals such as wheat and other cereals.

By the sixteenth century the Alentejo's vineyards were properly reestablished. There were as many of 3,000 ha of vines around Évora, and the most highly prized of these lay near the village of Peramanca. The name of the best wine which emanates from the region today also translates in this punning language as 'lame stone'. In 1590 students at the university wrote a parody of the first canto of Camões' *Lusiadas*, in which they alluded to the countrywide popularity of their Peramanca. Nothing, it seems, has changed.

The great reputation which Alentejo wines enjoy today is recent. It was wild country, as Borrow noticed. The Portuguese government was in the habit of banishing criminals to the region, and they slipped their chains from time to time and menaced the local landowners. Writing in the 1830s, the English writer found the wines 'muddy but strong'. At two estates the Reynolds family managed to make model wines in the middle of the century, largely as a result of their dependence on the Alicante Bouschet grape variety which was created at the time when the Reynolds laid out their vast domains of cork oaks. This great staining grape variety is now much despised in France, its country of origin, but works a treat at both the Quinta do Carmo and the Herdade do Mouchão, and elsewhere in the Alentejo.

George Borrow visited Estremoz, where many of the region's top wines come from today and stopped at an inn on the huge market square. There is still a cattle market here and I have bought excellent dried oregano from the stalls on occasion. He found it so vast that he imagined an army of ten thousand performing their evolutions there. He made no comment on the wine.

Wine was clearly being made. At the same time as Évora students were writing about Peramanca, the wines from Beja, Vila de Frades, Borba and Redondo were achieving fame. Things looked set to continue in that way until land reform in the 1830s scattered the small holders and opened up the region to the *morgados* or large-scale landlords, who planted cork oaks and sowed grain instead. There was a revival of viticulture in the second half of the nineteenth century, but the contemporary enthusiasm for Reguengos wines, for example, was quickly slapped down by the first sightings of phylloxera.

Even at the end of the nineteenth century, the region was still not considered a civilised place. In Queiroz's *The Illustrious House of Ramires*, Titó disdains 'the Alentejo as a thin skin of land of poor quality which, apart from a few leagues around Beja and Serpa, would never repay the effort put into it, and whose granite showed through at the slightest scratching of its surface.

'My brother João has an enormous estate there, absolutely huge, and all it yields is 300 *mil reis*!'

The administrator, who had formerly been a lawyer

in Mértola, protested in annoyance. 'The Alentejo! It is a province that had been abandoned, it's true. Abandoned disgracefully for centuries, through the imbecility of governments... But rich, nevertheless, rich, fertile land.'

The two men continue to argue. Tító insisting it was a wilderness, the other, a granary.

Cooperatives were formed at the end of the century, once again pointing to relatively small quantities of grapes being produced on the farms, which made it uneconomic for them to vinify themselves. The Republic which came into existence in 1910, revived the fight against the vine in the Alentejo, advocating wheat farming instead. The same argument was pursued under the *Estado Novo*. For Salazar wine was to be produced in central Portugal. Like Queiroz's Administrator, he thought the Alentejo was the nation's 'granary'. It remained a region notable for the size of its estates and the wealth of its *morgados* who were often to be seen amusing themselves in Lisbon, scattering money in expensive restaurants such as Gambrinus, in the centre of town.

What winemaking did exist, was virtually confined to a series of well-equipped cooperatives built with Salazar's blessing in the sixties. It was these institutions that spearheaded the revival of Alentejo wines from the seventies onwards. There were exceptions, however, one of these was Tapada de Chaves, which was available in bottle from the sixties.

Naturally the landlords came under fire at the time of the 1974 Revolution. Many upped sticks and fled to Brazil and the larger estates were confiscated. They were returned to their owners only a decade later. The committees which ran them in the intervening years managed them poorly, and created considerable damage, not just to the wine, but also to the reputation of the Portuguese corks which had been the real mainstay of the estates.

The fortunes of the Alentejo's wines have revived. There is now a wine school in Évora and since 1984 the region has been often cited as the most promising part of Portugal for wine production in the foreign press. In 1988 the first five Alentejano sub-regions were made into IPRs: Portalegre, Borba, Redondo, Reguengos and Vidigueira. In 1991 there were another three added to the list: Évora, Granja/Amareleja and Moura. Finally in 1995, plus the original five, they were elevated to regional elements in an all-embracing Alentejo DOC.

The Alentejo is hot, as hot as the Douro, but it lacks the rocky soils and it cannot boast the same dramatic scenery either. It can freeze in winter, especially at night, and I have known it bitterly cold in mid-April when I have come underdressed and left with a snivelling cold; but that is Portugal's charm: the climate is capricious.

White Alentejo wines fail to match up to the reds in general, but there are good things for all that, especially now some of the freshness is locked in by the use of stainless steel vats and air-conditioned cellars. The principal grapes that give character to the whites are Perrum, an ancient cultivar, which is probably present in Andalucia; Antão Vaz, which is indigenous to the Alentejo; Roupeiro (Siria in the Dão), Arinto and Rabo de Ovelha. Of these the Roupeiro is by far the most widely planted, accounting for nearly a quarter of all the green grapes in the region. Diagalves comes next, but that is not considered to be a very distinguished grape – better for eating.

The white wine which captures the Portuguese imagination more than any other, is Cartuxa from Évora. Based on Antão Vaz, Perrum and Arinto, it combines a mineral element with the aroma of apricot kernels, a little like the French Viognier variety. It is very powerful and intense.The model for others in the know is the basic white from Vidigueira, with its fresh hay scent derived from the predominant Antão Vaz. The Herdade Grande is another fine demonstration of this. It is a big white, with plenty of flavour. Monsaraz is pleasing, tobacco-scented wine from the co-op in Reguengos. Like a lot of the better and best wines it is made by João Portugal Ramos's consultancy business in Estremoz. At Roquevale, they add a little Fernão Pires to the brew to make quite a rich, flavoury wine.

The reds are generally made from a trinity of grapes: Trincadeira, Castelão and Aragonez – the Tinta Roriz of the north or Tempranillo of Spain. Officially the three must represent eighty percent of the grapes used, but as yet there is not so much of the Tinta Roriz to go round. The Trincadeira provides the structure and body, plus a certain herby character; the Castelão a fruitiness which tends to game with age, and the Aragonez the silky fruit which is characteristic of the very best wines of the Alentejo. In places there is a little Alicante Bouschet used too.

The taste of the best red wines can only be described as rich. They have fruit sweetness on the nose, but somehow veer away from that 'portiness' which is often considered a fault in the trade - the taste of port wine in something unfortified. The heat of the region has much to answer for. It means that the grapes ripen very rapidly. The harvest here takes place 85-90 days after bud burst, as opposed to around 100 in most other quality regions. From one day to the next, a grape might become overripe and begin to shrivel, a speedy decision to pick can be crucial.

Cartuxa

These days the most sought after wine in the Alentejo is Pera-Manca from the Fundação Eugénio de Almeida. Almeida, Conde de Villalva, had inherited it from his family, who had bought the former church lands when they came up at auction in 1869. In 1950 he replanted the vines which had disappeared at the time when phylloxera cut its vicious swathe through the vineyards at the end of the nineteenth century; in the generation or so when it had been planted with grapes in the nineteenth century, it had always been a forward-looking estate with an excellent reputation for its wines.

Eugénio de Almeida installed modern equipment in the former chapel, and reused some of the remaining equipment discarded by the nineteenth-century winemakers. In 1965 he took the decision to leave the estate to charity. It amounted to an impressive 6,500 ha of land around the city of Évora. This is run as an educational foundation which has so far funded a school and a department of the local university.

The winery occupies the buildings of a former Jesuit seminary (although the name celebrates a charterhouse: the Carthusians had a monastery nearby), which was disbanded when its inmates were banished by Pombal in 1776. There are 265 ha of vines and production is increasing significantly with each vintage. The wines are designed by Professor Francisco António Colaço do Rosário of the University of Évora. Sixty percent of the estate's production goes into the excellent Cartuxa. The rest is incorporated into the second wine. Only a tiny amount is creamed off for Pera-Manca, the fruit coming from the small Herdade dos Pinheiros estate. Like its northern equivalent, Barca Velha, Pera-Manca is only made in great years.

Eighty percent of Cartuxa is made from Trincadeira, Aragonez and Castelão, with a little Alfrocheiro Preto and Tinto Cão. It is a heady, hot country wine: a touch of caramel, leather, black fruits – blackberries, blackcurrants and black cherries – and tobacco.

Pera-Manca commemorates a wine popular in the sixteenth century, that was briefly revived in the nineteenth, until the vines were wiped out by phylloxera. Borrowing its label from the nineteenth-century incarnation, the first of the new Pera-Mancas was made only in 1986 and was put on the market in 1990. Only four have been released to date, but there are high hopes for both the 1997 and 1998 vintages. With production at just 1,000 cases, it is terribly rare now that it is one of the most sought after wines in Portugal with prices as high as 50,000 escudos a bottle for some vintages. I find it not unlike a very great Saint Emilion. The colour is brick red, and there are notes of orange and lemon, typical of the wines of the region. On the palate black fruits predominate, coupled with a hint of something gamey. It is a huge full wine. The perfect match for a woodcock, or a partridge at the very least.

Boutique Wineries and Co-operatives: Évora

Every year now, more and more small estates spring up in the Alentejo, selling the fruit of their plots of vines. Because the region was little involved in the bulk wine business before 1970, it has found it much easier to adapt to a style that resembles the rest of Europe, where small domaines make *vins de terroir*. Tapada de Coelheiros is another model wine from Évora. There are 14 ha of vines. There is a little Cabernet in the red, flanking the Trincadeira and Aragonez, making an intensely smoky, richly fruity wine with immense length; and a bit of Chardonnay in the white. Monte do Pintor (the painter's farm) near Évora is vinified by the same Dr Rosário who lends his skills to Pera-Manca. It is owned by Luis Saraga Leal, who has a modest, 12 ha estate. It is notably good value for a dark staining wine with a full, morello cherry taste.

The cooperatives still have a good deal to say. Redondo cooperative has 282 members farming 1,500 ha of vines of which about 20% is DOC. The best wines are called Porta da Ravessa. Also in the region is Roquevale, an enterprising company making a range of wines from its 160 ha of vines. Roquevale's reds are toasty and list to gamey aromas with age, but there is plenty of complexity from the sun-baked chocolate and marmalade character of the wine. Some of the wines are made in *talhas* and therefore labelled Tinto da Talha. They are very fairly priced, particularly the Terras do Xisto. The name obviously refers to the schistous soils.

From Estremoz comes Quinta do Mouro, a really lovely wine made by the dentist Miguel de Orduna Viegas Louro with a meddly of fruit aromas: cooked plums and cherries with a lacing of vanilla from the oak. A second wine from the dentist is the Monte dos Pelados, which has a little Cabernet Sauvignon in it. It is also highly impressive.

Ramos makes his own Alentejo wines outside the co-operatives at his spanking new winery down the hill from Estremoz. From the outside it looks innocuously like a little manor house. Inside it is about as modern as you can get, with great banks of stainless steel vats and plenty of new oak *barriques*. He vinified a million kilos of grapes here in 1999, bought in from various places together with the produce of his own vineyards. Ramos likes to play with new oak casks: French, American and Portuguese. He is careful not to oak the wines for too long. In a climate such as the Alentejo's, that could lead to dried out, stringy wines. They taste a little dumb after bottling, but they rally superbly.

The rich, silky Marquês de Borba with its reserve range is only made in the best years. The fruit can be sweet and smoky, with a whiff of tobacco. Elsewhere Ramos plays the varietal card. He bottles Aragonez, Trincadeira and Tinta Caiada (Bastardo) separately ageing them in 100% new oak. There is also a Vila Santa range in which he blends cultivars: Trincadeira with Aragonez; Alicante Bouschet with Cabernet etc. He is a great believer in Alicante Bouschet. He grew to love it during his years at the Quinta do Carmo.

Reguengos, Portalegre and Borba

Ramos advises the cooperatives at Reguengos and Portalegre in the north-east of the region. The current craze for Alentejo wine began with the products of the co-operatives, and they are still impressive although the better wines from many of them have shot up in price after rave reviews in a Portuguese press which has become avid for novelties.

There are around 500 grape-growing members of the

Reguengos *adega*. The best red from Reguengos is the Garrafeira dos Sócios. Again the citrus fruit character dominates, there is even a nuance of pineapple.

The top reds from the *adega* in Portalegre are made in tiny quantities and tend to be expensive. There are a couple of regional wines - Terras de Baco and the robust Conventual - and a DOC. The cooperative has 150 active members with a total of 600 ha.

Another famous – and expensive – wine from the Portalegre is the Tapada de Chaves, a small estate, once the property of Joaquim da Cruz Baptista Fino, a rich builder who planted the property with vines in the 1920s. In the sixties, his daughter, Gertrudes Fino, began to bottle the wine and sell it to the better Lisbon restaurants. João Portugal Ramos was brought in as long ago as 1987 to redesign the wine. In 1994 a new cellar was built. There are whites and reds. The latter contains 60% Trincadeira. The red from Tapada de Chaves has a bouquet of woodsmoke and cherries, great length and remarkable elegance. It is certainly among the Alentejo's and Portugal's greatest wines.

Also from Reguengos is José de Sousa, now an outpost of the J.M. da Fonseca empire. These rich red wines are made entirely by the traditional method: in huge clay amphoras. They have nice citrus flavours. The wines are made from Trincadeira, Tinta Roriz and Grand Noir. J.M. da Fonseca also makes the wines from Jorge d'Avillez's estate near Portalegre. D'Avillez was formerly involved with the company. The wines tend to be leaner and more elegant than many other Alentejo reds. The *garrafeira* is particularly good, an elegant wine that is far less of a thunderer than the wines from the south of the province.

One of the most modern estates in the region is Esporão, the 2000 ha (500 ha of vines) property of the Roquette family. Since 1992 the wines have been made by the Australian David Baverstock. The domaine was put together just before the Revolution, but the owner had to make a hurried departure soon after aided by one of the local communists, who tipped him off that he was about to be arrested. It was a while before planting, and the building of a proper winery could begin. In the meantime the grapes went off to the cooperative in Reguengos. It was not until 1987, fourteen years after the establishment of the domaine, that the first estate wines were released.

Roquette had conceived his estate like a French château. It was to make three wines only from its 500 ha, as well as around 200 ha of bought in fruit. The cheapest wines were issued under Alandra label. Monte Velho and Vinha da Defesa – a reference to the old, defensive role of the estate – were regional wines. Then came Esporão, the varietal wines and the *reservas*.

There has been a slight change of direction lately. Baverstock likes to use a lot of American oak on the wines and has started planting new varieties. He has some Alicante Bouschet, and some Syrah which is coming on stream now. He does not use Castelão, as it does not provide him the results he is looking for.   He has also planted a few foreign white grapes: Marsanne and Roussane from France's Rhône Valley and Semillon from Bordeaux.

The white Monte Velho is cast as a crisp summer

wine made from Roupeiro, Rabo de Ovelha and Perrum. More complexity is found in the half litre bottlings of Roupeiro, or the much richer, barrel-fermented, white Esporão.

The red Monte Velho is quite a simple wine, but a very pleasant one. Baverstock makes varietal wines too: an excellent Aragonez, a text-book Cabernet Sauvignon, and a prune-like Bastardo. The Esporão has more leathery, regional character to its fruit, while a new wine Quatro Castas (four varieties – Touriga Nacional, Aragonez, Trincadeira and Cabernet) has more complexity, and is wrought in a fruitier, more modern style.

Borba is one cooperative which is not in the Ramos stable. Here the wines are made by Manuel Domingos Ganhão Pinto. There are 300 members covering some 2,700 ha of vines. The wines are remarkably attractively priced. The basic red is quite tarry, while Montes Claros is a big, gamey blackstrap reeking of leather and coffee. It is a name with history. The *adega* acquired it some years back from another winemaker in Borba, José Mendonça, and made it their own. The top wine is the Reserva, which spends six months in oak and two years in bottle prior to release. They also make an interesting, pineau des Charentes-style *mistelle* called 'Licoroso'.

Vidigueira

The cooperative at Vidigueira rules over some 600 ha of vines, which with 549 members means a little over a hectare each. The most sought after estate in Vidigueira is Monte da Ribeira in Marmelar. The 25 ha of vines are superintended by João Ramos; they include some Cabernet Sauvignon besides the usual Alentejo grapes. There is a regional wine called Pousio. The *reserva* is called Quatro Caminhos (four tracks). It is notably orange-like in its fruit, with a taste on the finish reminiscent of blackcurrants.

Also in the region is Cortes de Cima, owned by the Dane Hans Kristian Jørgenson, who used to be a rubber planter in Malaya. He bought 375 ha of land near Vidigueira in 1988, and planted 40 ha with vines. His first bottles were released in 1996, and very rapidly became cult wines in Portugal. I have tasted the normal cuvée in Évora: with all its aromas of citrus fruits and tobacco, it smells sweetly of sun. The wine which excites the most coverage nationally, however is the Syrah, named Incognito: it is deep coloured, with a honey-like scent, and tastes of rich, stewed plums.

Also from Vidigueira is Herdade Grande, a reliable wine cut in the 'Periquita' mould. Naturally being Portugal, other companies bottle wines from the Alentejo. One of the most successful of these has been Sogrape, who made a first punt with Vinha do Monte in 1991 and since then have planted 37 ha at the Herdade do Peso.

The Legacy of the Reynolds Family

The two large model estates were both formerly in the possession of the Reynolds family: the 700 ha

Herdade de Mouchão and the 1,000 ha Quinta do Carmo – a former royal hunting lodge built by Dom João V. The Reynolds came to Portugal from Britain some time after 1811, where they had connections with the wine trade. Some of them went to New Zealand where they found little to do (possibly New Zealand was 'closed' then as now) came on to Portugal via Australia – bringing the eucalypt with them in their baggage. They have certainly altered the face of the country in the last century and a half: the roads of Portugal are now lined with eucalypts and whole forests are planted with them for the use of the paper industry.

In the Alentejo, Robert Hunter Reynolds married into the Spanish nobility, founded a cork company and bought large tracts of land which were planted with cork oaks. One of these was the 700 ha estate at Mouchão. Wine was only a very small part of their business, vines were planted on red limestone soils to provide *consumo* for the estate workers. The vat house at Mouchão was built between 1901 and 1904, and with its great stone *lagares* it remains largely unchanged today.

Members of the Reynolds family remain at Mouchão and Carmo – Mrs Richardson of Mouchão was born Reynolds. The Rothschilds from Château Lafite now have a 50% shareholding in Carmo which they bought from J.P. Vinhos of Azeitão. The other half still belongs to Julio Tassara de Bastos, who also descends from the Reynolds family on his mother's side.

Mouchão went through a difficult time after the Revolution, when the estate was managed by the local communists who seem to have helped themselves to stocks. From the 120 ha planted with vines at Mouchão in the nineteenth century, only 23 remained when they got their land back. The estate was in a lamentable state, and for the past two decades they laboured to replant the vines and at the same time satisfy their many fans. Fortunately one or two of the estate workers knew how things had been done in the past. Continuity was assured. Recovery has been hard and slow, severe droughts in 1992 and 1993 and frosts in 1994 and 1995 have plagued them. From the look of the 1996 vintage, however, Mouchão is certainly back on course. The wine is made from 80% Alicante Bouschet, with a little Trincadeira and Castelão, giving it a huge expression of leather, plums, tobacco and dried herbs. It is truly one of Portugal's greatest wines. There is a second wine called Dom Rafael.

In the past Carmo was famous for its fantastically concentrated *garrafeiras*. These were early works of the talented motoring winemaker, João Portugal Ramos. Carmo went through a difficult time soon after the sale. Ramos was given his cards, and its French owners counselled by their French winemaker, Arnaud Warnery, took objection to the presence of the pariah-grape Alicante Bouschet on their land, and ripped most of it up, planting fashionable French cultivars in its place. The wines suffered as a result. In recent years they have gone back on this policy, and the 1996 Reserva, I thought a return to form – it is a silky, rich, almost sweet wine with masses of concentration.

In 1998-1999, Lagos produced no DOC white and 290 hls of red; Portimão 75 hls of white DOC wine and 490 of red; Lagoa 2,238 of white 6,960 of red. Tavira made nothing at all. There were 533 hls of regional Algarve wine made that year.

The maximum yields for Lagoa are 60 hls/ha for red and white alike. Red and rosé wine require at least 12% alcohol, the white 11.5. Lagoa, Tavira and Portimão whites must be made from Siria (Crato Branco) while Lagos whites use Boal Branco. Algarve DOC reds should be made from Castelão or Negra Mole.

The regional appellation allows for red, white or rosé wines with minimum alcohol content of 11%. The list of recommended cultivars betrays a conservatism not encountered elsewhere. As yet no foreign cultivars are acceptable.

The Algarve with its golf courses, its holiday villas and its Jaguar salesmen with Buffy Frobisher moustaches, seems an odd place to cultivate the vine now, but it pays to remember that the holiday camp of the region is only a few decades old, and the Algarve's importance goes back to the Phoenician tradesmen who came here in pursuit of metal and may well have planted a few vines while they were at it.

algarve

The Moorish presence was long drawn out, and probably many Christians converted to Islam. Where vines existed they were there to make a little wine for home consumption. The region was one of poor farmers and fishermen. The arrival of the whitewashed municipal cooperative was a revolution in its time, for it meant income for grape growers and properly made wine for peasants and seafarers. Then came the tourism boom, and money came into the region. When that happened the pittance to be earned from vines suddenly began to look paltry. With more cash in their pockets the men of the Algarve could buy wine from elsewhere in Portugal – or the world – from the new supermarket.

It is therefore hardly surprising that there is currently a small crisis affecting viticulture in the Algarve. The snake may be shedding its skin, however, but a new one is growing. The municipal cooperatives constructed during Salazar's time - an era before the hotels and golf clubs – are beginning to look shabby and underused as they are not getting enough business. The European Union in its desire to reform peasant viticulture has been offering subsidies to vignerons who consent to rip up vines in areas which are not considered choice land. So far they have paid out nearly two million pounds in this way. The children of the old viticulturalists who have no interest in wine, see the possibility of making a few bob and liberating the soil for building and rush to cash in. Meanwhile only a scant basketful of licences to plant have been issued, with grants totalling £90,000. The licences have become hot property, and there are substantial amounts of money to be earned for anyone in possession of one. A hectare of vine land will cost £15,000: twice as much as it does in the Alentejo.

Down in the region they complain that Lisbon is indifferent to their needs. For many years the Algarve was encouraged to produce oranges. Now the production is too high, and the growers have difficulty selling them. To add insult to injury, Portugal is actually importing Spanish oranges, while home-grown produce rots in the sun.

In the late nineties the vines were in a miserable condition. There was a considerable need to replant and rethink the grape varieties used. By 2001 300 ha of the Algarve's vineyards had been replanted and some of the top names in Portuguese oenology had lent a hand in recreating the image of the local wine: Professor Rosário of Pera-Manca fame, David Baverstock from Esporão, and João Portugal Ramos. Under their guidance the Algarve is set to move upmarket.

The basic grape variety is the Tinta Negra Mole, best known, perhaps as the also-ran cultivar on the island of Madeira – the one which is never mentioned on the bottle. It does well on the predominantly sandy soils of the region, although the grape rarely produces wines with any body. There are several variations of Negra Mole, running from the more concentrated form, with small berries, to a pale-skinned big grape which is better employed for making rosé wines.

As in parts of the Languedoc, sandy soil tends to leach colour from the wine, making reds which are little more than pink. At Listel near Montpellier they plant their vines ungrafted, directly into the sand, as phylloxera cannot survive in this kind of soil. It would be interesting to try a similar experiment here in Portugal, but I am told that this way you lose an important subsidy from the EU, which will not advance money for ungrafted vines.

There are also some patches of deep red and yellow sandstone soils which look more promising than the sandy ground close to the coast. In the new plantations there are some surprising choices of grape: Syrah, Trincadeira (called Crato Preto here) and Touriga Nacional. David Baverstock is very keen on getting some Mourvèdre for the Algarve. At the cooperative in Lagoa they made some experiments with it in the sixties. The director says he tasted these wines recently, and the results were impressive.

For the white wines the first choice is Crato Branco, the Siria of the Dão.

There are four DOCs in the Algarve. Production is not enormous from any of them. Not so long ago the question was raised of demoting them to IPRs. One of them has *de facto* ceased to exist.

Lagoa

The star oenologists are being employed by a group of local plutocrats who want to see an improvement in the quality of the Algarve's wines and have the will and the money to have their plans set in motion. One of these is Vasco Pereira Coutinho, who has brought in Professor

Nuno Magalhães, the brother of Sogrape's Vasco. Ramos is working with a 12 ha property called Matamouros. Near Lagoa is the Quinta do Moinho, home for some of the year of the vintage British crooner Sir Cliff Richard, a born-again Christian and close friend of the British prime minister Tony Blair and his wife Cherie.

Richard is being advised by David Baverstock from Esporão. So far he has 10 ha, but he wants more, and there are rumours that a substantial purchase is about to be made. As Richard puts it, his name on the label will more or less guarantee the sale of the wine. Baverstock is currently vinifying Richard's grapes in the Alentejo by special dispensation in order to show him how good the wine might be.

Baverstock has his fingers in various pies in the Algarve. He advises the 20 ha Quinta dos Álamos and is currently looking for a buyer for another 27 ha property. There is a feeling that the cooperatives are not the ideal places to make the wine for these boutique properties, and Baverstock is hoping to set up a more modern installation soon.

Most of the wine is still made in the big, whitewashed cooperative on the edge of the town where a 25% bounty is paid to receive the best grapes. The whites are heavy and sappy, but not at all disagreeable, a little like some of the pungent white wines of Corsica. The regional appellation is Porsche's – nothing to do with the tank designer and car manufacturer Dr Porsche, or the Queen of

England's horse trainer for that matter. Both the DOC white and Porche's have definite character, and in the old days they were rather more famous than the region's reds. Now, however, few people seem to want to drink white wine, even when they are shovelling down plates of clams or lobster. Fish or fowl, in Portugal the call is for red wines.

Porche's red is made from Negra Mole with Periquita. The sandy soil eliminates much of the colour, and the wines are almost pink. They are best drunk chilled. The Lagoa wine tends to be fuller and longer. The best is obviously the reserve wine which gives off a whiff of blackberries. Lagoa wines are apparently quite long lasting, but the problem is the absence of body in the Negra Mole. Periquita is meant to provide that; Trincadeira could add a little complexity too.

Trincadeira gives the body to the most concentrated wine made by the Lagoa cooperative: Seleccionada. The *garrafeira* is rather more traditionally designed and smells of boiled sweets and red peppers.

Lagoa makes a couple of fortified wines: Algarseco and Algardoce. The former is like a dry oloroso sherry. It is quite brown and nutty and would go nicely with a piece of blue cheese. They make just 4,000 bottles a year. Algardoce is a *mistelle*. The fermentation is stopped when the wine has just five degrees. It is the colour of teak and tastes similar to a pineau des Charentes.

There is one successfully exported Algarve wine which is made in the Lagoa cooperative under instructions issued by José Neiva of DFJ. That is Esplanada or Cataplana, a blend of Negra Mole and Crato Preto. It smells a little like a freshly dug road, but there is a pleasant blackberry fruit too.

Portimão

In Portimão the situation is worse. The cooperative is currently closed. On the other hand there is a silver lining to the cloud. One grower who has 100 ha wants to remedy the situation by building his own winery. This will then become part of a new generation of Algarve quinta wines. Two further estates of between 20 and 30 ha are likely to come in on any scheme of this sort. Both are owned by industrialists and both want to create their estate wines which reflect their positions in society.

One man who is already making his own wine in a purpose built winery surrounded by 30 ha of vines is João Mendes at the Quinta da Torre. About a third of them are quite old, another third four years old and the rest recently planted. He has planted Touriga Nacional, Aragonez, Trincadeira and Mourvèdre and keeps yields down to a reasonable six tons a hectare.

The estate is in flux, as he has now installed his winery in the old farm buildings, but the wreckage from the works is still strewn around the place: tangled skeins of wire and heaps of rubble piled up outside abandoned workers' cottages and farm buildings. Once you enter the winery, however, there is instant order, cleanliness, shiny vats and – a local touch – some big earthenware *dolia* in which he ages a part of of the wine.

Mendes makes his white wines with Arinto; they have decent body and seem quite sophisticated. The reds are made from Cabernet Sauvignon, Castelão and Trincadeira. They are quite sweet-smelling, good even.

Another viable property is the Morgado do Reguengo. There are 900 ha of land with a 38 ha vineyard including Touriga Nacional, Tinta Roriz and Trincadeira. For the time being the wines are made in the cooperative in Lagoa.

Lagos

The cooperative is the usual building from Salazar's time. The municipality is still fiercely communist, despite the vast amounts of money which course through its streets as a result of the tourists. Up in the tasting room the most prominently displayed wine is from the 1974 vintage, the year of the Revolution.

There have been problems with the management of the *adega* but the situation seems more settled now. The labels celebrate Henry the Navigator, who planned the discovery of the world from not far away in Sagres, and the top wines are called O Infante. Again the grapes used are Negra Mole and Castelão, although in the past they had Bastardo. They tend to be light, summer reds. The regional Gil Eanes has more body. The best is the Lagos DOC, which has a distinct spiciness rather like cold mulled wine. Two fortified muscats are made. The best is the sweet one: a winter warmer for Hyperboreans marooned on a semi-tropical coast.

Again there is a clear move towards creating quinta wines. A Dutch group has bought up a 600 ha property called Corte do Bispo in Lagos to build a hotel and golf club. They also plan to plant 30 ha of vines. On the outskirts of town 12.5 ha have already been put down in what will form a 20 ha vineyard. I was taken out to see the first plantings. A Portuguese German living in South Africa has obtained leases for 20 ha, and there are two or three more wine estates of this size about to begin production.

José Lopes has a pretty quinta (Quinta dos Lopes) up in Bensafrim, a wild and rocky part of the Algarve behind Lagos. He has grafted 12.5 ha over to Trincadeira, Castelão and Touriga Nacional. His production is organic, and part of the vineyard is on sand, the other part on clay. There are some heady whites and light reds from Castelão grown on sand. Those grown on clay have more colour and depth of flavour.

Tavira

Tavira's *adega* has been sold and there is nowhere to take the grapes any more. The mayor would like to see viniculture revived. For the time being the only possibility is to transport the bunches to the winery in Lagoa. It is an awful situation, but as I say, there are remedies at hand.

From the Azores, the fortified wine of Biscoitos must be 16% alcohol. Yields are limited to 50 hls/ha made from Arinto, Terrantez da Terceira and Verdelho dos Açores. Graciosa has a maximum yield of 70 hls/ha and a

minimum alcoholic content of 10.5 %. It is made from Arinto, Boal, Fernão Pires, Terrantez and Verdelho dos Açores. The fortified wine of Pico is limited in production to 50 hls/ha and must have 16% alcohol. It must be

the islands

made from Arinto, Terrantez and Verdelho dos Açores.

In 1998-1999 the production for the Azores IPRs was 149 hls of fortified white Biscoitos, 629 hls of fortified white Pico, and 151 hls of unfortified white Graciosa.

There are other table wines produced in Portugal, many of these are unabashed *consumo* made for family consumption. On Madeira the quality grapes go to make the fortified wines, but there is a decent rosé made by the Symingtons, the owners of the Madeira Wine Company. For the rest there are still a lot of American vines in production, and on the family plots where they grow, the vines have to fight hard to find a square inch of earth which is not also feeding beans, courgettes, melons, marrows and potatoes.

The Symington rosé is the only non-fortified wine bottled on Madeira. Similarly there are table wines such as Graciosa and fortified wines like Pico and Biscoitos produced in the Azores, but none of these is normally shipped to the mainland, even if they are enjoyed by the many tourists who visit this last outpost of Europe before you reach America.

It is believed to have been the Franciscans who planted vines in the Azores, as early as the fifteenth century, as they lacked what they needed to celebrate the Eucharist. Azores Verdelho was famous in its time, and was even exported to Czarist Russia.

Picos and Graciosa wines are grown in *currais*: small plots framed by walls made of loose pebbles. These are important to protect the vines from the fierce Atlantic winds. *Biscoitos* or 'biscuit' refers to the little mounds of rocky earth in which the vines are planted. Lajido from Pico resembles a medium-sweet sherry, while the unfortified Graciosa Terra do Conde is austerely dry, and reeks of seaweed.

At present there are just three bottlers in the Azores, one per appellation.

food in the
wine country

Henry Vizetelly visiting northern Portugal in 1880 found the rural Portuguese subsisting on *caldo* soup and a little dried cod. Both are still common. The soup, with its turnip top broth thickened with a little mashed potato, is still as popular as ever; but the dried cod has grown so expensive of late that many rural Portuguese can no longer afford it.

Borrow also noted the prevalence of 'salt sardinhas', and the fresh fish is still one of the favourite foods of coastal Portuguese. On 23 June – Oporto's great night – the eve of the Feast of the city's patron saint, St John the Baptist, the inhabitants set up little grills in the streets to cook sardines. It is a great moment to be in Oporto. The locals let their hair down and stay up to all hours coshing one another with pots of basil or gaudy plastic hammers.

The hammers and the basil represent anointing or baptism. In the old days people you didn't like were swiped with some garlic flowers. If the smell got in your hair it took a few days to wash it out. The hammers are now considered kinder.

At midnight there is a magnificent firework display from the bridge which connects Oporto to Gaia, and that is followed by much merriment in the streets. The next day, the saint's day proper, there is the famous race on the estuary when the port companies pitch their ponderous, lumbering *barcos rabelos* against one another. They are heavy, keelless single masters that used to bring down the young port from the Douro in the days before the roads. If there is no wind they merely sit in the water, but there can be fun if they are carried by a breeze.

The boat which is most feared is Malvedos, one of several Symington-owned vessels. Once it gets a little wind in its sails, there is little to stop it and it glides all the way to the winning post. For the crews, made up of guests of the port houses, there is little to do besides scoffing *bolinhos* and *pasteis* and drinking frequent glasses of white wine or port.

Such foods are universal. It would be hard to get through the day without seeing at least one dried cod and potato ball. These are called *bolinhos de bacalhau* in northern Portugal and *pasteis de bacalhau* in the south. Other titbits which are pretty widespread are *rissois*, they are generally filled with either prawns or chicken.

The Minho

The Minho with its humidity and its fertile little plots of land is good growing country for almost everything. The minhoto prides himself on his self-sufficiency. A Minho staple is the excellent corn bread called *broa*. Maize was introduced in the sixteenth century when the Portuguese explorers brought back samples of 'Indian corn' from the Americas. Minho corn bread is very heavy, and a big slice is practically a meal in itself. It comes in a grey and a yellow version. The theory is that it cleans your teeth when you eat it, for it is full of benign enzymes which attack the bacteria which cause decay.

The classic minhoto soup is *sarrabulho*: coarse and porridgy it should contain the blood and offal of a freshly slaughtered pig. This makes it fairly seasonal. Pigs in the Minho, like everywhere else, are traditionally killed in the run up to Christmas. There is a lot of more genteel *caldo verde* on offer – kale broth thickened with potatoes and chouriço. Another local soup is *canja*, which is a basically chicken with rice. Much of the Minho is within striking distance of the coast on the Costa Verde with its down-to-earth seaside resorts. Viana do Castelo in the north was the first place to receive shipments of Newfoundland dried cod. Here the romance began. The Minho, like the rest of Portugal, still consumes vast amounts of *bacalhau*, despite today's frighteningly high prices.

At the bottom the Minho touches the outskirts of Oporto and its upmarket coastal suburb of Foz do Douro. Here there are a few pleasant restaurants to be found right down on the beach, where vinho verde is drunk with hake balls and *pataniscas*: salt cod and shrimps in batter. You will find an *arroz de marisco* virtually anywhere; a shellfish stew served mixed in with rice. If you are lucky you will find excellent seabass, served simply with boiled potatoes and a few *grelos* or turnip tops. Everywhere you go you will find a simple dish of *polvo* or octopus with a few chopped onions and the greenest of olive oil. The weather tends to be erratic when it comes to olive cultivation, but this does not put the minhotos off. They merely pick early. Like Tuscan oil it can be fiery.

In the first few months of the year the great speciality of the Minho is lampreys, these parasite eels which are generally stewed *a Bordalesa*; in a mixture of their own blood and red wine. They say that the January lampreys are for the rich, those of March and April for the poor, and after that, the lampreys are for the dogs.

The fishiness of the food disappears a little once you venture inland. In Amarante there are little bars where they will serve you a roll filled with smoked ham accompanied by a half pint pot of slightly fizzy vinho verde. Like that you may experience what vinho verde was, for so many ordinary Portuguese people: a pleasant refreshing drink. It is a pretty place in the centre, even if the outskirts have been ruined by the building of concrete slab blocks in the last twenty years. There is a lovely renaissance church at the head of the bridge. Here superannuated brides used to rub their naked flesh against the masonry of the tomb at biannual festivals in the hope of producing a child. At the same time they ate cakes baked by the local bakers called *testiculos de São Gonçalo*.

One of the region's specialities are huge and heavy, strong flavoured melons called *cascas de carvalho* – or oak bark. The flesh is translucent and it fizzes when you cut into it. It is often served with ham, or *presunto*. In the Minho they generally say the best comes from Chaves, a dusty town in Trás-os-Montes, up on the Spanish border.

The meat dish that everyone knows from the Minho, is *rojões*: cubes of marinaded pork cooked

with new potatoes. It can be greasy, and needs a wine with acidity to help it down. Red vinho verde is the thing. In Ponte da Barca I ate Barrosã veal, which is a local speciality. It comes from the larger animal which the French call *génisse* and the Italians *vitellino*; the flesh was a pale yellow colour but it had very good flavour. It was served with a deep dish of *friar* – black eyed - beans and rice. The same restaurant offered *cherne*, translated as 'Jew' or 'toad' fish on its English-language menu. I later discovered this was in fact a wreckfish of the grouper family (*Polyprion americanum*).

sangue or black pudding.

At the Quinta da Aveleda they make a firm, wax-bound cows' milk cheese on the estate, which often crops up in Portuguese shops abroad.

Two desserts are naturalized in the Minho: *filhós* are pumpkin cakes (pumpkin is used in a great many Portuguese puddings); *rabanadas* is a local name for French toast.

Douro

The quintas of the Douro Valley possess some of the best preserved eighteenth- and nineteenth- century kitchens in Europe. I have seen one or two good ones in the port lodges in Vila Nova (Taylors is a case in point), but they are paltry beside the old kitchens at Quinta do Valado, or, for example, the Symingtons' harvest kitchen at Bonfim.

Here you will see the great banks of shiny copper pans which feed the five hundred at harvest time. After all, it is hungry work bringing in the heavy loads of grapes from these steep, schistous slopes, or treading the sticky wine in the granite *lagares*. The latter is particularly tiring: a martinet calls out a marching beat – '*Um, dois! Um, dois!*' as the treaders perform. Every now and then there is a moment of relaxation when there is music and dancing in the *lagar*. In the old days *bagaceira* was handed out. Now it is more likely to be *água pé*, 'foot water', a thin wine made from the second pressing of the grapes.

The harvesters gather in the kitchens for their

August 16 is the anniversary of the death of the novelist Eça de Queiroz who lived in the Lower Douro and whose house is now preserved as a museum. At the Quinta da Covela nearby, they served me his favourite dish: an *arroz* of peeled broad beans with *salpicão*, or smoked pork loin, chicken and *chouriço de* meals. Under the great chimney there is room to set up half a dozen tripods so that some hearty stew can be simmered over the embers. A spit is nearby; ready to take a piglet or two, or a kid at the very least. Above the fire, hanging from an iron pole, are half a dozen smoke-blackened hams and many more sausages. Everything is in place to cook the timeless meal, a meal – sadly – never experienced by the hardy tourists who stray up the Valley. It is experienced less by the locals now that a greater deal of automation has crept in. Very few quintas these days press the grapes by foot.

I remember a near perfect Douro lunch at Valado: *caldo verde*, that kale soup thickened with potatoes which seems to unite central and northern Portugal – once you have crossed the Tagus you are in *açorda* country. The soup was followed by salt cod, broad bean mash and small, waxy potatoes baked in the oven then 'punched' before being bathed in olive oil. We finished up with 'Romeo and Juliet': local cheese with quince paste or *marmelada*.

Barrosã and Miranda beef have many fans in the region and I have often seen large carp pulled from the river. There are also fresh ewe's milk cheeses. The classic dishes in the quintas, however, tend to have a slightly international allure.

In Trás-os-Montes, 'new Christians', or reluctant Jewish converts, made sausages out of chicken called *alheiras* when they were obliged by the Inquisition to hide their true faith. These are still popular in the Douro, where they are hung up to smoke in the great chimneys. There is a non-Kosher version called a *farinheira*, which is made from pork.

Dão

My most abiding memory of Viseu, the capital of the Dão, is the old covered market, which like that of Oporto, is housed in galleries around a central courtyard. The market women used to carry prodigious loads on their heads, a trick, I was told, they had learned from long contact with Africa. On this occasion I went upstairs and found a man washing tripe. The intestines were all over the floor, and he looked as if he were repairing the inner tube of some monstrous bicycle.

Later, taking a break from winemaking, we went to the Grão Vasco, the old fashioned hotel in the centre of town which had a reputation for its local dishes. There we ate a proper *cozido*, the equivalent of a Spanish *olla*, or an Italian *bollito misto* where a variety of meat, sausages and vegetables stew up together.

'Punch' potatoes are not exclusive to the Dão – I have eaten them in the Douro too - but they are quite delicious and look as easy as pie, but like that, they are not. I have tried to reproduce the flavour several times in London, and so far without success. I suppose this is true of most things which come under the banner of 'heroic simplicity'. Alvaro Castro at the Quinta da Pellada has grown bored with the eulogies I have made to his wife's potatoes when I lunched in their house. They accompanied some simply baked *bacalhau*.

One of the most striking dishes I have eaten in the Dão was *bacalhau na broa* – dried cod cooked inside a hollowed out loaf of *broa* or corn bread. There were other things besides: onions cooked in wine, lots of garlic and some potatoes in their skins, which were possibly unessential. The fish was then covered in a layer of breadcrumbs.

There is a sort of meat pie, called variously *bola de carne*, or *queque do visconde*, the equivalent of a Spanish *empanada*. Other hors d'oeuvres found in the more mountainous regions are slices of excellent black pudding flavoured with cumin and padded out with rye bread.

The Dão is famous for game and wild mushrooms in the autumn. One of the more memorable meals I have eaten in the region was at the Clube dos Caçadores or hunters' club in the outskirts of Viseu where they not only eat animals shot locally, but advertise imported crocodile, kangaroo and ostrich on the menu. We sat under a boar's head, in a cloud of cigarette smoke with mobile telephones going off at regular intervals, so that the place looked like a cross between a smoke house and a telephone exchange.

After some sardines in vinegar, which we devoured from head to tail, and some crunchy pigs' ears, we had a clear partridge broth with pasta and little strips of partridge in it. The flesh of the same bird had found its way into an *arroz* with some wild

mushrooms. Next came some slices of wild boar seasoned with fresh lemon juice with broccoli and more 'punch' potatoes.

The Quinta de Cabriz is a restaurant owned by Dão Sul, so there should be no surprise about what you drink there. The food is good. We had some *aperitivos* or hors d'oeuvres of *farinheira* (see Douro p152), some juicy *morcela preta* or black pudding, and *chouriço*; *bolinhos* and *croquetes* and *chora do mar*, a mixture of sea food and noodles. The name means 'lament for the ocean', a complaint that the people of the region are too far from the sea. This was followed by roast kid with fried potatoes, *migas* (bread and oil paste), *feijão* (beans with rice) and *nabiça* or turnip tops. Kid should be cooked in a bread oven, like the baby lambs across the border in Spain. It is often served with roast potatoes; sometimes with a few red peppers cooked alongside. Kid, strong flavoured lamb and beef – particularly from Lafões – are all recommended in the region.

The pudding was sweet pumpkin, fresh ricotta-like cheese and an eggy pudding. Not all puddings are made of egg yolks. I have had very nice pears stewed in wine in Viseu and sweet chestnuts are a speciality. Mangualde makes bean cakes. Esmolfe is famous for its apples.

Beira Interior

Dão and the Beira share the honours when it comes to Portugal's greatest cheeses. They used to be made by women, and the warmth of their hands was a vital element in the cheesemaking process. This is *serra* country, ewes' milk cheeses which liquify in winter and have to be unloaded from their cloth bound interiors with a spoon. Producers have taken to freezing them now and then bringing them out at all times of the year, but in their purest state they are like the magnificent Vacherin Mont d'Or from Franche Comté, a proper seasonal delicacy for which one happily waits all year.

There is a local watercress soup, called *agrião*. At the meal I ate in the region it prefaced what is

pretty well the Portuguese national meat dish, *arroz de pato* or *pato ao forno* – duck cooked and layered with rice, then baked in the oven. The local *enchidos*, or salami-style pork sausages, are famous: it's both high and dry here. Chick peas are cooked with pork crackling. The region also makes a sort of haggis by stuffing the *buchos*, or stomachs of sheep or goats, with different sorts of meats. Otherwise lamb or goat is generally roast.

An *arroz de carqueja* finds a use for the red gartered coot (*fulica armillata*). *Bacalhau* is served with plenty of oil and potatoes or cooked with milk in the oven.

Bairrada

Vegetarians and creatures of a delicate sensibility are warned to stay clear of Bairrada. The roads would be quite enough to reduce them to quivering wrecks. On all sides you are assailed by images of ecstatic pigs hurling themselves onto spits or forks, or gaily bedding down on glowing embers in preparation for the feast; and they are not just any pigs: life expectancy in the porcine world is short. The weaners of the Bízaro breed are snatched away from their mothers when they are under ten weeks old when they weigh between five and ten kilos. This race is favoured for its longer back and larger rump, which makes it ideal for the spit. A special *molho*, or marinade is then smeared inside the rib cage. It is made of fat with spices and garlic and a great deal of salt. Then the piglet is sewn up again and impaled on a spit before cooking. Originally the locals cooked the beasts over vine prunings, but these days they favour a bread oven. To ensure a properly crispy skin, the piglet is removed from the oven when it is nearly cooked, and left for a while in the open air.

After about three hours in the oven it is crunchy. It is served with boiled potatoes or slices of orange, a salad and a bottle of the local sparkling wine. The guts form a side dish, or are cooked later with beans in a *feijoada*. There can be no other region in Europe where white sparkling wine is seen as the ideal accompaniment to meat, but the men of Bairrada are categorical on this subject. I put their theories to the test at the restaurant Mugasa in Ancas, at the heart of the region.

Bairrada suckling pig is popular. In the high season people come up from Lisbon or down from Oporto just to eat it and the pigs come from farther afield, and may not be *Bízaro*. I have even heard one story – I am sure it wasn't true – that Spanish pigs have been used *in extremis*.

There is much grumbling in Bairrada at the moment, as the heavy-handed European Union has decreed that restaurateurs may not despatch their own pigs, but must buy them from an abattoir instead. This, argue the locals, is a recipe for disaster. The next thing they know will be imported deep frozen hogs – from Spain.

Pig killing was a joyful time in Bairrada, as it is everywhere else in Europe where poorish families depend on pigs for sustenance throughout the winter months. Prosperity used to be measured by the number of pigs killed in the year. The first were despatched at Martinmas (November 11), but more often families waited to nearer Christmas time to slay the hog.

That day there was vegetable broth laced with olive oil for breakfast. For pudding that evening there would be a variant on *sarrabulho*, a curious dish made from eggs, sugar and boiled pig's blood. Most of the flesh was put into Aveiro salt to be made into hams and gammon. The brains were eaten with scrambled eggs; the trotters boiled up in a stew with garlic and vegetables; or with butter beans; lean meat *rojões* were preserved in lard like a French *confit*. As in the Minho they were eaten with boiled potatoes.

Sausages were made from meat marinaded in red wine with paprika, pepper and garlic. More blood went into the black puddings. The sausages were above all used as a flavouring and garnish for hearty soups.

Despite all appearances people here can be made to eat other things than pork. Bairrada has another dish: *chanfana*. This is made from mutton, or more often oldish goat, stewed in sealed clay pots for hours with plenty of local wine, onions, paprika, bacon and garlic until the meat drops off the bones. Traditionally the beasts were sold at the market in Oliveira do Bairro. *Negalhos* were pieces of goat belly stuffed with sausage, bacon and mint and slowly cooked in an airtight black clay pot.

'Bairrada food is neither varied nor rich' is the candid observation of one book on the region, but there are other things to recommend besides suckling pig and mutton stew. For a start the coastal region near Aveiro is famous for its rice fields. Vegetables grow well here and a simple soup was made from black eyed beans and cabbage.

Corn bread – *boroa or broa* – was taken out into the fields for a mid morning snack with some sardines or *bacalhau. Bacalhau* was served in a variety of different ways. Towards the coast at Aveiro, there is naturally more fish on the menu as well as eels taken from the salt marshes. These were often presented with the suckling pig sauce (see above).

Aveiro has *ovos moles*, a pudding famous throughout Portugal made of sweetened egg yolks. Sweet rice is also popular as is *aletria doce*: thin vermicelli boiled in milk and sugar and perfumed with lemon peel and cinnamon.

Estremadura

The Estremadura naturally focusses on Lisbon, and the capital is clearly one of the best places to eat. In Oeste chicken is cooked in clay, and by the sea there are sardines and more sardines. From the marshes come eels, which are served up stewed in Óbidos. Pigs are big: There is a pork *arroz* in Bombarral and a bloody slaughterman's *arroz* in Torres Vedras. From

Alcobaça, Caldas da Rainha, Torres Vedras, Peniche and Bombarral come 'convent' puddings of various descriptions – as the name suggests the recipes derive from the old nunneries and convents.

Ribatejo

Close to Lisbon far from the sea and mountains alike, the Ribatejo is not the region for startling culinary discoveries. I have eaten surprisingly good sea bass in Rio Maior, and had the usual staples – *caldo verde* and strong flavoured local lamb – elsewhere. When I ate with José Lobo de Vasconcellos he served the lamb with *pommes allumettes* and mint sauce. The latter, I suspected, had been made in my honour.

The river fish enjoys a certain fame, especially the shad, which is eaten in the spring – often as part of an *açorda* (see p159) – or which gives its roes to an *arroz* in winter. Fish stews are popular as are eels and lampreys. The former are often made into an *ensopado*: a bready stew, or simply fried. Soups also figure largely on menus here. One famous concoction is the *sopa de pedra*. The story is a long one – the tale of a shaggy beggar, who claimed he could make soup from a stone. He boiled the stone but called in turn for other ingredients – beans, *chouriço*, pigs' ears, black pudding, bacon, vegetables, herbs – the stone was good, but these things, he said would make it even better. Finally the soup was declared delicious and the beggar rejoined: 'See what you can do with a stone!'

The ribatejanos eat kid like most other Portuguese, but their dish adds *chouriço* and red peppers. I have found very good local, waxed-rind ewes' milk cheeses. These are consumed, after the Portuguese practice, with bread before a meal. There are the usual eggy puddings: *fatias de Tomar*, for example, use 24 yolks and a kilo of sugar! The only other ingredient is water.

The local olive oils are good and are protected by a DOP - the equivalent of a wine DOC. The variety is the Galega, which was first planted in the Ribatejo some two thousand years ago.

Setúbal Peninsula

George Borrow ate well in Pegões in the Setúbal Peninsula. The company danced and sang while he demolished a plate of rabbit with olives. Indeed, he noted that rabbits were about the only thing to eat in Pegões: 'produced in abundance on the moors around. We had one fried, the gravy of which was delicious, and afterwards a roasted one, which was brought up on a dish entire; the hostess, having first washed her hands, proceeded to tear the animal to pieces, which having accomplished, she poured over the fragments of a sweet sauce... Excellent figs, from the Algarves, and apples concluded our repast...'

Borrow also noted the *porco preto* pigs in Palmela and revelled in their flavour. 'Gallant swine they are, with short legs and and portly bodies of a black or dark red colour; and for the excellence of their flesh I can vouch, having frequently luxuriated upon it in the course of my wanderings in this province; the *lombo*, or loin, when broiled on the live embers, is delicious, especially when eaten with olives.'

On the coast fish is more in vogue, especially the sardines and red mullet of Setúbal, which are grilled or roasted in the oven. There are also numerous fish stews. The ewe's milk cheese of Azeitão is one of the most celebrated in Portugal, and there are typical desserts such as egg yolks with cinnamon, or Setúbal orange cakes.

Alentejo

The practice in the Alentejo today is to spread the table with tempting *acepipes* which are called *petiscos* here: *porco preto* ham; *enchidos* or salame; *chouriço* doused in olive oil from Moura or Elvas; pigs' ears with the ubiquitous coriander; onions and black-eye beans; *bacalhau* with red peppers; hake roes; octopus drenched in bright green oil; green chilli peppers; omelettes with red peppers; whole, fresh ewe's milk cheeses from Serpa or Évora; fresh crab or little mackerel. In other places these have been more banal: I have had cheese toasted with oregano and mushrooms with coriander.

One of the loveliest first courses I have enjoyed in the Alentejo, was the *tubera* I ate at the delightful São Rosas restaurant beside the castle in Estremoz, which had the texture of a potato, but which tastes of ceps. It must be a member of the truffle family. Some

raw ones were brought out for me to examine, they grow beneath the scrubland and are in season in the late spring.

Coriander is everywhere, but not just coriander, purslane goes into soups, and there is a local version of the Andalusian gaspacho flavoured with excellent local oregano, but also adding sausage or fish at will. The most popular soup – *açorda* – is frequently offered outside the region – is composed simply of stock, stale bread, roughly crushed garlic, coriander, olive oil and a soft boiled egg. Another is *calducho*, which includes *bacalhau* or sardines, possibly both. Spring soups are based on fresh vegetables: *alcobaças* (like watercress), *cardinhos* (from the artichoke family), or wild asparagus cooked with eggs and slices of *chouriço*.

Chick peas are widely grown on the clay soils of the Lower Alentejo. Chicken is served up in little pies. There are hearty stews, generally made from lamb and the famous dish of pork and clams, which was first made in Lisbon, but which is now available all over its region of adoption.

Porco preto or Iberian pork is now quite readily available. It is roasted or fried and served with *migas*. Its trotters are submerged beneath heaps of coriander and bread to make *pézinhos*, one of the region's favourite meals.

The Alentejo's favourite seafood is dog-fish, which is served in a vinegary bread soup littered with coriander. *Bacalhau* is naturally another favourite, served with butter and parsley. Another main course was a loin of native pork with spinach flavoured with coriander. The Alentejanos are fond of earthy foods: a vast dish of pigs' ears is served in a sort of eggy soup. Delicious was a pigeon consumed at São Rosas in Estremoz, it was cooked with cabbage, garlic in its skins, thyme and tomatoes. I have eaten super kid too, quite crisp, with crunchy roast potatoes.

The leitmotiv which binds all Alentejano meals together (although 'light' it is not) are *migas*. This is a bread dish made with olive oil, a little like an *açorda*. They can, of course, be quite delicious, but they are filling, and function in the same way as the famous Yorkshire pudding, that was designed to stop British people from eating too much beef. Olive oil is everywhere, but it is some of the best in Portugal, especially when it comes from Moura and the north of the region.

Pork – basted with red pepper paste – beef (*carne Alentejana*) and lamb (*baixo Alentejo*) all have a national reputation and are protected by statute; as are the sausages of Portalegre and Barrancos ham, which is made from *porco preto*. Sausages are also a speciality in various parts of the region: *botifarra* from Azaruja, *cacholeiras* from Crato or bacon pasties from Arraiolos.

The most famous cheese is the Serpa, but also not to be spurned are the good cheese of Nisa and Évora.

The *queijada*, or cheesecake, was a well-established Alentejano sweetmeat then as now. Nuns, disenfranchised by the recent dissolution of the monasteries, survived by baking them. Borrow found them 'delicious'. They are particularly good at Easter, when they can be bought from the cafes on the great square in Évora with its houses shorn up by huge buttresses. They tend to be among the most reliable of the region's desserts. Many of the others are variations on egg yolks, like the rich *morgado*, or landlord's pudding, or the *barriga de freira*, or nun's belly. *Pão de rala* means grated bread (it contains pumpkin), while *pão de ló* is a sponge cake with eggs eaten at Christmas.

Algarve

Fresh fish is the thing in the Algarve, although providing you are in a smart hotel almost anything might be procured. In the days before tourism, Portimão and its fishermen survived by canning sardines and tuna. *Xarém* is an interesting thick, green cockle soup made with maize flour with the consistency of runny polenta. It is flavoured with coriander. Squid is stuffed with its own tentacles in the ordinary way, but some chopped *chouriço* is added to provide some spice.

Fresh produce can be exciting here: the oranges in mid-winter, pineapples, bananas – even sugar canes, grow and ripen in Portugal's southernmost province. Figs are abundant, and along the coast they are turned into little cakes to the joy of schoolchildren.

practical hints for the traveller in the wine country

The Minho

Oporto is a useful starting point for exploring the Minho, indeed, the *comissão* is based here, in a lovely nineteenth-century house overlooking the Douro, built by a man who had made a fortune in Brazil and came home in triumph. Oporto is the biggest city in northern Portugal; and there are naturally plenty of hotels here. I well remember the first one I stayed in, near the suburban station. I was kept awake all night by motorbikes without silencers which sounded like dentists' drills and a curious duel between a parrot and an Alsatian dog. The one barked and the other squawked, neither wanted to other to sleep; and presumably that was their attitude towards the inhabitants of the hotel as well. One old port shipper took pity on me, and moved me into the Lawn Tennis and Cricket Club, a well-appointed island of Britishness between the centre of town and Foz.

More recently I have sometimes had the luck to stay at the Infante Sagres (351 22 339 85 00), the best and most Iberian hotel in town. Vila Galé (351 22 519 18 00) is an international style four star, similar to the Ipanema Park (351 22 610 41 74) on the other side of the city. Quietly old fashioned is the Grande Hotel do Porto (351 22 200 81 76) where I once witnessed an extraordinary performance of women modelling underwear. Cheaper and quite central is the Hotel da Bolsa (351 22 202 67 68).

The Taberna de Bebeobos (351 222 053 565) is

under the arches on the quay opposite Gaia. The food is rustic and homely. The Bull and Bear (351 22 610 76 69) is Oporto's most modern restaurant. I have had good cep soup there. It is close to Foz where there is a good seafood restaurant right down on the beach called the Praia do Ourigo. The place to eat seafood is the port suburb of Matosinhos which is a warren of decent little restaurants, all, it seems, as good as one another.

Some people swear by the Casa Aleixo (351 225 370 462), which is virtually next to the Campanhã railway station, where I was the reluctant witness to the fight between the dog and the parrot. It tends to be clubby, but I had a good meal there recently of octopus and hake in batter, *arroz de feijão* and big hunks of roast veal and potatoes. The waiters need to be checked when it comes to the wine. What you order and what they bring can be wildly different.

A useful place to stay near Barcelos, is the Quinta da Franqueira, a former convent with nicely furnished rooms around the old Franciscan cloister (351 253 831 606). The owners are English producers of vinho verde. Another old estate with rooms to let is the Solar das Bouças: (351 253 909 010) .

Barcelos is within striking distance of Braga with its cathedral, convent of Nossa Senhora da Oliveira, and mediaeval palace of the dukes of Braganza. Nearby is Bom Jesus do Monte, a sanctuary 600 metres high with 14 stations of the cross. There is a brace of hotels right and left of the church if you should need a rest after the climb. Guimarães is the birthplace of the Portuguese monarchy and has two castles and many baroque buildings. There are a couple of pousadas here, including a mediaeval building in the old city - Nossa Senhora da Oliveira (351 253 514 453) – in which I ate and stayed a couple of decades ago. I still have a note of the meal: pork with lemon, bay and olives and a 1966 Dão garrafeira.

Nearby is the Casa de Sezim, an excellent estate with rooms (351 253 523 000). The Pinto de Mesquita family have lived here since 1376.

Before the motorway reduced the journey time to Pinhão to an hour and half, the port wine trade used to stop in Amarante for lunch half way, before continuing their journeys up to the Douro. Vinho verde was still brought from the cask then, if you were not lucky it was murky and flat. In the old days the town was famous for its fresh savel, or shad, which comes up the river to spawn in spring. It is a long time, however, since I have seen it on an Amarante menu: better to stick to the more rustic bars hung with hams and sausages where a mug of frothy vinho verde is accompanied by a doughty ham roll. I have bought excellent honey from the Serra do Marão here, crudely packaged in a giant instant coffee jar.

There are lots of cafes where you may eat sweet,

eggy cakes such as *amarantinhos* or *papos d' anjo* – angel's breasts. They can be quite heavy, and tend to go best with a slug of tawny port.

The town was torched by the French two centuries before it was mauled by developers, but the Gauls failed to reach the area across the Tamega, up by the monastic church of S. Gonçalo. There are some pleasant cafes there with seats outside, ideal for a quick coffee if you are travelling towards the Douro. The Pousada de S. Gonçalo (351 255 46 11 23) high up on the Serra do Marão was built during the war and must have felt chic in its day; the last time I stayed there it was in distinct need of a refit. I am happy to hear that this has now taken place.

For the vinhos verdes which abut the Douro, there is a charming rococo coaching inn with features culled directly from Borromeo close to the junction of River Tamega called the Casa da Cocheca in Baião (351 255 55 11 74), run – with her husband – by a lady who descends from Dona Antónia Ferreira. There is a dastardly collection of ancient weaponry. All four rooms are very comfortable, and there are local products for sale, including the pottery made by Isabel, the daughter of the house. There is no dining room, but the breakfasts are sumptuous, with home made jams and delicious fruit from the trees outside.

Where the Douro meets the Tamega at Entre-os-Rios there is the estalagem Porto Antigo (351 255 560 150) which can rustle up a decent trout. They are four and half hours from Oporto by boat and the inn

is popular with trippers making their way up to Pinhão through the various locks and impediments set up in the last fifty years. It takes another couple of hours to reach the centre of the port wine producing area. A restaurant which is recommended in Baião is the Pensão Borges (352 255 541 322). They make the traditional dishes of the Lower Douro.

Viana do Castelo is the port on the Lima whence the first exports of Portuguese wine were despatched to Britain. There is a Relais et Châteaux hotel, the Estalagem Casa Melo Alvim, in an ancient house in the centre of the town (351 258 808 220). Lima has a famous old bridge with 27 arches. A stop in Valença is also advised, as this was the stronghold against Spaniards wishing to cross the Minho. The fort was built in the style of the French military engineer Vauban in the seventeenth and eighteenth centuries.

The Quinta de Luou is a well preserved old property, also offering bed and breakfast (351 226 163 308).

In the far north, just outside Monção I have stayed in a gorgeous old house called the Solar de Serrade (351 251 65 40 08) complete with chapel and rooms with four poster beds. It is popular for marriages among the immigrants, but there is no restaurant as such, and guests are obliged to go into town, where there are plenty. The Palacio da Brejoeira looks older than it is, but that doesn't stop it from being an impressive testament to Brazilian wealth in the nineteenth century. The mansion contains a museum (351 251 66 61 29).

Melgaço has pretty granite buildings in the

centre. There is also the granite Solar do Alvarinho (351 251 410 195) behind its renaissance arcade, where you may sample different wines from the region.

Many restaurants by the riversides specialise in lampreys in season. One which is recommended is O Moinho beside the ancient market hall in Ponte da Barca (351 251 42035 or 42 514).

For more information contact the Gabinete da Rota dos Vinhos Verdes in Oporto: (351 226 077 315).

Douro

The unspoilt nature of the Douro Valley can have its disadvantages: there are probably no more than 200 beds in the whole area, and only a handful of restaurants worthy of the name. For most of us who have some contact with the wine trade, there is the option of being put up in a comfortable quinta and being waited on hand and foot in a way which has virtually disappeared in other European countries. For those who lack that advantage, there are some budget hotels in Régua and one or two beds and breakfasts in Pinhão. Added to these there are three pousadas: Solar da Rede (351 254 89 01 30) near Mesão Frio – which looks magnificent from outside – at the beginning of the wine country; The Barão de Forrester (351 259 959 215) at Alijó in the middle; and Santa Catarina (351 273 43 12 55) at the far end of the Valley.

The opening of Vintage House (351 54 73 02 30) in Pinhão by Taylor, Fladgate and Yeatman has been a positive development: it is a four star Relais et Châteaux hotel on the site of an old lodge I stayed in once, when it was occupied by half a dozen twelve-year-old boys, a cook and about the same number of servants. The boys treated me very well and took me on a boat trip on the river, carefully covering me with a plaid lest I be splashed by the water, although I was no more than twenty-five at the time.

It has been an odd experience to see it now dressed up as a hotel, complete with exotic interior decoration carried out under the eye of Gilly Robertson, the wife of the chairman of the company. The rooms too have many flamboyant touches. The only disappointment I experienced in the beginning was in looking at the menu, which proposed a sort of modified international cooking which owed little to Portugal, and even less to the Douro. More recent experience has been cheering. I have had good *enchidos* and some local partridge wrapped in cabbage and served with a creamy, grain mustard sauce. I also tasted some good wild boar, another thing which is plentiful in the Valley. The wine list is good; Taylor's, making no table wine, can afford to be impartial here. There are indications that more port houses are looking at the possibility of attracting wine tourists. Royal Oporto certainly has plans to convert one of its quintas into a restaurant.

There is another possiblity: renting air-conditioned rooms or even an estate cottage at the Quinta de la Rosa (call +44 (0)1296 748989 in England). The quinta is only a couple of kms from Pinhão and you can easily walk in to buy provisions from a handful of good local shops. A little farther away is the German-owned Casa do Visconde de Chanceleiros (351 254 730 190).

As the capital of the Upper Douro, Pinhão is not an inspiring place. The only things of beauty it airs are the tiles in the railway station. There are a few places to eat, however, of which the best is thought to be the Clube Pinhoense on the 'river beach'. More exotic is a bar nearby which is allegedly run by an Australian, although on closer enquiry he turns out just to be a Portuguese who has been to Australia. Others say that the restaurant operated by the local firemen is worth a punt. There are quite a few places selling souvenirs now, and at least two which sell wine. Not far away, in Vale de Mendiz, is the Sandeman-owned *lagares* museum (351 22 370 22 93) containing the only round *lagares* in Portugal.

A French winemaker working in the region has discovered a louche bar in Tarouca, not far from Lamego.

The Douro is still a wild place – which is much of its appeal – and the monuments to past civilisation are few and far between. Mesão Frio is a pretty old town, filled with noblemen's houses with enormous escutcheons. Nearby is the charming old spa town of Caldas de Moledo. It looks a little dilapidated these days. I suspect few people come to take the waters.

Régua is not beautiful, but just outside Vila Real to the north is the Italian Nicola Nasoni's eighteenth-century gem, the Casa de Mateus, known worldwide from its guest appearance on the labels of the famous Sogrape rosé. Diogo Cão, who discovered the mouth

of the River Zaire, was born in Vila Real in 1482; Fernão de Magalhães (Ferdinand de Magellan) was born in Sabrosa not far away. He was the first man to circumnavigate the globe, in 1522.

Lamego is a pleasant old cathedral city. Provesende, above Pinhão, owes its distinction to the marquês de Pombal, who banished seven noble families there, all of whom constructed magnificent houses in the village. They are mostly romantic ruins these days, although one or two of them could still be repaired given the will to do so. Nearby in Casal de Loivos is a useful bed and breakfast with stunning views over Pinhão Valley (351 254 732 149).

In the Cima Corgo there is also S. João de Pesqueira. As its name implies, the inhabitants used to trade in fish. There are a few pretty old buildings. At Murça, to the north, is the famous prehistoric granite boar. More prehistoric art works are to be found in the Serra de Carlão near Alijó. Very recently archaeologists uncovered another important site in the Vale do Côa which was then threatened with destruction by dam building. The figurative scratchings from twenty thousand years ago have now been saved. There is a museum at Quinta de Ervamoira, owned by Ramos Pinto.

In the Upper Douro there are attractive small towns at Vila Flor, Torre de Moncorvo and Cinta; but the chief charm of the region is the landscape with its whitewashed port wine quintas. The best of these is Vesúvio, down by the river, opposite Senhora da

Ribeira. In the modest restaurant in Senhora da Ribeira the former British prime minister John Major ate lunch, and the feast – chicken and chips and white wine – is recorded on a brass plaque. He was staying at the Symington Quinta dos Malvedos at the time. A strange tramp haunts the quayside, wearing a Portuguese flag on his head. No one appears to know if he was conjured up by Major or not.

For further information call the Gabinete da Rota do Vinho do Porto (351 254 320 146).

Dão

The old world place to stay in Viseu is the Grão Vasco in the centre of the city (351 232 42 35 11). Some people prefer the modern Montebelo (351 232 420 00 00), which is a little way out of town, but has very comfortable rooms with large balconies. It has been a while since I have visited the city centre, but I recall it used to be marvellous place to buy huge, thick black canvas shepherds' umbrellas with great wooden shafts carved with what looked like primitive runes.

The chief attraction is the great granite cathedral and the 16th century museum devoted to the local master of the international gothic style, Vasco Fernandes, or 'Grão Vasco'.

There are large numbers of dolmens to see once you reach the higher parts of the region. One of the best examples is in Orca dos Juncais.

There are baroque palaces at Mangualde (the condes de Anadia) and at two wine estates: the Casa da Insua and the Casa de Santar and a magnificent twelfth-century Cistercian abbey church with baroque additions at S. Cristovão de Lafões. In the old spa town of Caramulo there are two museums, one dedicated to modern art, the other to ancient motor cars.

For more information: Gabinete da Rota do Vinho do Dão (351 232 410 060).

Beira Interior

So far there is not a great deal of infrastructure in this remote region by the Spanish frontier. Great rolled stones are everywhere, looking as if some Sisyphus had abandoned them and his labours, there on the hillsides. More likely, however, that they were dumped by some Ice Age glacier. The landscape is populated by flocks of sheep, which justify their presence by their splendid cheeses, conceived on the high slopes of the Serra da Estrela. A few predators are heard by night. It is here that the last of Portugal's wolves make an occasional sortie in search of dinner.

Just every now and then you glimpse a decent sized vineyard. Most of the vines, however, are clustered in tiny pockets. In the old days the farmer would make some primitive brewage for his own comforts and needs, now he takes the grapes to one of the cooperatives.

The ever present granite had its uses in the rare towns in this part of Portugal. It went to construct the great cathedral at Guarda, built 1,000 metres above sea level over a period of 150 years and finished with a flourish of Manueline art. Portugal's oldest city, *Guarda,* has more besides, such as the colonnades of the old ghetto and the Solar dos Alarcões.

Castles are everywhere. This was the first line of defence against the ever-intrusive Spaniards: the bleak Marialva, Longroiva - built by Portugal's first king Afonso Henriques - Meda, with its panoramic views; or Trancoso, Sabugal, Sortelha, Pinhel and the strange Roman tower at Centum Cellas are just a handful of the best known.

In Belmonte was Portugal's concealed Jewish community, posing as 'new Christians' yet maintaining, over the long drawn out centuries, as many of their religious rites and traditions as they could remember. Officially they were expelled in 1497, more than half a millennium ago. In recent times they have opened their own synagogue.

Belmonte is not solely *marrano,* the contemptuous name for the converted Jews, here and in Spain. It was also the birthplace of Pedro Alvares Cabral, the man who discovered and colonised Brazil.

In Sabugal, in the shadow of one of the Beira's most grandiose castles, the young men of the town practise a *capeia*, a primitive form of bull-fighting designed to test the virility of youth. An angry bull is pushed back by a crowd of youths until his strength gives out.

The border fort of Almeida is situated at a height of 800 feet above sea level. It achieved its present Vaubanesque form in the seventeenth century. All remains of the original castle were destroyed by an explosion in a powder magazine during the French invasion of 1810; there was a massive loss of life.

Inside the walls of the castle at Castelo Rodrigo are the remains of the palace of Cristovão de Moura, who was believed to have sympathized with the Spanish takeover. In 1640 the local people set fire to his home. During the nineteenth century the townsfolk quit the place en masse and settled at Figueira de Castelo Rodrigo at the bottom of the hill.

In Pinhel there are a couple of Manueline treasures in the Igreja da Misericordia and the castle keep.

The best place to stay is the Hospedaria do Convento (351 271 31 28 27), just outside Castelo Rodrigo. It was formerly part of the Cistercian abbey of Santa Maria de Aguiar, founded in the mid twelfth century. It is owned by Dr António Alberto Galhardo Simões, a Coimbra-educated banker who spent a year reading PPE at Balliol College, Oxford. At the Convento, the wing constructed in the 1830s following the dissolution of the monasteries, has been partly converted into a very comfortable hotel. There are just seven, very comfortable rooms, but more are planned for the surviving mediaeval range which abuts the simple twelfth-century church. The church is typically austere and Cistercian, although there is an elaborate sixteenth-century retable, which

somehow enlivens the place. There is a marvellous vaulted sacristry next door, which is currently filled with rubble. The gothic vault is supported by massive columns – it should provide a ravishing communal space once the conversion is finished.

For more information call the Gabinete da Rota dos Vinhos da Beira Interior (351 271 22 41 29).

Bairrada

There is no denying the glory of the Palace Hotel in Bussaco (351 231 93 01 01). With its crazy Manueline twirls and nautical motifs designed by the Italian theatre architect Luigi Manini, it sits on a steep knoll in the middle of a primaeval forest. At 547 metres, the hotel is visible for miles around.

The interiors are wonderful: there are exterior walls covered with *azulejos* depicting scenes from the plays of Gil Vincente and inside are painted episodes from Portuguese history. On the stairs are displayed some of the great moments from Wellington's victory over the French. There are knights in armour standing guard, and their eyes light up behind their visors at night. The rooms have charm and are filled with old furniture (some of it seemingly on its last legs), although a lick of paint here and there would not go amiss. The kitchens too could do with an overhaul. Anyone going through Bairrada should stop for a suckling pig or two somewhere else and sleep at the Palace.

Another place to stay is the spa town of Luso, where there is an old fashioned grand hotel owned by the same group as the Palace in Bussaco (351 231 93 03 50). Curia is naturally another spa town, this time specialising in urinary disorders (you are advised to drink a lot of water). It, too, has a palatial Grande Hotel (351 231 51 21 85). Near Anadia is the eighteenth-century mansion, the Paço da Graciosa, which has long been famous for its wines.

I remember the Quinta das Lágrimas (351 44 16 15) in the Oxford of Portugal, Coimbra, in its romantic, unreformed state. Here was the site of the trysts between the king, Dom Pedro and his mistress Dona Inês immortalized by Camões. I am not sure I like what they have done to it by turning it into a hotel. The signs directing you to the different buildings are reminiscent of a ward guide to a hospital, and the air conditioning ducts have wrecked the ceilings in the main corps de logis. The restaurant is good, so is the wine list, and that is some solace. A long time ago I stayed in Astoria (351 239 82 20 55), a cousin of the

Palace in Bussaco. I had a delightful, 1940s suite which cost next to nothing then.

You might prefer to stay in an old house. António Afonso Navega's lovely Quinta do Carvalhinho in Ventosa do Bairro has rooms (351 231 28 93 43). If you do, do not miss the office he has created in his winery. It is a comfortably furnished old tun. Diogenes never had it so good.

As far as suckling pig is concerned, visitors are stuck for choice: there are some 50 suckling pig joints along the main road. Every restaurateur, it seems, is named dos Leitões: 'of the suckling pigs'- Vasco dos Leitões, Manoel dos Leitões, etc. Meta dos Leitões in Mealhada makes his own wines, and these have a large following. Everywhere you look there are roadhouses advertising baby pigs. This form of marketing was lifted from Pedro dos Leitões who started the piglet cult in the years before the Second World War. He is now honoured with a granite statue for his role in the development of the region.

The best places to scoff a piglet these days, I'm told, are the more discreet restaurants, undistinguished on the outside and well hidden from the main road. I found one place called Mugasa (351 234 741 061) in Ancas where the pig was just so. I was relieved to see that the owner of Casa de Saima and his wife ate there every day. That must be a recommendation.

Ancas (haunches) is one of the anatomical names which distinguishes the smaller towns of the region.

Two more are Bustos (breasts) and Nariz (nose). Naturally a name is not enough to draw visitors to a region, but there is plenty to offer in Coimbra with its two cathedrals, ancient university quadrangle and exotic botanical garden, before you start branching out into the vines.

For more information call the Gabinete da Rota do Vinho da Bairrada (351 231 51 01 80).

Estremadura

Lisbon naturally has a wealth of hotels and restaurants. The most central hotel of all is the Avenida Palace (351 213 46 01 51), where the fictional Felix Krull, in Thomas Mann's novel of that name, worked as a liftboy, waiter and thief! No danger, I am sure, of that sort of thing going on today. There is no restaurant anyhow. The Parque Real (351 213 57 01 01) is a simple four star with good views over Lisbon from the top of its ten storeys.

I have never eaten at Tavares (351 213 42 11 12), Lisbon's most famous, nineteenth-century dining room, much frequented by Eça de Queiroz and literary lions of his sort. Gambrinus (351 21 342 14 66), is a posh old *cervejaria* designed in a curious old Nordic style where the rich *morgados* used to gather before the Revolution. It is chiefly notable today for the high prices of the wines and the curious ballet performed by the waiters. Gambrinus is in Baixa, where most of the restaurants offer a pretty standard sea food menu. The windows are piled high with crabs, rock lobsters, sea bass and monk fish, as well as a few baby lamb and kid carcasses. In the old days most of the crustaceans were still alive and suspended on strings so that you could choose the perkiest one. Now only a few restaurants continue this practice.

I also have the impression that the great spider crab or *santola* is becoming a rarity. These days restaurants offer the more common or garden *sapateira*. A Berlenga (351 213 42 03 46) is as good a place as any to enjoy this food. They have other things besides: suckling pig, wild boar chops with *fines herbes* and a wine list with omissions. A good place to eat a variety of *açordas* is naturally Papa'açorda (351 213 46 48 11), where the bread and oil is mixed with eggs and coriander. Watch out for their Pedron peppers, they can be very hot.

More soigné is the plush Vela Latina by the Torre de Belem (351 213 01 71 18) where I have had excellent lobster soup and turbot accompanied by prawns wrapped in a cabbage leaf. O Funil (351 217 96 60 07) is in the drab business quarter of Lisbon, near the bullring, but here I ate a wonderfully spicy *arroz de polvo* and a *pato ao forno* which was exceptionally moist and good. The wine list is extensive.

There is naturally a huge number of simple restaurants where you may eat homely, unsophisticated things for under £10 a head. Everyone's list would be different. There is no real Lisbon food. As one waiter from Trás-os-Montes put it 'All they know how to do here is to slam a steak down on the grill!' That was at Transmontana (351 213 42 03 00), where you may eat good roast lamb and kid and drink from a small selection of Alentejo wines just up the steps from the Rossio. Again in the Bairro Alto is Floresta da Cidade (351 213 46 06 21), which has quality fish and meat as well as good *toucinho do céu*.

At the small, unpretentious Gamba d'Ouro in the Bairro Alto I tried the *cozido* or stew. I counted up the various ingredients: the whole snout of a young pig, and an ear from an older beast, and a cheek from the same; a piece of beef; several chunks of bright red *chouriço* and black pudding; two pieces of chicken; haricot beans, rice, a turnip, a large potato and half a cabbage. That was for one.

For some people the best Lisbon restaurant of the traditional type is Tia Matilde (351 217 97 21 72), which is in a funny little lost part of town, bisected by a railway line not far from the Gulbenkian museum. It started out as a cafe. The butcher across the way used to bring in some meat so that Matilde would cook it for his lunch. It looked so appetising that more people demanded food. Then the butcher went into business with Matilde and this swish restaurant was born. I had dinner there once in early January: lovely *porco preto* ham (at a fraction the price you'd pay in Spain), huge tiger prawns with butter and garlic; rabbit stew; *arroz de frango* cooked with the chicken's own blood; *serra* cheese and *toucinho do céu*. The wine list is also excellent.

Many might wish to stay in the posher villages and

resorts to the west of Lisbon. In Sintra – Byron's 'variegated maze of mount and glen' – is the Quinta de Seteais (351 219 23 32 00), or of 'seven sighs'. It used to be known as 'da Alegria' – of happiness. It was renamed because it was believed that the Convention of Sintra had been signed here in 1808, which allowed the French to leave Portugal with their arms and booty. With its directoire public rooms, it is one of the most ravishing hotels in Europe, with lovely views over the formal gardens and out to sea. The food, however, is disappointing. It is better by far at the Tacho Real up a hill in the centre of town (351 219 23 52 77). There is an old-fashioned presentation here, and good Chaves hams are served as well as delicious fresh cheeses, *chouriços* and bready *farinheira* sausages. A few dishes contain memories of the Portuguese past. There is a green prawn curry served with poppadoms, for example.

There is plenty to see in Sintra. The old royal palace with its curious kitchen chimneys, where Dom João wore down the tiles as he paced his way through the years of captivity. The Paláclo da Pena is a further example of the rich imagination of the king consort Ferdinand, who also inspired the plans for the Palace Hotel in Bussaco. There are handicrafts of interest, like the majolica made by the prisoners at Sintra. Sometimes this is made in pure blue and white and decorated simply with coats or arms, which makes a change from the more elaborate styles of Portuguese majolica.

The cooking at the Fortaleza do Guincho (351 214 87 04 91) a few miles north of Cascais is quite the opposite to the simple, homely style encountered in most Portuguese restaurants. It is a seventeenth-century fort on the beach, placed there to protect the coast from marauding Barbary pirates. Beyond a vaguely renaissance door, some pepperpot towers and a gallery on squat doric columns, the architecture is so primitive it could be African. From the rooms you look straight down from your terrace on to the breakers below. The hotel and its kitchens are French managed. It comes as a surprise, and to an extent a delight, to see such sophisticated French food in Portugal. The menu one evening offered an exemplary pâté en croûte, some gilthead bream cooked with caramelised onions and apple crumble. Indeed one of the chef's signature dishes – a parmentier aux truffes - I had last enjoyed in Paris's newest three star restaurant (the stars, that is, the restaurant itself is over two centuries old), the Grand Véfour. There is an excellent list of Portuguese wines and a very knowledgeable wine waiter.

The Fortaleza is situated on the first unbuilt up stretch of coastline west of Lisbon. Around it are some of the city's very smartest restaurants. In Cascais and Estoril are the villas inhabited by many of the deposed monarchs of Europe after 1918, the kings of Romania, Bulgaria, Spain, Italy, not forgetting the Duke of Windsor.

Just outside Lisbon is the rococo gem of Queluz,

with one of the country's swankiest restaurants installed in the kitchens (Cozinha Velha in the Pousada de D. Maria 1 – (351 21 435 61 58). It was built as a palace for Dom João V, but chiefly enjoyed by Queen Maria. The design is by the Frenchman Jean-Baptiste Robillon, but the works were continued under a local architect, Mateus Vicente do Oliveira. Even so, it has always struck me as looking more German than anything else.

The architect of the most impressive edifice in the region was indeed German – Ludovic or Ludwig who designed Mafra: the Portuguese Escurial: half palace, half monastery. It was built for João V, the king who - according to Voltaire – amused himself by watching religious processions and took a nun for a mistress. The place is so immense that it took 50,000 men 13 years to construct.

There is plenty to see beyond Lisbon, especially in the seaside region the Portuguese call 'O Oeste'. Like the capital itself, Alenquer was destroyed by the 1755 earthquake, but Portugal's first Franciscan friary, built in 1222, was miraculously saved from the blast. There is a Manueline church at Sobral de Monte Agraço, where Wellington also resided in the fort as he tended his complex of defensive lines emanating from Torres Vedras.

In Torres Vedras itself is the Fort of S. Vicente. The parish church is also worthy of a visit. The town

museum is installed in the old Graça Convent. Here you may study Wellington's defence of Lisbon, and the defences which extended from the Tagus to the coast. In around a year 152 forts had been equipped with over 600 cannons. When he saw how well Wellington had protected the capital, Masséna made his excuses and turned back towards Santarém. He took French leave and left via Spain.

There are relics of an earlier French invasion at Vimeiro, close to the coast with its pretty fishing villages. Nearby is the walled seaside town of Peniche and the chapel of Nossa Senhora dos Remédios, with its lovely *azulejos*. From there the natural punctuation marks for travellers are Óbidos and the spa town of Caldas da Rainha ('the queen's springs')

Óbidos is rather cute and touristy – a bit like Rye or Les Baux de Provence- but it possesses a ravishing, fifteenth-century *pousada* within its circuit of mediaeval walls where I once ate suckling pig moistened by a bottle of 1967 Colares. Caldas commemorates Dona Leonor, the wife of Dom João II, who found that the waters here relieved her rheumatism. There is a Manueline church dating from a few years later.

At Bombarral you can stay at the Quinta dos Lorridos, owned by J.P. Vinhos. Call 351 262 605 240.

Also unmissable is the wonderful Cistercian monastery at Alcobaça: the largest and grandest in Portugal, with its Manueline door in the form of two trees with interlacing branches and the tombs of Dom

Pedro and his mistress, Inês de Castro. Sublime too is the Brobdingnagian kitchen. Nearby is the National Wine Museum (351 262 58 22 22).

For further information telephone the Gabinete da Rota do Vinho do Oeste (351 262 95 50 60).

Ribatejo

The region extends either side of the Tagus, which begins broad outside Lisbon then shrinks to a manageable size as the traveller proceeds towards Tomar in the north of the region. Many of the towns, such as Rio Maior, or Almeirim, are bustling, modern places, and anything but picturesque. To the south, at least, the Ribatejo is quite flat; it only develops some interesting relief as you reach Abrantes – incidentally the name of the dukedom granted to Marshal Junot who did not live long enough to enjoy it. It is rather better remembered as the name of one of the riper mistresses of Honoré de Balzac.

At Cartaxo there is a museum dedicated to wine and rural life (351 243 70 02 65) in the Ribatejo. Nearby Santarém is Portugal's gothic town, with the important churches of S. João do Alporão and Graça, in the latter is the tomb of Cabral, who discovered Brazil in 1500. Even more impressive is the Manueline church by Diogo Boitaca at Golegã.

On the south side of the flood, Almeirim played an important and tragic role in Portuguese history when the Cortes met here in 1580 to decide the country's fate after the death of Dom Sebastião in the Magreb. It was the beginning of sixty years of Spanish captivity.

The Museum in Patudos, built in 1905, brings together an interesting collection of carpets, porcelain, furniture and paintings by Rembrandt, Dürer, Zurbaran, Delacroix and José Malhoa – one of the most important Portuguese painters of the nineteenth century.

This is bullfighting country, and as a consequence of this, a breeding ground for the dapper, little Lusitanian horses which are used in the ring. In Salvaterra de Magos occurred the most celebrated combat in Portuguese bullfighting history, when the handsome conde dos Arcos, one of the country's best horsemen, was killed by the bull before the eyes of his father, the marquês de Marialva and the king, Dom José I.

The old marquis stepped into the ring, and despatched the bull on foot, as was the practice among nobles. The king was so shocked by the event that he banned royal bullfights for the duration of his reign.

For lovers of horses the Companhia das Lezírias has a show-jumping circuit at Coudelaria, with a restaurant (351 353 63 64 3 12).

Towards Tomar is the castle of Almourol, romantically sited on an island in the middle of the Tagus. It was built in 1171 by the Templar Gualdim Pais. Constância lies at the confluence of the Tagus and the Zêzere. This was once the home town of Luis de Camões.

The Templars had their Portuguese stronghold in Tomar until the extinction of the order, when the buildings passed into the hands of the Order of Christ. The site is justly famous. It is possibly the most beautiful collection of religious buildings in Portugal and the Manueline window designed by Diogo de Arruda should certainly not be missed; nor should the renaissance cloister constructed by Philip II of Spain.

The little town lies at the bottom of the hill. There is a series of homely restaurants by the river side, and Portugal's best preserved mediaeval synagogue. The town hall is a little gem, as is the parish church, with its Manueline door.

Not far from Tomar is the great abbey church of Batalha. It was constructed at the end of the fourteenth century to celebrate the Anglo-Portuguese victory over the Spanish, and English architects played an obvious role in the design of the nave. Where the style is purely Portuguese is in the unfinished, Manueline chapels and the Royal Cloister. Here is buried the Unknown Warrior who died in the First World War.

There are rooms at the Quinta do Casalinho in Almeirim (351 243 52 96 18).

For more information, the Gabinete da Rota do Vinho do Ribatejo (351 243 33 03 30).

Setúbal Peninsula

This is the Costa Azul, or Blue Coast, famed for its beaches. In Vila Nogueira de Azeitão there is not only J.M. da Fonseca to visit, but the old palace of the dukes of Viseu. To the south is the national park, which has fortunately preserved a long stretch of coastline. In the midst of this is the Franciscan friary of Arrábida; the only eyesore being a huge cement works. It was on the road driving north from Setúbal, that the unconventional South African poet, Roy Campbell, met his death in a car crash in 1957.

The Quinta da Bacalhôa in Azeitão is a renaissance palace which once belonged to Afonso de Albuquerque, first Viceroy of India. It is filled with precious *azulejos* and was lovingly restored by the American, Elizabeth Scoville, whose family acquired it in 1937. For the wine see p124 above.

The westernmost point of the peninsula is the Cabo Espichel with its pilgrimage church of Nossa Senhora do Cabo which boasts an impressively long range of eighteenth-century dormitories, built for the pilgrims.

The fishing port of Sesimbra has a moorish castle, captured by the Portuguese in 1165. Setúbal is rough and industrial, but there are good things for all that, especially Diogo Boitaca's Igreja de Jesus of 1491, one of the most important works of the Manueline style.

The best places to stay are the pousadas at Palmela (351 212 35 12 26) or Setúbal (351 265 52 38 44). Both are splendid old castles, and from the heights of Setúbal you look out from the crenellated terraces down on the town and right out to sea. Palmela's past is a little gory, but that seems to put no one off his sleep nowadays.

For further information: the Gabinete da Rota dos Vinhos da Costa Azul (351 265 59 31 27).

Alentejo

The Alentejo is a large region. Its head lies in Portalegre, some of which is actually to the north of Lisbon, while its tail, mostly denuded of vines, rests against the scorching sands of the Algarve.

The Moors were here for longer, and their influence can still be seen in some of the many castles which rise out of the arid landscape. There is plenty of Christian history too; and landmarks in the story of Portugal. Near Portalegre, for example, is Avis, where the second royal dynasty was founded once the Burgundian line died out in 1385. Dom João I had been master of the military order which was based in the town.

The man who buried the dynasty – the last of the Avis monarchs – was Dom António, prior of the Order of Saint John, who reigned briefly after the death of Dom Sebastião. The Spanish Philips came next. António's monastery has now been skilfully converted into a pousada (351 245 99 72 10).

Nearby is Alter do Chão, the royal stud founded in 1748 where the Lusitanian breed of horses was traditionally raised. Portalegre itself is a pleasant jumble of baroque buildings around a whitewashed cathedral. Castelo de Vide preserves an ancient ghetto together with a thirteenth-century synagogue.

The best hotel in Évora is clearly the Pousada dos Loios (351 266 70 40 51), which is in the most literally heavenly place, in the old monastery right next door to the remains of the Roman Temple of Diana.The rooms are in the former cells; but it's a great deal more comfortable than it sounds, and the neighbouring cell to the bedroom is now a bathroom. There is a decent restaurant in the cloister next to a sacristy with a magnificent Manueline door, serving *porco preto* ham on the bone and pork with clams, cooked – so they say – the Alentejo way. Puddings include *morgado*, an allusion to rich landowners, and *pão de rala* or grated bread, which contains big bits of sweetened pumpkin.

Da Cartuxa (351 266 74 30 30) is a cheaper modern hotel, just three years old, built just inside the city walls with extensive gardens and a pool. The bedrooms have terracotta floors, and there are lots of pretty, brightly coloured pots around the public rooms. The cooking in the restaurant is fine, and there is a sommelier who is more than keen to show his mettle.

Évora's most famous restaurant is Fialho (351 266 70 30 79), a pretty little place filled with old majolica where the chef once worked with the legendary Paul Bocuse. The owner of A Tasquinha d'Oliveira formerly worked as a waiter at Fialho. His wife does the

cooking. It is a tiny space, a former shop with four or five tables, but the food can be stunningly good. The restaurant Lis (351 266 771 323) is a decent standby with ample portions of good food. Only its location and design leave something to be desired.

There is an excellent covered market in Évora selling *porco preto* hams, pigs' ears, honey and lovely local ewe's milk cheeses. Before you leave the city you should take in its most macabre monument, the Capela dos Ossos, or 'chapel of the bones'. It was decorated in the sixteenth century with more than 5,000 skulls. A legend over the door reads ' *Nós, ossos que aqui estamos, pelos vossos esperamos*' (Our bones are here, hoping for yours).

In Estremoz there is the sublime Pousada da Rainha Santa Isabel (351 268 33 20 75) in the fourteenth-century castle keep with antique four-poster beds in the rooms. They can be a hardship for those who are not 'vertically challenged', but the hotel none the less allows you to buy postcards of your bed to send to your friends at home. The food can be disappointing. I ate the simplest Alentejano soup: bread, eggs, oil and garlic followed by a stewed partridge with mushrooms and raisins.

The best restaurant in Estremoz is São Rosas (351 268 33 33 45), a stone's throw away in the castle bailey. More basic is Zona Verde (Largo Dragões d'Olivença 86). It doesn't look like much, but there is *porco preto* loin and local rabbit as well as a curious eggy pudding called *sopa dourada* made from stale bread and almonds. The great square has market stalls selling excellent dried oregano, fresh cheeses and sausages, and the town is also reputed for its pottery.

Between Estremoz and Vila Viçosa are the marble quarries which – they say – export their stone to Carrara and elsewhere, to be sold as native products. There are coarse ceramics to be found all over the region. Those from Redondo are well known, with their simple fish and cockerel motifs. They can be remarkably good value. A huge salad bowl cost me no more than £4.

At Vila Viçosa is the enormous sixteenth-century palace of the Braganzas which also harbours a coach museum. The fortress town of Elvas is famous for its sun-dried plums, which were formerly a sweetmeat consumed by English families at Christmas.

The southernmost part of the Alentejo producing decent wine is the area around Vidigueira. There are no large towns here, but the settlements have much charm with their collections of whitewashed houses all set off by a strip of colour at the base. In Viana do Alentejo is a castle constructed by Dom Dinis, with a Manueline church. The castle in neighbouring Alvito has been turned into a pousada (351 48 53 43).

The region possesses many impressive Roman ruins, such as the villa at São Cucufate near Vidigueira or the castle at Lousa on the River Guadiana. Vidigueira itself conjurs up memories of Vasco da Gama, who, though born at Sines on the coast, was given the title of 'count' of Vidigueira as a reward for his epic journey.

J.P. Vinhos maintains a hotel in Arraiolos, Portugal's carpetmaking town (351 212 19 80 60).

For further information: the Gabinete da Rota dos Vinhos do Alentejo (351 266 74 64 98).

Algarve

A region you either love or loathe is the Algarve. Towards the coast it is monstrously built up with high-rise blocks, but there are simple villages filled with one-storey houses which have plenty of charm, and from time to time a magnificent castle such as the bright red structure at Silves, behind Portimão. This was the last stronghold of the Moor. When it fell a cathedral was erected in thanksgiving.

There is an impressive castle at Aljezur and Lagos retains its mediaeval walls. From here the unfortunate D. Sebastião set sail for Alcacer Quivir, and the battle that would cost him his life, and Portugal its independence. From Lagos it is a short distance to Sagres, from the fort of which Prince Henry directed operations which were to lead Portuguese mariners to uncover the secrets of the world.

The fanciful chimney pots of the region enjoy some fame. Their strange forms are also supposed to go back to the time of Moorish dominion.

Lagoa has some rustic charm, and a famous old gate. O Lotus (351 282 35 20 98) is a handy restaurant for the cooperative in Lagoa and for the official, government, tasting centre nearby.

Denominações de Origem

Appellations D'Origine / Designations of Origin

Vini Portugal

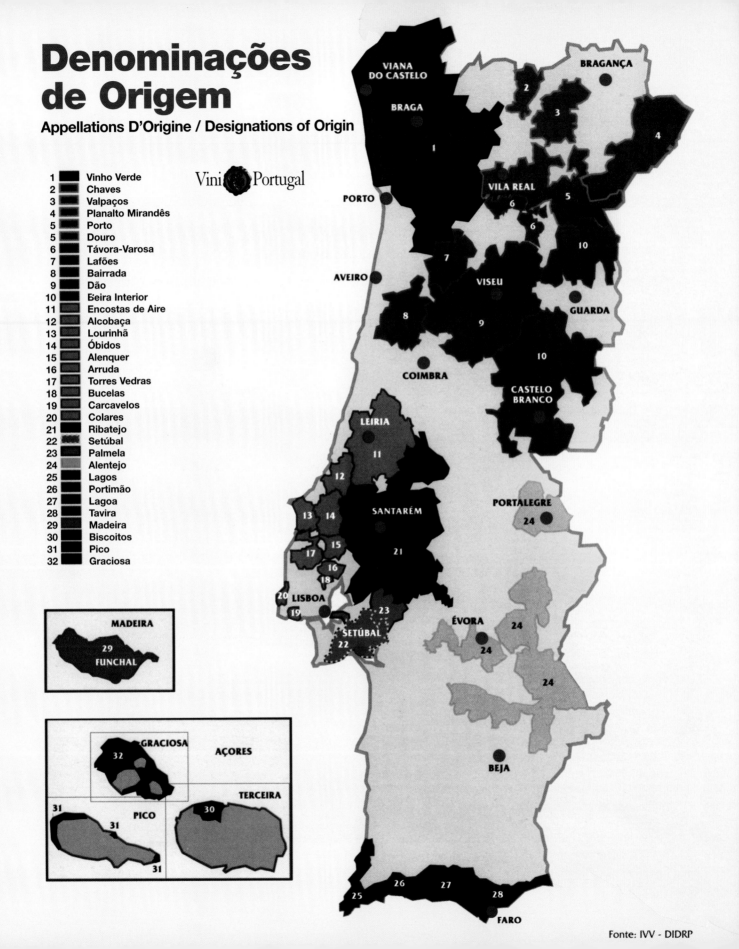

1 Vinho Verde
2 Chaves
3 Valpaços
4 Planalto Mirandês
5 Porto
5 Douro
6 Távora-Varosa
7 Lafões
8 Bairrada
9 Dão
10 Beira Interior
11 Encostas de Aire
12 Alcobaça
13 Lourinhã
14 Óbidos
15 Alenquer
16 Arruda
17 Torres Vedras
18 Bucelas
19 Carcavelos
20 Colares
21 Ribatejo
22 Setúbal
23 Palmela
24 Alentejo
25 Lagos
26 Portimão
27 Lagoa
28 Tavira
29 Madeira
30 Biscoitos
31 Pico
32 Graciosa

MADEIRA
29 FUNCHAL

GRACIOSA
AÇORES
32
TERCEIRA
31
PICO
31
30
31

VIANA DO CASTELO
BRAGANÇA
BRAGA
2
3
4
1
VILA REAL
6
5
6
10
7
VISEU
8
9
GUARDA
10
COIMBRA
CASTELO BRANCO
LEIRIA
11
12
PORTALEGRE
24
13 14
SANTARÉM
15
17
21
16
18
ÉVORA
20 LISBOA
19
23
24
24
SETÚBAL
22
24
BEJA
25 26 27 28
FARO

PORTO
AVEIRO

Fonte: IVV - DIDRP

wine classifications

Portugal has the oldest demarcated wine region in the world: the Douro Valley. This was originally mapped out in the 1760s, more than a decade before its nearest rival, Tuscany. This first controlled appellation naturally omitted much and included the odd patch which had little to do with the Douro. The most notable example of the latter was the marquês de Pombal's own estate at Oeiras on the coast near Lisbon. Later this became the base for another fortified wine of the port type, Carcavelos.

The Douro was demarcated for port. It was not until 1998 that further legislation was passed for the table wines of the region that made a clear difference between the two wines. Elsewhere the Portuguese were among the pioneers when it came to protecting regional typicity in wine. In the last years of the monarchy statutes were passed in the parliament building in S. Bento which protected vinho verde, Bucelas, Colares and Carcavelos. Sadly, the process stopped there, and it was not until after the end of Salazar's dictatorship that further real progress was made in isolating local characteristics in wine to bring Portugal into line with the European Union.

Portugal currently has 33 demarcated quality wine-producing regions known legally as *vinhos de qualidade produzidos em regiões determinadas*. The best are the **DOC**s, or *Denominação de Origem Controlada*. These stipulate the place, grape varieties, yields and minimum alcoholic strengths and bottle age of a wine. Rather less stringent are the **IPR**s or *Indicação de Proveniência Regulamentada*, which have allowed a certain number of foreign varietals to be tried out in Portuguese soil. Two acronyms which you will still meet on Portuguese labels are **VQPRD** and **VLQPRD**. VQPRD was the old umbrella term for what has since been split between DOC and IPR when the law was updated and no longer figures on new labels, but don't be confused by old stock and vintages. VLQPRD (*vinhos licorosos de qualidade produzidos em regiões determinadas*) referred to the classification which protects Portuguese fortified wines: port, Madeira, Moscatel de Setúbal, and the Pico. These have now all become DOCs or IPRs as well.

How to Read a Portuguese Wine Label

Below the IPR comes the *vinho regional*, again there is more fluidity here. In the Douro, for example, anyone seeking to make wine from a non-permitted variety such as, say, Syrah, would have to use the regional label: *vinho regional, Trás-os-Montes, Terras Durienses.*

Vinho de mesa refers to an ordinary table wine with no pretensions to quality.

QUINTA DO BARÃO[1]

DOURO[2]

Denominação de origem controlada[3]

1997[4]

Reserva[5]

Vinho tinto[6]

13%vol. Produto de Portugal 75clE[7]

Produzido e engarrafado na Quinta por

João Soares Albuquerque dos Reyes, Vila Soeiro,

Rezende, Portugal[8]

[1]The name of the estate. A *quinta* is a substantial farm. Other words encountered are *tapada*, meaning a walled estate, like a French *clos*; *palacio* or *paço* mean palace, *solar* designates a manor house. A *casa* or *casal* is a large house. *Vinha* means vineyard. In the Alentejo the vocabulary is different: *herdade* or *monte* both designate a farm.

[2]Douro is the region of origin.

[3]In this instance the Douro is a DOC, demarcated region.

[4]The vintage year. The wine must all be from the year. Sometimes the word *colheita* is found. It means vintage.

[5]*Reserva* means a 'reserve' wine of particular quality. The best wines are labelled *garrafeira*. Like the German word *Kabinett* this refers to the cellar, i.e., put it away.

[6]Red wine; *branco* is white; *rosado* is rosé. Other words which might figure on the label are *doce* for sweet, *seco* for dry, *licoroso* for fortified sweet wine, *bruto* for dry sparkling wine and *método clássico* indicating the champagne method, etc.

[7]Alcoholic strength, and bottle size.

[8]The name and address of the producer.

glossary

adamado: sweet

adega: winery

aguardente: grape spirit or brandy used in fortification

ânfora: large clay vessel used for fermenting and/or storing wine

armazém: literally meaning a warehouse, *armazém* is also the name for a building in which wine, especially Port and Madeira, is matured

branco: white wine

bruto: dry sparkling wine

carvalho: oak

casa: large house

casta: grape variety

clarete: light red or dark rosé

colheita: literally meaning 'harvest' or 'vintage'; also denotes a style of Port

DOC: Denominação de Origem Controlada (see above)

doce: sweet

escolha: choice or selection

espumante: sparkling wine

estágio: period of ageing

estufagem: the heating process used to age Madeira

garrafa: bottle

garrafeira: a red wine from an exceptional harvest that has been aged for at least two years before bottling, followed by a further year in bottle before sale. White *garrafeiras* must age for at least six months before bottling, followed by a further six months in bottle. Both red and white wines must have an alcoholic strength at least 0.5%/vol. above the legal minimum to qualify.

IPR: Indicação de Proveniência Regulamentada (see above)

lagar: a large, low sided vessel, usually made from stone, where grapes are foot-trodden and fermented

leve: Literally meaning 'light'; low in alcohol

licoroso: fortified sweet wine

lodge: an English term used by Port and Madeira shippers to denote a building where wine is stored and matured

maduro: old or matured

metodo classico: champagne method

pipe: English corruption of Portuguese term 'pipa', meaning cask or barrel. In the Port trade a pipe is also a standard unit of measurement

quinta: farm or estate

reserva: reserve

rosado: rosé wine

seco: dry

solar: literally a manor house or 'mansion'; sometimes used to denote a wine from an estate (see also; quinta)

tapada: walled estate

vinho: wine

vinho de consumo: everyday wine

vinho generoso: fortified wine

vinho de mesa: table wine (see above)

vinho regional: regional wine (see above)

vinho tinto: red wine

stockists

ATLÂNTICO (UK) LTD
Unit 21, Summerstown Ind. Est.
London SW17 0BQ
☎ 020 8946 0707/Fax 020 8946 0808
atlantico@aol.com

BERKMANN WINE CELLARS LTD
12 Brewery Road
London N7 9NH
☎ 020 7609 4711/Fax 020 7607 0018
postmaster@berkmann.co.uk

C & D WINES LTD
Amapola House
25 Metro Business Centre
London SE26 5BW
☎ 020 8778 1711/Fax 020 8778 1710
helen@candwines.co.uk

BEN ELLIS & ASSOCIATES LTD
Brockham Wine Cellars
Wheelers Lane
Brockham
Surrey RH3 7HJ
☎ 01737 842160/Fax 01737 843210
lance@benelliswines.com

BIBENDUM WINE LTD
113 Regents Park Road
London
NW1 8UR
☎ 020 7722 5577/Fax 020 7722 7354
sales@bibendum-wine.co.uk

**CHARLES HAWKINS FINE FRENCH
& NEW WORLD WINES**
Hall Gardens
56 High Street East
Uppingham
Rutland LE15 9HG
☎ 01572 823030/Fax 01572 823040
charles@charleshawkins.demon.co.uk

D & D WINES INTERNATIONAL LTD
Adams Court
Adams Hill
Knutsford WA16 6BA
☎ 01565 650952/Fax 01565 755295
ddwi@ddwinesint.com

EHRMANNS LTD
29 Corsica Street
London N5 1JT
☎ 020 7418 1800/Fax 020 7636 7289
ehrmanns@ehrmanns.co.uk

EUROPVIN LTD
55 Penn Road
London N7 9RE
☎ 020 7607 9673/Fax 020 7700 6519
julia.wilkinson@europvinuk.fsnet.co.uk

FORTH WINES LTD
Crawford Place
Milnathort
Kinross-Shire KY13 9XF
☎ 01577 866001/Fax 01577 866020
enquiries@forthwines.com

D & F WINE SHIPPERS LTD
Centre House
St Leonard's Road
London NW10 6ST
☎ 020 8838 4399/Fax 020 8838 4500
dfwineship@aol.com

ENOTRIA WINECELLARS LTD
4-8 Chandos Park Estate
Chandos Road
London NW10 6NF
☎ 020 8961 4411/Fax 020 8961 8773
marketing@enotria.co.uk

FIRST DRINKS BRANDS LTD
Imperial House
Imperial Way
Southampton SO15 0RB
☎ 023 8031 2000/Fax 023 8031 1111

FREIXENET (DWS) LTD
Freixenet House
Wellington Business Park
Berkshire RG45 6LS
☎ 01344 758500/Fax 01344 758510
prowles@freixenet.co.uk

HOUSE OF HALLGARTEN
Dallow Road
Luton
Bedfordshire LU1 1UR
☎01582 722538/Fax 01582 723240
cliff@vitisvinifera.demon.co.uk

JOHN E FELLS & SONS LTD
Fells House
Prince Edward Street
Berkhamsted HP4 3EZ
☎ 01442 870900/Fax 01442 878555
info@fells.co.uk

**MAISON MARQUES ET
DOMAINES LTD**
Burleigh House
17-19 Worple Way
Surrey TW10 6AG
☎ 020 8332 2223/Fax 020 8334 5900
maison@mmdltd.co.uk

MORENO WINE IMPORTERS
26 Macroom Road
London W9 3HY
☎ 020 8960 7161/Fax 020 8960 7165
sales@moreno-wines.co.uk

HWCG WINE GROWERS LTD
10-11 Twyford Centre
London Road
Bishop's Stortford
Herts M23 3YT
☎ 01279 506512/Fax 01279 657462
wine@hedleywright.com

LAYMONT & SHAW LTD
The Old Chapel
Millpool
Cornwall TR1 1EX
☎ 01872 270545/Fax 01872 223005
info@laymont-shaw.co.uk

MERIDIAN WINES LTD
Brook House
Northenden Road
Gatley
Cheshire SK8 1ZZ
☎ 0161 9081350/Fax 0161 9081355
sales@meridian.co.uk

MORRIS & VERDIN LTD
Unit 2, Bankside Industrial Estate
Summer Street
London SE1 9JZ
☎ 020 7921 5300/Fax 020 7921 5333
info@m-v.co.uk

OAKLEY WINE AGENCIES
PO Box 3234
Earls Colne
Colchester CO6 2SU
☎ 01787 220070/Fax 01787 224734
oakleywine@btconnect.com

PRIVATE LIQUOR BRANDS LTD
Dorset House
High Street
East Grinstead
West Sussex RH19 3DE
☎ 01342 318282/Fax 01342 314023
general@plb.co.uk

STEVENS GARNIER LTD
47 West Way
Botley
Oxford OX2 0JF
☎ 01865 263305/Fax 01865 791594
vdp@stevensgarnier.claranet.co.uk

WITHERS AGENCIES LTD
1 South Street
Lewes
East Sussex BN7 2BT
☎ 01273 477132/Fax 01273 476612
david@vicawines.co.uk

PORTUGALIA WINES (UK) LTD
Unit 6, 90-92 Queensbury Road
Wembley
Middx HA0 1QG
☎ 020 8997 4400/Fax 020 8997 3222
sales@portugaliawines.co.uk

RAYMOND REYNOLDS WINES
Station Road
Furness Vale
High Peak
Stockport SK23 7SW
☎ 01663 742230/Fax 01663 742233
info@raymondreynolds.co.uk

WALTER S SIEGEL LTD
Regent House
123 High Street
Odiham
Hants RG29 1LA
☎ 01256 701101/Fax 01256 701518
wine@walter-siegel.co.uk

Photograph captions

Tinta Barroca grape,1; Quinta Napoles, Douro 2; Quinta da Grima, Bairrada, 3; Great casks still in use, Setúbal, 8; Fernão Pires grape, 12; Baga grape, 13; Vines in the Douro, 14; Vintage Niepoort, 17; Potes tradicionais, Alentejo – José de Sousa, 18; Warre, Porto/Gaia, 21; Palacio da Brejoeira, 25; Garrafeira de Velhos, 28; Arinto grape, 36; Roupeiro grape, 37; Castelão grape, 40; Touriga Francesca grape, 41; Torres Vedras, 45; Douro, 46; Torres Vedras, 49; Granite posts to stretch the vines, 52; Quinta da Covela, 58; Alvarinho vines, 61; Rural scene near the Minho river, 62; Vesúvio-Lagares, 68; Trincadeira Preta grape, 73; Douro, 74; Harvest baskets, Douro, 75; Douro, 76; Vines of S.João da Pesqueira, 79; Old vine, Dão 81; Modern and old, Bairrada, 83; Quinta Velha, 84; Modern winery, Dão, 89; Velha vines, Bairrada, 90; Baga grape vine, 93; The river Dão, 94; Caves São João, Bairrada, 100; Modern winery near Lisbon, 103; Quinta da Romeira, 104; Alenquer, Estremadura, 105; Winery in Cartaxo, 108; Wines ageing in wood, 111; Vineyard in 'Campo', 113; Vineyard in 'Charneca', 114; Moscatel de Setúbal, 117; Adega Cooperative, Palmela, 118; Sandy soil in Pegões, Setúbal, 121; Wine tourism in Alentejo, 125; Grapes in 'Tegão', 128; Vineyard in Alentejo, 133; Cartuxa winery, 134; Touriga Nacional grape, 138; Harvest, 140; Vines grown in 'curraletas', Azores, 144; Quinta Roriz, Douro, 146; Verdes, 147; Quinta Vila Beatriz, Vinho Verde, 150/151; A typical house, Óbidos, 153; Vinha Velha, Alentejo, 154; Aguardentes ageing in cask, 157; Casa de Santar, Dão, 161; José Maria da Fonseca, the oldest producer in Setúbal, 162; Palácio da Brejoeira, Minho, 165; Casa de Santar, Dão, 166; Sala de Saima, Bairrada, Enotourism, 167; Esporão, Alentejo, 170; Lusitanos horses, Ribatejo, 173; Chaves, Alentejo, 177; Quinta de Roriz, Douro, 181; A modern winery for the Bordeaux-type 'half casks' made of oak, Alentejo, 183; Quinta Nova, Dão, 184.

statistics

Units: 1000 hl
(*): Provisional data
Source: Portuguese
Wine Institute

NATIONAL WINE PRODUCTION

	1997/1998	1997/1998	1998/1999	1998/1999	1999/2000*	1999/2000*
	'000 hl	%	'000 hl	%	'000 hl	%
Wine category:						
DOC+ IPR	2,280	37	1,910	51	3,616	50
Regional wine	1,005	16	564	15	998	14
Table wine	2,839	46	1,276	34	2,616	36
Total	6,124	100	3,750	100	7,230	100

Units: 1000 hl
(*): Provisional data
Source: Portuguese
Wine Institute

Vintage 1999/2000* according to regions

Wine Regions	Total	DOC+IPR	Regional Wine	Table wine
Minho	**1.400**	**1.395**	**4**	**1**
Trás-os-Montes	**1.700**	**1.322**	**58**	**320**
Douro	1.550	1.300	32	218
Other sub- regions	150	22	26	102
Beiras	**1.300**	**2528**	**201**	**571**
Dão	400	322	37	41
Bairrada	500	176	49	275
Other sub-regions	400	30	115	255
Ribatejo	**900**	**34**	**123**	**743**
Estremadura	**1.100**	**29**	**220**	**851**
Terras do Sado	**250**	**34**	**118**	**99**
Alentejo	**500**	**216**	**274**	**10**
Algarve	**10**	**5**	**1**	**4**
Madeira	**50**	**50**	**0**	**0**
Açores	**20**	**3**	**0**	**17**
TOTAL	**7.230**	**3.616**	**999**	**2.616**

Units: 1000 hl
(*): Provisional data
Source: Portuguese
Wine Institute

COMPARISONS BETWEEN VINTAGES

Wine Regions	Total (1000 Hl) (*)	Total (1000 Hl) (*)	Total (1000 Hl) (*)	Growth %	Growth %
	1998/1999 vintage	Average vintage 95/96, 96/97, 97/98	1999/2000 vintage	98/99 - 99/00 vintage	Average vintage 95/96, 96/97, 97/98
Minho	603	938	1,400	132	49
Trás-os-Montes	961	1,548	1,700	77	10
Douro	897	1,359	1,550	73	14
Other sub- regions	64	189	150	134	-21
Beiras	339	892	1,300	283	46
Dão	107	269	400	274	49
Bairrada	87	297	500	475	68
Other sub-regions	145	326	400	176	23
Ribatejo	530	869	900	70	4
Estremadura	686	1,390	1,100	60	-21
Terras do Sado	201	326	250	25	-23
Alentejo	239	443	500	109	13
Algarve	5	15	10	100	-33
Madeira	43	50	50	16	0
Açores	14	15	20	43	33
TOTAL	**3,621**	**6,486**	**7,230**	**100**	**11**

Note that in the above chart the data related to the 98/99 vintage is still based on provisional data, although on the first chart, final data is presented.

The amount of Portuguese wine production in **1999/2000 was 7.5 million hectolitres**, twice the amount of **1998/1999 vintage, which was 3.750 million hectolitres**. This was above the average production of the last three vintages.

Number of growers in Portugal: 300,000

Total ha of vineyard in Portugal: 252,709 ha

Consumption per person in Portugal: 52 litres

bibliography

Richard Ames, *The Bacchanalian Sessions*,
London 1693.
– *The Search After Claret*, 1691.
– *A Farther Search After Claret*, 1691.
*Anuário 1999-2000 Vinhos e Aguardentes de
Portugal*, Lisbon 1999.
Udal Ap Rhys, *A Tour through Spain and Portugal*,
1750.
Joseph Baretti, *From London to Genoa*, London 1770.
David Birmingham, *A Concise History of Portugal*,
Cambridge 1993.
George Borrow, *The Bible in Spain*, London 1843.
Eduardo Brazão, *The Anglo-Portuguese Alliance*,
London 1957.
Duarte Calvão, *Rotas do Vinho - Portugal*, Lisbon 2000.
Manuel Carvalho and João Menéres, *Colours of Vinho
verde*, np, 1998.
Camillo Castelo Branco, *O Vinho do Porto*, Oporto 1884.
Marcus Cheke, *Dictator of Portugal: Marquis of Pombal*,
London 1938.
William Colbatch, *Account of the Court of Portugal*,
London 1700.
John Croft, *Treatise on the Wines of Portugal*, 1788.
Richard Croker, *Travels through Several Provinces of
Spain and Portugal*, 1799.
William Dalrymple, *Travels through Spain and Portugal
in 1774*, London 1777.
Daniel Defoe, *Trade with France, Italy and Spain*,
London 1713.
John Delaforce, *Joseph James Forrester*, London 1992.
– *The Factory House at Oporto*, London 1983.
David Erskine, Ed., *Augustus Hervey's Journal*,
London 1953.
H.E.S. Fisher, *The Portugal Trade: A Study of Anglo-
Portuguese Commerce 1700-1770*, London 1971.
A.D. Francis, *The Methuens and Portugal*, London 1966.
John Hampton, *History of the Lisbon Chaplaincy*,
Lisbon 1989.
John Healy, ed, Pliny the Elder, *Natural History*,
Harmondsworth, 1991.
José Hermano Saraiva, *Portugal, A Companion
History*, Manchester 1997.
*The Diary of John Hervey, First Earl of Bristol, With
Extracts from his Book of Expenses, 1688 to 1742*,
London 1894.
Edward Hyams, *Dionysus, A Social History of the Wine
Vine*, London, 1987.
Marion Kaplan, *The Portuguese: The Land and Its
People*, Harmondsworth 1998.
Alex Liddell and Janet Price, *Port Wine Quintas of the
Douro*, London, 1992.
H.V. Livermore, *A New History of Portugal*, Cambridge
1966.

Rose Macaulay, *They Went to Portugal*, London 1946.
Richard Mayson, *Portugal's Wine & Winemakers*,
London 1992.
Richard Mayson, *Port and the Douro*, London, 1999.
Kenneth Maxwell, *Pombal, Paradox of the
Enlightenment*, Cambridge, 1995.
João Paulo Martins, *Vinhos de Portugal*, Lisbon 1998
and 1999.
Mercator, *Letters on Portugal*, London 1754.
A. Moreira da Fonseca et al, *Port Wine, Notes on its
History, Production and Technology*, Oporto, 1998.
James Murphy, *Travels in Portugal*, London 1795.
Clara Roque do Vale, Joaquim Madeira, António Homem
Cardoso, *Alentejo Wines*, Lisbon 1996.
Ramalho Ortigão, Eça de Queiroz, *As Farpas*,
Oporto 1885.
Rod Phillips, *A Short History of Wine*, London 2000.
Peter Russell, *Henry 'The Navigator'*, London and
Newhaven, 2000.
José Salvador, *Roteiro does Vinhos Portugueses*,
Oporto 1999.
Mário Saraiva Pinto, António Fevereiro Chambel, António
Homen Cardoso, *Bairrada Wines*, Lisbon 1999.
Adam Smith, *The Wealth of Nations*, London 1838.
M. de Puymaurin, *De la Fabrication de vins en
Angleterre*, 1811.
Cyrus Redding, *Modern Wines*, 1833.
Jancis Robinson, *Vines, Grapes and Wines*, London, 1987.
A.J.R. Russell-Wood, *The Portuguese Empire, 1415-1808*,
Johns Hopkins, 1992.
Baron Edouard de Septenville, *Etude Historique sur le
marquis de Pombal*, Brussels 1868.
Desmond Seward, *Monks and Wine*, London 1979.
André Simon, *A Dictionary of Wines, Spirits and
Liqueurs*, London, 1958.
André Simon, *Bottlescrew Days: Wine Drinking in
England in the 18th Century*, London 1926.
André Simon, Ed., *The Bolton Letters – The Letters of an
English Merchant in Madeira 1695-1700*, London 1928.
Dan Stanislawski, *The Individuality of Portugal. A Study
in Historical Political Geography*, Austin, Texas, 1959.
Dan Stanislawski, *Landscapes of Bacchus: The Vine in
Portugal*, Austin, Texas and London 1970.
Jonathan Swift, *Journal to Stella*, London 1766.
Jorge Tavares da Silva, Norma Stanway, Jacques
Maréchal, *Bussaco*, Brussels 1997.
J.B. Trend, *Portugal*, London 1957.
Richard Twiss, *Travels through Portugal and Spain*,
London 1775.
Edite Vieira, *The Taste of Portugal*, London 2000.
Henry Vizetelly, *Facts about Port and Madeira*,
London 1880.
William Warre ed., *Letters from the Peninsula by
Lieut.-Gen Sir William Warre CB, KTS*, Staplehurst 1999.

Private papers relative to the history of the Reynolds family
were kindly communicated to me by Iain Richardson.

index